ETHICS AND
AGENCY THEORY

Ethics and
Agency Theory
AN INTRODUCTION

Edited by
NORMAN E. BOWIE
R. EDWARD FREEMAN

New York   Oxford
OXFORD UNIVERSITY PRESS
1992

Oxford University Press

Oxford   New York   Toronto
Delhi   Bombay   Calcutta   Madras   Karachi
Kuala Lumpur   Singapore   Hong Kong   Tokyo
Nairobi   Dar es Salaam   Cape Town
Melbourne   Auckland

and associated companies in
Berlin   Ibadan

Copyright © 1992 by Oxford University Press, Inc.

Published by Oxford University Press, Inc.,
200 Madison Avenue, New York, New York 10016

Oxford is a registered trademark of Oxford University Press

Library of Congress Cataloging-in-Publication Data
Ethics and agency theory : an introduction /
edited by Norman E. Bowie and R. Edward Freeman.
p.   cm.—(The Ruffin series in business ethics)
Includes bibliographical references and index.
ISBN 0-19-506798-3
1. Business ethics.   2. Executives—Professional ethics.
3. Corporate culture.   4. Agency (Law)   I. Bowie, Norman E.,
1942–   .   II. Freeman, R. Edward, 1951–   .   III. Series.
HF5387.E825   1992
174'.4—dc20   91-23384   CIP

9 8 7 6 5 4 3 2 1

Printed in the United States of America
on acid-free paper

Dedicated to
Maureen Burns-Bowie
and
Maureen Wellen

PREFACE

This book is based in large part on a conference "The Implications of Agency Theory for Business Ethics" held at the University of Delaware June 10–11, 1987 under the sponsorship of the Center for the Study of Values. The authors gratefully acknowledge support from the Exxon Education Foundation and the Franklin J. Matchette Foundation, which made the conference possible. The authors also wish to express appreciation to the conference coordinator, Mrs. Sandy Manno and to the following conference participants who provided helpful comments on the papers that appear in this volume: Professor Eric Noreen (University of Washington), Professor Tom Dunfee (University of Pennsylvania), Professor Victor Goldberg (Northwestern University), Dr. Roy Radner (Bell Laboratories), Professor Daniel Hausman (Carnegie-Mellon University), Professor Joseph Galaskiewicz (University of Minnesota), and Professor Edward McClennen (Bowling Green State University).

During the development of the volume we wish to thank The Darden School Foundation, the Olsson Center for Applied Ethics, and the Carlson School of Management. We especially appreciate the support of John Rosenblum, Robert Fair, Charles Fitzgerald and Robert Harris of The Darden School and the fine work of Patricia Bennett, Henry Tulloch, and Karen Dickinson of The Olsson Center. Andrew Wicks and Melissa Kupperinc assisted with the proofreading and the index. Herb Addison, Stanley George, and Mary Sutherland of Oxford University Press have provided their usual outstanding support.

CONTENTS

CONTRIBUTORS

John R. Boatright
John Carroll University

Norman E. Bowie
University of Minnesota

J. Gregory Dees
Harvard University

Richard T. DeGeorge
University of Kansas

Ronald F. Duska
Rosemont College

R. Edward Freeman
University of Virginia

Kenneth Koford
University of Delaware

William E. Lawson
University of Delaware

Gary Miller
Washington University

Barry M. Mitnick
University of Pittsburgh

Lisa Newton
Fairfield University

Mark Penno
University of Chicago

Wanda A. Wallace
The College of William and
Mary

ETHICS AND
AGENCY THEORY

1

Ethics and Agency Theory: An Introduction

The purpose of this volume of essays is to begin a conversation between business thinkers who urge that we adopt a "principal-agent" view of the modern corporation and ethicists who insist that we need to examine the moral assumptions and implications of such a view. It is essential that this dialogue take place. The real world of the modern corporation is rapidly changing. Leveraged buy-outs, hostile takeovers, greenmail, poison pills, and other corporate governance issues are often evaluated in terms of principal-agent theory. Are actions really in the interest of shareholders (principals), or do they represent self-dealing by management (agents)? Can we understand recent corporate restructurings as a realignment of monitoring costs among principals and agents? These questions are central to today's debates about corporate governance, yet there is a curious lack of moral language in this debate.

It is plain that corporate action is in the moral realm. Even a dyed-in-the-wool free market economist such as Milton Friedman argues that managers' obligation to maximize shareholder wealth is a *moral* one, placing the corporation squarely within the moral realm.[1] Therefore, it is extremely surprising that a recent statement of agency theory is void of moral language. Pratt and Zeckhauser's book, *Principals and Agents*, intended as a way to make recent advances in agency theory accessible to managers, virtually ignores the moral implications of the theory.[2] Agency theory is put forth in a straightforward and scientific manner, as if its assumptions are void of moral content, and as if its implications are no more than technical adjustments between managers and stockholders.

This volume intends to correct this misunderstanding, and to place agency theory squarely within the discourse of morality. We see agency theory less as a scientific theory subject to rigorous empirical examination than as a narrative—a story that we can tell about how we are to understand our corporations. There are many characters in this narrative, and the plot is complex. Before it unfolds, let us try to understand the context of the story we call "agency theory" and give it square footing on the intellectual and practical landscape.

Modern agency theory is usually dated to S. A. Ross's influential article in 1973, "The Economic Theory of Agency: The Principal's Problem," and the paper by Michael Jenson and William Meckling, "Theory of the firm: Managerial behavior, agency costs and ownership structure" in 1976. Subsequently, scholars have traced the intellectual roots of the issue to the "property rights" tradition that emerges from the work of Ronald Coase in the 1930s, and later to a seminal article by Armen Alchian and Harold Demsetz in 1972.

The basic problem for economists is to understand the black box that is the firm. Opening the lid, we find immediate conflict. Shareholders and managers each want to appropriate as much of the residual value of the firm for themselves as possible. If we come to see managers as agents, acting for shareholders, the economic problem becomes how to develop the proper system of incentives so that the interests of managers comes into alignment with the interests of shareholders. Or, framed differently, under what set of conditions will managers act in the interests of shareholders? Or, what is the optimal level of monitoring that shareholders must do, if they are to be assured that managers act in their interest? Indeed there are a number of ways to frame the question, but each way has common assumptions.

First, economists assume the worst about human behavior. The agency problem exists in part because managers and shareholders are self-interested. While self-interest undoubtedly plays a large role in human motivation, the adoption of this assumption in a wholesale manner is problematic, as a number of scholars have shown.

Second, the currently accepted doctrine in economics contains its own notion of original sin. In a world in which economic actors have perfect information and therefore can bargain in a costless way, agency problems simply don't arise. But, alas, such a Garden of Eden exists only in textbooks, journal articles, and on office blackboards. Sadly, to hear economists, we are confronted with a "real world" in which markets do not work in this Newtonian, frictionless way. Information is costly. Using the price mechanism itself is costly. Bargaining is not free. We are then thrust into the problems of finding second-best solutions. While a thorough critique of the foundations of eco-

nomics is well beyond our present scope, it is worth pointing out that
the agency problem exists in part because we have *chosen* to describe
economic activity in a particular way. The tropes of economics are
the issue rather than some discovery of the essence of human nature.[3]

Finally, each way of modeling the agency problem still greatly sim-
plifies the so-called "real world." Many managers, as well as employees, are also shareholders of their firms, at least through their pen-
sion plans. And most managers and employees have not one but
multiple principals. They act in the interests of their families and
communities, their customers, other employees, suppliers, and
shareholders. The managerial task in today's real world is to balance
the interests of a host of stakeholder groups, each of which could be
understood in terms of the agency relationship. There is little schol-
arship available in economic theory that deals with the "multiple
principal" problem.[4]

While this concern with agency relationships is relatively recent in
economics, it is quite different if we turn to political theory. One way
of understanding the emergence of the modern nation-state is as an
entity that acts in the interests of its citizens. Certainly the social contract tradition from Hobbes, Locke, and Rousseau sees the state as
acting in the interests of its members, and in Hobbes's case, doing
what individual members cannot do: restraining the use of force.

Curiously, the multiple principal problem has been central to political discussions, especially recently. How does a public official balance the competing demands of a host of interest groups? What systems are in place to assure some minimal level of minority rights?
Thus, while the explicit use of agency theory models is a compara-
tively recent phenomenon in political science and due in large part
to the work of Mitnick, the traditions are quite old.[5] Moe has recently documented the development of agency theory in this literature.[6]

An even older tradition of agency theory can be found in the law.
The law recognizes that agency relationships pervade modern life.
In their comprehensive treatise of the law of agency Conard, Knauss,
and Siegel argue as follows:[7]

Agency embraces all kinds of agents—from the disappearing domestic
servants, who may be directed in every move, to employees of businesses
of all types, to the professional lawyer or broker, who may be advising his
"principal" what ought to be done for him. An organizational entity itself
may be an agent. Agency involves all kinds of employers, from the news-
boy who pays a helper to a corporation which pays thousands of employees in skilled and unskilled capacities. . . . It involves all kinds of jobs,

from the degrading to the ennobling—from Oliver Twist picking pockets for Fagin to Lee Iacocca donating Chrysler funds to restore the Statue of Liberty. . . . The common element of agencies is that the main benefit or detriment of the act is intended to fall upon one of the parties, while the other is a mere instrument. In the terms of a metaphor as old as civilization, one party is "over" the second, and second is "under" the first. (p. 3)

The key legal issue is the nature of the relationship between principal and agent, and revolves mainly around responsibility for any wrongdoing, or an interpretation of the nature of the agreement.

Now agency theorists would have us believe that by telling a story about the organization of economic activity in the language of principals and agents we are really promoting a world in which there is a great deal of free contracting. The essence of the agency relationship, according to theorists, is the voluntary nature of the agreement when principal hires agent and when agent agrees to work for principal. But tradition tells us otherwise.

Agency law is derived from two sources. The first is, in fact, the tradition of contract from English common law. But the second and more interesting historical connection comes via a later development, the law of torts. The question of responsibility in agency relationships arose over whether or not a "Master" was responsible for damages due to acts committed by his "Slaves," or his "Servants." Ferson claims that the master-servant relationship is defined as follows:[8]

One who procures, or even accepts, the services of another person and the right to control that person while he renders the services, is put under a master's responsibility.

If we substitute the notion of "right to monitor" for "right to control," we have a definition of the employment relationship that should please most agency theorists. Indeed, even today, the language of agency law (cf. the latest American Law Institute restatement of agency law)[9] is still replete with the "Master-Servant" metaphor, which conjures an image most ironic for the agency theorists who believe that the essence of their theory is the notion of free contracting.

The issue in both of these legal traditions is that of vicarious liability. Can the principal be said to be responsible for the acts of an agent, simply because she is his agent? The essence of the modern corporation is that in most cases vicarious liability holds, and the action of the employee is imputed to the employer.

We find this notion articulated in Jones v. Hart (England, Court of King's Bench, 1698).[10]

If the servants of A. with his cart run against another cart, wherein is a pipe of wine, and overturn the cart and spoil the wine, an action lieth against A. So where a carter's servant runs his cart over a boy, action lies against the master for the damage done by this negligence: and so it is if a smith's man pricks a horse in shoeing, the master is liable. For whoever employs another, is answerable for him, and undertakes for his care to all that make use of him.

As well we find the notion clearly articulated in the Code Napoleon, article 1384.[11]

A person is responsible not only for the injury which is caused by his own act, but also for that which is caused by the act of persons for whom he is bound to answer, or by things which he has under his care. . . . Masters and contractors, for the damages caused by their servants and employees in the functions for which they have employed them;

To avoid vicarious liability under the law of agency, a purported tort feasor must show that the agent in the principal-agent relationship is an independent contractor rather than a servant. If this can be shown then vicarious liability may not apply. If we distinguish between the notion of a "generalized agent" and "specific agent" in the law of contracts,[12] then we have a similar situation whereby we hold principals responsible for the promises of their generalized agents, but not their specific ones. Unfortunately, for agency theorists recommending this way of talking, almost all employment relationships could be said to be generalized and to be principal-agent rather than principal-independent contractor. So it looks as if the doctrine of vicarious liability applies full scale.

Additionally, there has been a recent move by some legal scholars to claim the law of torts is the only one that matters. Contracts are to be reduced to torts, since the major legal question is one of who pays, not what was promised. Such a utilitarian reduction proposed by McNeil and others fits nicely into the agency model, for the question becomes one of finding the most efficient mechanism for accomplishing a particular economic activity, bypassing abstract and tedious issues of consideration.[13]

There is a great deal of irony with this line of argument, for the traditions of the notion of agency are steeped in the language of morality from the fourteenth century to modern times. It is only in the period of the last twenty years that a small group of so-called "social scientists" have attempted to abstract the notion from these traditions and present it as a scientific and value-free way of understanding economic activity.[14]

The essays in this volume seek to correct the misconception that agency theory and ethics have little in common. We intend to begin

a conversation that enriches this powerful analytical tool for understanding economic activity with the traditions of moral philosophy,
and in doing so, begin the return of the agency notion to its roots,
wrestling with the difficult issues of moral responsibility.[15]

We have assembled this book of original essays for three audi-
ences. The first is practicing managers who are interested in how to
better understand the moral dilemmas that they face. Undoubtedly
some of the language is technical and there is some jargon, but we
have tried to be as clear as possible about the practical implications
of the connections of agency theory and ethics. Second, we hope to
reach a wide audience of faculty in the world's colleges of business
and departments of economics who are already familiar and comfortable with agency theory, but who may be extremely uncomfort-
able with ethics and the connection to agency theory. Finally, we
believe that moral philosophers and other ethicists will gain immensely by understanding how social scientists like economists can
develop such powerful models as agency theory, and by seeing what
ethicists have to offer in the conversations that these models engen-
der.

WHAT AGENCY THEORY AND ETHICS
CAN LEARN FROM ONE ANOTHER

Agency theory can easily become a path into the forest of theoretical
economics. After all, the free will literature refers to agency theorists, the notion of promising (contract making) is central to normative ethical theory, and deontologists are certainly comfortable with
a view that takes obligations or duties to others as its essential concept. However, upon setting out on the path, the ethical theorist
becomes disoriented and anxious. Agency theorists provide no familiar landmarks and actually seem indifferent or hostile to ethics.
Instead of a familiar path into the forest of economics, the business
ethicist may believe that he or she is the fly about to be devoured by
a Venus's-flytrap.

The first two chapters in this book help us to understand how
agency theory can be seen as both a familiar path and a Venus's-
flytrap for business ethicists. Both Gregory Dees and Richard De-
George spell out the central assumptions of agency theory, show its
relevance to ethicists, and demonstrate that ethicists have something
important to contribute to agency theory.

Both Dees and DeGeorge find much to admire in agency theory
as it has developed. Dees argues that the agency theorist's commitment to efficiency should remind ethicists that the implementation
of ethical ideals takes place in a world where people have imperfect

knowledge and where implementation has costs. Agency theory can even provide models for implementing an ethical ideal. DeGeorge is impressed with the descriptive power of agency theory. Agency theory has something important to say about incentives and sanctions and about decision-making in conditions of uncertainty and asymmetry of information. However, both Dees and DeGeorge insist that agency theory has normative implications when it is used as a framework for decision making.

Dees asks, "Is there some risk that this tool [agency theory] will lead to decisions that run counter to, or threaten to undermine, ethical values?" Dees thinks the answer is yes because agency theory is vulnerable to abuse and inappropriate application. One of the dangers in the use of agency theory in decision making is that it contains four major biases. Dees cites the fact that agency theory (1) treats obligations as one-way—agent to principal; (2) encourages excessive distrust and disrespect for agents; (3) ignores important issues of fairness; and (4) limits solution possibilities so as to exclude ethical norms.

DeGeorge points out that ethical norms are overriding and that any agency relationship is subject to moral scrutiny. For example, no agent is ethically permitted to do what the principal is morally forbidden to do. Agents cannot escape moral blame for an immoral act by claiming that they were merely acting on behalf of the principal. Neither can a principal escape responsibility for the actions of an agent when the agent is acting on the principal's behalf. Hence the agency relationship does not define the moral relationship but rather takes place within a moral milieu.

This point is important because in the standard economic literature the ideal agency relationship is always evaluated in terms of what would be most efficient. But, as DeGeorge points out, efficiency is only one value and it is seldom the overriding or primary value when an ethical decision is to be made. Suppose that polygraph tests were determined to be an efficient monitoring device to keep employees honest. Other values, e.g., privacy rights, might preclude the use of such tests even if they were the most efficient monitoring device.

Finally, DeGeorge insists that the economist's assumption that both the principal and the agent are self-interestedly motivated be subjected to analysis. DeGeorge agrees that in the abstract self-interest is ethically neutral, but it does not follow that principals and agents always act in their self-interest. Whether a person should pursue self-interest in a given case is a matter for ethical analysis.

Dees also is concerned about the self-interested assumption of agency theory. Dees points out that attributing all human behavior to self-interest is adopting a worst cast scenario: A person will always put her own interests ahead of the interest of others whenever she can get away with it. If people act on that assumption, trust is undermined and the worst case scenario could become self-fulfilling. Whether or not agency theory requires such a worst case scenario as an assumption will be the focus of our attention in Section Four.

HOW GOOD A THEORY IS AGENCY THEORY?

Those approaching agency theory for the first time might think that "agency theory" really represents one relatively simple theory. Barry Mitnick reminds us that if we speak of "agency theory" we must remember that contemporary agency theory has at least three different ancestors—the theory of the firm, decision theory, and sociological and organizational theory. The point of this analysis is to show that failure to appreciate the importance of all three theoretic ancestors contributes to the impoverished discussion of much contemporary work on agency theory. This is particularly true, Mitnick argues, with agency approaches in organization theory.

Mitnick's first target is the economics-based approach to agency. He rightly criticizes the notion that a sufficient test for a good theory is predictability. Predictability does not provide explanation. Mitnick indicates that he can predict that it is morning when his daughter comes into the bedroom to watch early morning cartoons. But surely the daughter "theory" is no theory at all. The arrival of his daughter does not *explain* the fact that it is morning. Philosophers of science who criticize Friedman's approach point out that a scientific theory must provide a causal explanation. Apparently Mitnick wants agency theory to be a full-blown mature theory. If so, it must do more than simply predict. He notes with approval that Fama and Jensen "attempt to explain the appearance of the corporate form with a controlling board of directors separate from management."

However, when contemporary agency theorists take explanation seriously, their scope of explanation is too limited. Even if Mitnick's daughter theory could explain morning, the theory would be of no use in cases where there is no early-rising child. On a more practical note Mitnick criticizes those who treat agency problems as simply problems of X, insurance for example. In addition, the economic approach focuses exclusively on individuals when it should focus on organizations as well. Mitnick wants agency theory to be a widely encompassing theory.

If the dangers of the economics-based approach are to be avoided and if agency theory is to become a theory in the full-blown sense, where should we look for assistance? Mitnick has several suggestions in this regard, but his overall approach is truly interdisciplinary. He recommends the literature in human judgment theory; the sociological literature on norms; the organizational, social control, and authority relations literature; exchange theory; transaction costs; incentive system literature; the sociological literature on networking; the studies on boundary-spanning and inter-organizational relations; the literature on compliance and implementation; and finally the law of agency.

Ordinary scholars understandably turn pale when faced with Mitnick's challenge. The task appears Herculean. To what end should it be undertaken? Mitnick argues that agency theory should apply to all relations that are "analytically concerned with acting for and control." Agency theory should *explain* those relationships and serve as a higher order theory for derived theories. Mitnick also insists that it should bridge the gap between theory and application. In terms of the philosophy of science, Mitnick does not want agency theory to be a purely formal exercise. He wants it to apply to the world, which means that agency theory should both entail observation statements and predict.

Whereas Barry Mitnick criticized the economic model of agency theory on the grounds that the model was defective as an acceptable theory, others criticize the model on normative grounds. This line of analysis is taken up in the paper by Lisa Newton.

Newton claims that agency theory rests on a very traditional and now morally discredited conception of the corporation: The purpose of the agents of the corporation is to pursue profits for the stockholders (principals). Newton views that conception of the corporation as morally discredited because corporations organized so that corporate agents pursue only the interests of the stockholders (1) violates the rights of the agents to be treated as full persons rather than as a means for achieving the interests of the stockholders, (2) infringes the right of the community to have all institutions serve the overall common good, and (3) abridges the right of the environment to have its resources conserved and its ecosystems protected from damage. Since the underlying conception of the corporation is morally flawed, the agency theory derived from it is similarly flawed. When you apply agency theory to individual actors within the corporation you overlook certain essential facts about a corporation— facts that have a moral significance. Relationships among individuals in the corporate world are better described as ones of cooperative mutual dependence. Such individuals function as a team. To look at these individuals as simply agents of the stockholders is to miss some essential facts about the behavior of such individuals. Moreover, if one insists on agency theory, why not expand the number of principals to cover all the stakeholders (groups whose existence is necessary to the survival of the firm).

IS EGOISM A NECESSARY ASSUMPTION
OF AGENCY THEORY?

A common criticism of agency theory that is present in the analyses by Dees, DeGeorge, and Newton is the egoistic assumption of agency theory—an assumption found in orthodox economic theory. Psychological egoism is a theory that says that every person *always* acts so as to achieve her own perceived best interest. Psychological egoism makes a factual claim about human behavior. Ethicists insist that if one takes the moral point of view one must be prepared to allow the interests of others to override one's own interest. If psychological egoism is true, advocating the moral point of view is pointless. Gary Miller opens the third section of the book by tracing out the implications of an assumption of psychological egoism in economics. The main implication is that under traditional economic theory ethics has no place. First of all, ethics tries to tell economic actors to do what in fact economics says economic actors don't do—namely to act in a way contrary to their perceived best interest. If the ethicist succeeds, she causes endless trouble for the economists. As Miller says, "If ethics were successful in getting economic actors to follow ethical rules at whatever cost, then it would require the abandonment of the discipline of economics as we know it. Neoclassical economists have invested a great deal of human capital that ethics is in some sense putting at risk."

Is psychological egoism true? Philosophers are virtually unanimous in their view that psychological egoism is factually incorrect. At first glance it seems that in some cases psychological egoism is clearly false. A mother rushes to save her child despite great danger to herself. An employee blows the whistle on an employer to protect the public and is fired as a result. Don't these examples undercut psychological egoism? No, the psychological egoist responds. Both the mother and the whistle-blower would have had great pangs of guilt if they had acted otherwise. In popular parlance, they couldn't have lived with themselves. This response has some plausibility, particularly in the case of the mother. It's not unreasonable to think that a mother wouldn't be able to live with herself if she didn't try to rescue her child, regardless of the magnitude of the danger to her. But what about the man who initially survived a plane crash in the Potomac River but consistently handed the rope to other passengers until he drowned? The other passengers were strangers, and he had a wife and children of his own. How was his act in his perceived best interest? No matter how altruistic the example, the psychological egoist will usually postulate some deeper motive (even an unconscious motive) of self-interest. At this point many philosophers think the psychological egoist is defeated. What looked like an empirical theory about human behavior now looks like a matter of faith. The psychological egoist will let nothing count against the theory, and hence has no empirical theory at all. After all, a scientist will submit a theory to testing and will give up the theory if the tests continually go against it.

Of course, the psychological egoist might contend that since both conventional self-interested actions and so-called "altruistic" actions are actions of the agent, that shows that all actions are self-interested. But now the psychological egoist is using "self-interest" in an ambiguous way. At first, "self-interest" meant acting exclusively on behalf of one's own self-interest. Now "self-interest" has been redefined to mean acting on any interest one has. But of course the main question still remains. Are there two different kinds of human motives? Do we sometimes have an interest in acting for ourselves and sometimes on behalf of others, or do we simply act for ourselves? We often do act in terms of our own self-interest, and often our interests and the interests of other coincide, but philosophy and psychology have yet to establish that we never act contrary to our perceived self-interest.

Another possible move for the economist is to give up the descriptive assumption of psychological egoism in favor of the normative assumption of ethical egoism. Rather than assuming that people *do* act in their perceived best interest, the economist would argue that people *ought* to act in their perceived best interest.

Miller's paper provides the underlying analysis for identifying two basic objections to this move. The first is metaphysical. It is generally assumed that you can only make moral judgments about a person's actions if she is responsible for those actions. That's why we usually don't morally blame people for getting sick. On the economists' model the competitive market is a deterministic mechanism that leaves no room for individual moral choice. Miller takes as his example worker safety.

> The individuals involved respond to incentives in ways that they must respond, disciplined by market competition. If a particular employee doesn't want to work at a dangerous job, even with the risk premium on wage, then he can quit. By definition, there are other potential employees willing to take over at that equilibrium wage level. If a manager doesn't want to supervise employees who are taking this risk, then she too can quit. The competitive labor market becomes a selection device by which risk-acceptant employees are sorted into high risk jobs (like skyscraper construction) paying a risk premium and risk-averse employees are sorted into low-risk, low salary jobs.

From the worker safety case and other similar examples Miller argues that the competitive market is a deterministic machine. In actuality that picture of the market is at best oversimplified. Even in the traditional analysis, the economic agent is free to leave a situation where the economic agent is asked to do something she believes to be morally inappropriate. A person can quit her job or refuse a perceived unfair offer.

But given the high costs quitting one's job entails, if quitting is a free act, making a tough anti-competitive moral choice is often a free act as well. The one seems no more coerced than the other. Thus the first argument *against* trading a normative ethical egoist postulate for a descriptive psychological egoist assumption fails.

But there is a better argument. Miller shows that on game-theoretic grounds, ethical egoism is self-defeating. If one recommends acting in one's perceived best interest, then others will respond appropriately, and no one including the ethical egoist will achieve her self interest. Consider a non-cooperative repeatable game where there are two equally feasible outcomes:

1. B announces her intention to be trustworthy as long as A trusts her and lives up to the trust. A should trust B as long as she behaves in a trustworthy manner.
2. B intends to honor A's trust two out of three times, and to abuse it once every three, as long as A continues to trust B. But if ever A chooses not to trust B, then B will abuse A's trust forever more, every time B gets the opportunity.

A's best response is to trust B and take his lumps every third round, because that is still better than taking the short-run alternative of just not trusting B. However, you can't get the requisite trust with an ethical egoist's "I will be trustworthy two-thirds of the time." You can't build a *reputation* for trustworthiness from that basis, and you get the highest payoffs when you have a reputation for trust.

In principal-agent relationships, you might need less in the way of monitoring devices if you have an established relation of trust. If the principal can be reasonably sure the agent won't take advantage of her when he could do so, there will be less need for monitoring devices and hence more "profit" for both the agent and the principal. Of course this assumes, contrary to traditional economic analysis, that the agent will not take advantage of each situation where he could gain at the expense of the principal. In economic terms, for the higher payoffs to eventuate the principal must assume the agent will not defect.

The totally self-interested assumption also receives explicit treatment in the article by Koford and Penno. As they indicate the severity of the mathematical model is extreme; it requires that the two situations, one that slightly enhances one's own good at a heavy cost to others and one that slightly decreases one's own good to the great benefit of others, a purely self-interested person would choose the former.

Koford and Penno argue that the assumption of self-interested behavior should be relaxed on the grounds of descriptive accuracy. Rather than assume that people are self-interested in the economic sense, they consider two other assumptions: (1) some people are ethical and others are not, and (2) any individual will be ethical in some situations and not in others.

Consider the first alternative assumption. As the proportion of ethical agents increases, the necessity and hence the cost for internal control systems decreases. That seems rather obvious.

Koford and Penno then consider corporations that desire to select for either purely self-interested or ethical agents. You might wonder why any corporation would want to screen out ethical agents. Consider a trucking firm that wants employees to violate federal regulations or a multinational firm that needs employees to bribe local officials. Hence we cannot assume that all corporations want ethical employees.

A complicating factor that Koford and Penno ignore is the following: Firms like those described above often forget that they pay a high price for selecting out ethical employees. Since by definition these employees are purely self-interested, they will take advantage of their boss and the company as quickly as they will take advantage of the government. Hence these companies will need to spend the maximum amount on internal controls. It might be cheaper for these companies to follow the rules than to screen out the ethical employees.

But assume most firms want ethical employees. Since even in a world where most people are ethical, the unethical clearly gain, what incentive can a corporation use to attract ethical employees? Koford and Penno suggest that we look at the utility function of ethical agents to see their preferences. Since they get pleasure from ethical actions, you can assume that they value social settings in which there is a high level of trust and responsibility—they enjoy being in a Kantian kingdom of ends or in a society characterized by a sense of justice. This information provides management with a number of incentives to attract ethical agents—for example, the existence of honor codes and a supportive corporate culture. Most important for traditional agency theory, these incentives would include the absence of detailed internal control mechanisms.

Koford and Penno then consider the other alternative—that all individuals are ethical in some situations but not in others. Why should agents be ethical in some situations but not in others? Citing the work of Radner, they argue that when the difference between ethical behavior and unethical behavior is sufficiently small, persons will make themselves worse off in the short-run but better off in the long-run. Koford and Penno then consider how accounting systems might encourage ethical decisions by agents.

Whereas Koford and Penno argue that agency theorists should give up the purely egoistic assumption, Ron Duska suggests that the traditional egoistic definition of business be changed. Duska defines an agency relationship as a "two-party relationship in which one party (the agent) is authorized to act on behalf of and under the control of the other party (the principal)." An efficient agency relationship is one where the agent carries out the *actual* wishes of the principal in the most effective manner. How does the principal ensure that result? He introduces monitoring and policing devices, although these devices are costly. How much should the principal spend? Certainly not more than he would lose if the agent cheated. But what should he assume about the agent's propensity to cheat? On the economic model agency theorists use the standard economic assumption that all persons are purely self-interested and will maximize their own self-interest at the expense of others when they can get away with it. It is this egoistic assumption that Duska finds normatively self-defeating.

First, Duska cites with approval the economist Eric Noreen, who points out that if you assume that agents are not purely self-interested you can spend less on policing and monitoring costs. Ideally, the principal would like to be assured that she has totally loyal agents. What reason would an agent have to be totally loyal?

Part of the answer depends on what the agent believes the motivation of the principal to be. If the motives of the principal are totally self-interested, as the economic model assumes, then the agent has no reason to be loyal to the principal. He should sacrifice the interest of the principal whenever he can get away with it because that is what the principal would do to him. Hence, if the principal is to develop loyalty and hence cut policing and monitoring costs, she must act contrary (or at least convince the agent that she would act contrary) to the egoistic assumption.

Moreover, the agent must be convinced that the business firm or corporation won't simply be a purely self-interested profit-making institution. Otherwise, as American managers are finding out, there would be no reason for employees to be loyal to it. Agents (employees) would only support the firm if it were in their self-interest. Monitoring and policing devices have as their point ensuring that it is in the self-interest of the agent to look after the interests of the principal. But, as American industry is discovering, the costs of such devices are high.

Is there an alternative? Duska argues that what is needed is a non-egoistic theory of business. And agency theory, ironically, provides that non-egoistic theory. In Duska's view, business becomes a cooperative relationship where all agents work toward the principal's interest of providing a good or service. However, note that the principal's interest is no longer profit but the provision of goods and services. Profit is merely a means for the system to bring that about. Profit is not an end in itself. From this point of view the manager is not simply an agent to the stockholders to increase their profits but primarily an agent of the public to provide goods and services. Duska argues that managers would then become professionals. Business would become a service.

The issues discussed in these papers are not mere academic exercises. If the psychological egoist assumption is dropped, or better, modified, there are major implications for professional business education. That issue occupies Wanda A. Wallace. Wallace begins her analysis by asking whether the denial of egoism would require a wholesale change in how accountants and economists view their disciplines. Contrary to some other contributors in this volume, she denies that any wholesale changes need take place. Wallace argues that standard utility theory can accommodate both egoistic motivation and altruistic motivation. Some people prefer to donate to charity; some don't. Both preferences can be understood by and present no theoretical difficulties for revealed preference theory. Wallace also argues that egoistic behavior (self-interest) is not inconsistent with the public interest. Specifically echoing Eric Noreen and philosopher Kurt Baier, Wallace recounts cases from decision theory (prisoner's dilemma situations), finance, and even tipping behavior where ethical behavior pays.

The relation of ethical behavior and self-interest goes back in the Western tradition to Plato. Plato argued that ethical conduct is always in the best interest of the individual. Ethical behavior pays. You might think you would be better being a tyrant, but Plato tried to argue that the tyrant's life is in fact a miserable one. Taking his argument to its logical conclusion, Plato argued that since ethical behavior always pays, the only reason people behave unethically is due to ignorance.

Wallace does not go as far as Plato in this regard, but she seems to think that there is considerable overlap between self-interest and altruistic behavior. She would certainly agree with the consensus of contemporary philosophers that ethical behavior does pay for society as a whole. Ethical and legal norms are devices that human beings have discovered to enable human beings with frequently competing interests to engage in cooperative behavior. An analysis of the standard prisoner's dilemma shows the utility of cooperation.

However, there is a gap between what is good for the individual and what is good for society. Undoubtedly, ethics does pay for society. But the very best world for any individual is a world where everyone else behaves morally except her. However, that is true of every individual. The problem for society is this: How can society capture the benefits of ethical compliance when each individual is tempted to cheat so that she can free-ride off the benefits of the ethical conduct of others? From this perspective society considered collectively and individuals within society can be considered as in a principal-agent relationship.

The implications of this for business education seem to be the following: It is a mistake to assume that people always behave in a way that maximizes their self-interest. People as a matter of fact behave in ways that diminish what they could achieve for themselves. However, it is also a mistake to assume that people will always act ethically because ethical behavior pays for society as a whole. How does society monitor and constrain behavior so that individuals will cooperate for the greater good (including in most cases their own) and not attempt to free-ride off the moral behavior of others? Wallace correctly sees that this question is unabashedly normative. In the remainder of her paper, she argues that agency theory provides an opportunity and a responsibility for raising these ethical issues in the business curriculum. She also provides some pedagogical tools for bringing that about.

CAN AGENCY THEORY HELP EXPLAIN A CONFLICT OF INTEREST?

The introductory papers in this volume by Dees and DeGeorge correctly point out that ethical theorists have much to learn from agency theory. Two philosophers, John Boatright and Bill Lawson, have attempted to use agency theory to shed light on the concept of a conflict of interest. Although Boatright finds the economic vision of agency theory unhelpful, he does think that agency theory as understood in the law can be of use in understanding the essential nature of a conflict of interest. (We are reminded again of Mitnick's assertion that agency theory is not one theory but several theories.) In the final paper, Bill Lawson uses the example of court-appointed credit committees in bankruptcy cases to show how even the legal conception of agent-principal relationships cannot fully elucidate the concept of a conflict of interest.

In his analysis John Boatright argues that agency theory can be of use to ethicists by providing a model that helps us to better understand some of the moral rules persons follow in business relationships. Specifically, Boatright argues that agency theory will enable us to better understand the notion of a conflict of interest in business.

Philosophers have found it extremely difficult to give an analysis of "conflict of interest" that isn't too broad. Boatright is well acquainted with that difficulty and argues that what is central in a conflict-of-interest situation is that the person with the conflict be under an obligation to act in the interest of another. Hence, "a conflict of interest occurs when a personal interest interferes with a person acting so as to promote the interest of another when that person has an obligation to act in that other person's interest." This definition coincides with the kind of conflict agents face. Indeed, the existence of such conflicts gives rise to what is commonly called the agency problem. Agents frequently have interests that conflict with the interests of the principal the agent is obligated to serve.

How will identifying conflicts of interest with the agency problem help provide an adequately narrow definition of a conflict of interest? First, Boatright points out that agents are not morally culpable when situations over which they have no control prevent them from pursuing the interest of their principals. Thus, accountants who face obligations to both reveal and not reveal confidential information about a client are not in a conflict of interest situation, contrary to the usual terminology.

Boatright's definition also helps explain why "abuse of position" is a conflict of interest. As an illustration, Boatright cites a Xerox policy statement that prevents an employee from using his position to benefit himself. For example Xerox would forbid an employee from sending new Xerox employees to his wife's real estate firm. Surely allowing the Xerox employee to do that would not hurt Xerox and if the real estate firm provided good services, the new Xerox employees and Xerox itself could benefit. So harming the interest of the principal is not the issue. Failing to serve the principal exclusively is the issue as Boatright sees it. A more common example of abuse of position is insider trading. Since using inside information for personal gain need not harm the principal, what's wrong with it? What's wrong is that an agency position is used for personal gain.

Boatright also argues that the injunction not to be involved if a conflict of interest continues after a person ceases being an agent. He cites Section 1.9 of the American Bar Association's *Model Rules of Professional Conduct* that protects former clients from a lawyer's divulging of confidential information. Although Boatright's conclusion is a plausible one, whether agency theory can help here depends on whether you are talking about agency theory in law or agency theory in economics.

In economics there is no assumption that the agent's obligations end once the relationship ends. However, in the law of agency, one obligation—the obligation to keep confidential information confidential—continues. Section 395 of the Restatement of Agency says not to use or to communicate information confidentially given him by the principal or acquired by him during the course of or on account of his agency . . . to the injury of the principal, on his own account or on behalf of another . . . unless the information is a matter of general knowledge.

Boatright cites the furor that erupted when Robert H. Mosley, president of American Express, allegedly used information obtained when he was a director on the McGraw-Hill Board to assist in American Express's attempted takeover of McGraw Hill. Mosley's behavior seems obviously wrong even though he was no longer on the McGraw-Hill Board when he gave American Express the information. Perhaps the legal analysis of agents is more satisfactory as a model than the economic analysis.

Finally, the agency analysis in law captures the concept of loyalty, which seems relevant in conflict-of-interest situations. In the law of agency, the duty of loyalty is explicitly proscribed. The problem with a conflict of interest is that it undermines loyalty. Abuse of position is wrong because it is disloyal. Again, Boatright shows how the agency theory in law is richer than the agency theory in economics. The presumption in economics is that the agent will be disloyal where disloyalty means putting his own interest ahead of the principal's interest. The law assumes that people can be loyal and enjoins them not to give in to the temptation to be disloyal in this sense. Boatright's analysis provides another reason why agency theory and egoism should be separated. Agency theory without egoism is a better theory.

Suppose we conclude from Boatright's discussion that the legal understanding of agency, but not the economist's understanding of agency, helps us define the concept of a conflict of interest. In his paper, Bill Lawson provides a case where the legal understanding of agency theory fails to encompass a conflict-of-interest case. The situation Lawson describes is a court-appointed creditor committee, one of whose members is at the same time an employee of one of the businesses affected by the bankruptcy proceeding. The creditors' committee is supposed to represent the best interests of the creditors. By statue the committee consists of creditors who have a fiduciary obligation to act for the best interests of its constituents and not for themselves. Often one of the creditors is a corporation that sends its credit manager to represent it. The credit manager is a legal agent of both the corporation and the body of creditors. And on at least three occasions, Lawson argues, the interests of the body of creditors conflicts with the interests of the committee member's corporation: (1) The debtor has been a bad client over and above the inability to make payments on time; (2) the debtor is a competitor; (3) the accounting department has determined that the company would get a better return—although other creditors may not fare as well—if the debtor's company were liquidated. Since the credit manager is a dual agent, what ought she to do? The legal theory of agency is of no help here.

The actual operation of creditor committees makes this dual role even more explicit. Each committee member votes twice. In the first instance she is supposed to represent her company. But how would such a dual voting system eliminate the conflict of interest? You might face a situation where you must work on a plan that is supposed to be for the good of all creditors, knowing full well at a later time you will vote against it.

Lawson's discussion brings us full circle. We began our discussion by pointing out the normative aspects of agency theory. Most agency theorists, despite the denials, make moral claims. Moreover, these moral claims are open to challenge. The egoistic assumption has been especially open to criticism. An adequate theory of agency needs assistance from ethical theory. What Boatright and Lawson have shown is that DeGeorge was correct when he said, ". . . agency is only a part, and a relatively small part of ethics and ethical theory."

NOTES

1. Friedman (1962; 1970; 1985). The bibliography at the end of this volume collects together all of the relevant references for the entire volume. Text and footnotes will use the encapsulated form, viz., Friedman (1962), and the bibliography will contain the complete reference.

2. Pratt and Zeckhauser (1985).

3. Donald McCloskey has been instrumental in arguing that the texts of economics are no different in kind from literary texts. See McCloskey (1986; 1990).

4. There is surprisingly little literature on the problem of one agent with multiple principals. Arrow's paper in Pratt and Zeckhauser (1985) is suggestive. One interesting line of thought is to see managers as the agents of multiple principles. See Aoki (1984) and Evan and Freeman (1988).

5. Mitnick's paper in this volume as well as Mitnick (1974) gives a more thorough account of the history of agency theory. Even though his work was done at the same institution and at roughly the same time as Ross, Mitnick is rarely given any credit for the development of modern agency theory.

6. See Moe (1984).

7. Conard, Knauss, and Siegel (1987), p. 3.

8. Ferson (1954), p. 13.

9. American Law Institute (1958).

10. Quoted in Conard, Knauss, and Siegel (1987), pp. 65-66.

11. Quoted in Conard, Knauss, and Siegel (1987), p. 77.

12. Means (1962).

13. McNeil (1980).

14. Again McCloskey (1990) is instructive.

15. For more on the notion of intellectual life as conversation see Mc-Closkey (1986; 1990) and Rorty (1989).

I

WHAT AGENCY THEORY AND ETHICS CAN LEARN FROM ONE ANOTHER

2

Principals, Agents, and Ethics

J. Gregory Dees

The discipline of economics has come to play an increasingly influential role in the way decision makers in public and private organizations define and resolve issues. Corporate strategists rely on analytic frameworks drawn from the economics of industrial organization and from game theory. Project managers and financial analysts lean heavily on discounted cashflow analysis to evaluate investment and financing decisions. Public policy analysts turn to cost-benefit analysis to support specific regulatory or legislative positions. Even judges are beginning to appeal more explicitly to notions of economic efficiency in their decisions.

Behind this growing influence lies a system of thinking that emphasizes notions such as scarcity of resources, distinctive competence, rational self-interest, and allocative efficiency. Efforts are made to give these concepts and the theories built around them precise specifications and, where possible, mathematical structure. Despite differences on specific issues, economists exhibit a remarkable amount of agreement on general theories and methods. Alone among the social sciences economics offers a systematic approach and analytic rigor that resembles the natural sciences. It is no surprise that decision makers faced with untidy issues appreciate the way economic approaches provide an order and logic for problem solving.

Until recently, however, economists had little to offer on what might be called "sub-micro" level issues, e.g., internal organization, management systems, and contracting arrangements. The growth of transaction cost economics, principal-agent analysis, and related extensions of game theory promises to change that. The economics of organization is emerging as an important new field of study.

In this volume our focus is on one of these recent developments in the economics of organization, the use of principal-agent models. These models offer insight into the complications of contracting for services, whether it is a firm contracting for labor from employees, or a patient contracting for medical services from a doctor. The models highlight potential information and incentive problems and, thereby, serve to guide decisions about monitoring behavior, evaluating performance, and structuring compensation.[1] Though work in this area is relatively new, talk of principals and agents is already becoming widespread in schools of management, law, and public policy.

What business is this of ethicists? Despite historical attempts to separate the two,[2] social science of any sort is inevitably intertwined with ethics. Social life has ethical dimensions. We expect others to conform to certain norms and share certain values. Common life would not be possible without some minimal level of ethics, and it would not be so attractive without shared values that go beyond these minima. To put it in an overly simple way, we want to promote such things as honesty, trustworthiness, fairness, justice, a sense of public duty, respect for the autonomy of others, and avoidance of gratuitous harm. The widespread use of a social science framework becomes the business of ethicists if there is some risk that this framework will lead to decisions that run counter to, or threaten to undermine, ethical values.

Does the use of principal-agent models pose such a risk? This chapter sets out to provide a defensible answer to that question.[3] It may be viewed as an essay on product safety, in which the product is principal-agent analysis. It asks economists working in this area and decision-makers who may use this analysis to step back and reflect on the limits and risks of abuse associated with this form of analysis. It poses the question whether use of the principal-agent approach might lead to ethically objectionable attitudes, policies, or behaviors. Its purpose is not to lay blame, but to identify potential problems and to foster constructive efforts for improved use of this method of analysis.

A case will be made that principal-agent analysis, in its current popularized form, does pose such a risk. This is not because the theoreticians developing the method have been unreflective about the limits of their work. Some are clearly sensitive to the concerns that I will raise, even though they may not label the concerns as ethical.[4] The problem is that principal-agent analysis is vulnerable to abuse and inappropriate application. It appears relevant to a wide range of transactions and relationships; its basic structure is relatively simple; and its deductive methodology gives the appearance of yielding highly scientific conclusions. For all these reasons it is tempting for decision makers to use it uncritically as a basis for policy decisions, overlooking its limits and biases.

Because its central finding has a negative tone, this chapter runs the risk of being viewed as simply another round in the academic blood sport of competitive discipline-bashing. I hope it will be understood that this is not what I have in mind. The objective here is to promote a constructive dialogue between disciplines. Though I express my ethical concerns as forcefully as I know how, this is done against a backdrop of respect for the intellectual effort that has gone into developing and refining principal-agent analysis, and with appreciation for the usefulness of this analysis when it is thoughtfully applied. I will not argue that the risk outweighs the benefit of continuing to do work in this area, but only that the risk is real and that with some effort (on the part of theorists, decision makers, and friendly critics) it can be kept to a minimum. I also believe that ethicists can learn something from principal-agent analysis and I will say something on this score as well.

HOW DOES PRINCIPAL-AGENT ANALYSIS WORK?

Principal-agent analysis is a diverse and rapidly developing field.[5] The field is commonly referred to as "agency theory," but I have resisted this label because I believe it is misleading. At this point in its development, the field exhibits less coherence and consistency than the designation "theory" connotes. It is more accurate to describe it as a modeling approach within which there are some common structures and assumptions but also wide variations.

All principal-agent models deal with contractual arrangements between two (or more) individuals.[6] One, the principal, wishes to purchase a service from the other, the agent. If terms are agreed upon, the agent will provide the service and the principal will compensate the agent. The principal's problem is to decide on the optimal way to compensate the agent. It is generally assumed in these models that the principal can dictate the terms of the contract, subject only to the constraint that the compensation offered must equal or exceed the agent's reservation utility, which is typically determined by the agent's next best known alternative. The value of the reservation utility is simply stipulated in the model. Agents will not accept contracts with expected values below the stipulated reservation utility. The principal's goal is to develop a compensation scheme that attracts a capable agent, and that most efficiently motivates the agent to do her best to deliver the level of service desired.

Economists working on this problem point out that this compensation decision becomes a non-trivial exercise when certain complicating, but common, conditions hold. These conditions are goal incongruity, uncertainty, information asymmetry, and agent risk aversion. *Goal incongruity* in principal-agent models refers to the fact that the agent's preferences regarding the performance of the service (in the absence of contract-based incentives) do not match the principal's preferences. The agent is not sufficiently motivated by the satisfaction of a job well done. She must be induced to provide the type and level of service the principal desires. *Uncertainty* in this instance refers to the fact that the observable outcome of the agent's work is not a perfect measure of the input. The observable outcome is a product of the agent's skill and effort, combined with factors beyond the agent's control. For instance, a business manager's financial performance may be affected by the general business climate, and a builder's success in completing a project on schedule may be affected by the weather. *Information asymmetry* refers to the fact that the agent has better information about her abilities, preferences, and level of effort than does the principal. As a result, the principal cannot easily identify the best suited agents, and cannot easily link compensation to agent input. This asymmetry can only be reduced by the principal's engaging in costly investigation, monitoring, or audit activities. *Risk aversion* on the part of the agent simply means that the agent prefers not to have her compensation vary, particularly if the variance is affected by factors not fully under her control. Accordingly, the agent would resist having her compensation simply be a function of the observable outcomes of her efforts.

These conditions create potential incentive problems and make it difficult to devise an efficient and effective contract. Some possible contractual arrangements create incentives for underperformance on the part of the agent, and some are likely to attract a poorly qualified agent. This first problem is typically referred to as *moral hazard;* the second is referred to as *adverse selection.* Principal-agent models are designed to help principals find their best contracting terms. The objective is to optimize the payoff to the principal, considering all the constraints that have been mentioned. This modeling approach has two aspects that make it particularly useful. First, it is amenable to rigorous analysis. By structuring the problem as an optimization problem for the principal, rather than as a two-person bargain with each party attempting to optimize her own outcome, it is more likely that analysts can find a definitive solution. By adopting simplifying assumptions, the mathematics are made more manageable. Second, the principal-agent structure appears to exist to some degree in a wide range of transactions, contracts, and relationships. Examples mentioned in the literature include (principal first) shareholders and managers, employers and employees, patients and doctors, citizens and public servants, creditors and debtors, customers and service firms, and so on. A case can be made that there is an element of the principal's problem in every exchange relationship in which the exchange is not perfectly simultaneous. The first party to deliver her goods must rely on the second party to keep her part of the bargain. For a time, the second party acts as the first party's agent.

Even though principal-agent models share this common structure, specific models vary along several dimensions. Some variations are due to the fact that different situations require different assumptions. Others are due to the advancing state of the art, and represent attempts to extend, refine, and improve upon models previously developed. Still others are a function of the modeler's preferences, technical skill, creativity, and judgment. Some models are static, looking only at short-term, one-shot contracts; others are dynamic, considering many periods and long-term relationships. Some include only a single agent; others include multiple agents whose independent outputs might be compared; still others include teams of agents who work together to produce a joint output. Some include monitoring; some do not. Some are purely descriptive or conceptual; some are intended to be prescriptive.

Assumptions made about the specific preferences of the principal and the agent can also vary from model to model. The common structure does not dictate these details. Nonetheless, certain assumptions have gained wide use. One is that the principal's single objective is to maximize her return, as determined by the utility of the service provided less the compensation paid to the agent, with no other internally imposed constraints. Another is that the agent has a negative utility for effort,[7] a positive utility for money, and no other relevant preferences. In some cases, it is assumed the agent is opportunistic. Opportunism is defined as "self-interest seeking with guile."[8]

Work in the field of principal-agent models varies in one other regard. It seems to fall roughly into two academic camps. One camp is highly technical, quantitative, deductively rigorous, and abstract. The other camp is more informal, qualitative, and applied. Work in the former camp is usually presented in a much more cautious, qualified way, and is typically performed by mathematical economists. Work in the latter is often more loosely argued, and, at the same time, more ambitious in its attempt to influence policy decisions. It is this latter work that is more likely to create the problems raised in this paper.

It should also be noted that principal-agent models have been criticized for a number of reasons that are independent of any ethical questions. The models are rarely tested empirically. The few empirical tests that have been conducted have had mixed results. The conclusions from specific agency models tend to be highly sensitive to the assumptions made. The contracts proposed are typically not very robust. To complicate matters more, the assumptions are not always intuitively plausible. The models are, of necessity, highly stylized. This raises questions about how sound it is to generalize the conclusions, since much potentially relevant contextual complexity has been left out. The confidence that is placed in this modeling approach, as Frank Easterbrook points out, "depends almost entirely on the power of deductive logic."[9] Finally, the models are very narrow in their scope, in that they typically do not account for possible externalities, nor do they include explicit consideration of the markets in which these contracting relationships may be taking place. Theoreticians working in this area are aware of these problems and are attempting to better define and remedy them, but they should be acknowledged from the start of our discussion.

Though the basic concepts behind principal-agent analysis were explored as early as 1921 by Frank Knight,[10] extensive work in this area did not get under way until the early 1970s with the publication of Alchian and Demsetz's now classic paper on the theory of the firm.[11] This is not yet a mature method of analysis. Nonetheless, it is being promoted widely, outside the safe confines of economic research circles, in professional schools and in publications aimed at institutional decision makers, as a potentially valuable guide for policymaking.

WHAT ARE THE ETHICAL RISKS?

Principal-agent analysis is best thought of as a heuristic device. It provides a way to simplify a complex problem (i.e., identifying the best contract for the provision of services) in order to make it more analytically tractable. Such simplification can provide a fresh perspective and important insights. However, as Wimsatt points out,[12] heuristics have some natural risks associated with them. In particular, they transform the complex problem at hand into a "nonequivalent, but intuitively related problem." This transformation may lead to errors if the user of the heuristic loses sight of the differences. Heuristics also tend to have systematic biases. The errors they cause tend to follow a pattern. To borrow a term from cognitive psychologists, heuristics can have "framing effects." By casting the complex issues in simpler terms, they may obscure some important aspects of the problem and lead to a restricted class of solutions.

All heuristics carry these risks, but nonetheless we use them. Often they are cost-effective and relatively accurate. They provide a valuable starting point for attacking complex problems. Yet, in the excitement associated with the development of a new heuristic, such as principal-agent analysis, there is a risk that some who are eager to put the heuristic to work will forget the limits and potential biases.

The case that I want to make regarding principal-agent analysis is that it has framing effects that could blind less cautious users to important ethical dimensions of contractual arrangements. I do not mean to imply that these effects are somehow intended by those who develop the models. It is true that some who promote the use of these models may do so with a specific ideological agenda. However, I am confident that much of the important work on principal-agent models is being done by social scientists who have no particular axe to grind.

What Question Does a Principal-Agent Model Answer?

Concerns about the limits and abuses of principal-agent models may be put into perspective by considering what sort of questions principal-agent models are best suited to answer. Suppose we are considering potential contractual arrangements between service buyer A and service supplier B. Questions arise at three levels:

Level 1. *Individual Preferences*
> What sort of contract would best serve A's interest, if she could dictate the terms?
> What sort of contract would best serve B's interest, if she could dictate the terms?

Level 2. *Likely Joint Solution*
> What sort of contract (if any) is likely to result from bargaining between A and B?

Level 3. *Ethical or Social Preferences*
> What sort of contractual arrangements would be best, from an ethical and social point of view?
> How can we get both parties to accept and honor these socially desirable arrangements?

While principal-agent analysis may provide some useful information at each of these levels, it is most relevant to Level 1 and goes only a short way to answering the Level 3 questions. One danger is that users of this analysis may get confused about just what sort of question they are answering. At any level, principal-agent models may blind us to relevant ethical dimensions of the contracting problem.

Principal-agent analysis is useful at the first level, but only if it is sensible to describe at least one of the parties as a principal and the other as an agent. If A is the principal and B the agent, the analysis provides advice to A regarding her most desirable contract. (If there is some ambiguity about which party is best modeled as the principal, separate models could be developed to answer this egocentric question for each party.) However, the advice provided by A's principal-agent model is only sound if the contracting situation is reasonably well represented by the assumptions of the model. A static model may yield poor advice when a long term relationship is involved. A single-agent model may yield poor advice when multiple agents are present. A model that leaves out of consideration the resentment and morale effects of intensive monitoring may provide poor advice on when and what to monitor. A model that exaggerates B's tendencies toward opportunism may lead to unnecessary and expensive protective measures. Including the ethical commitments and values of both A and B may be crucial even at this stage. The difficulty is that adding all potentially relevant considerations may make the model so complicated that the mathematics would be intractable, in which case this approach loses one of its main attractions, its rigor.

A principal-agent model based on common assumptions, as outlined in the previous section, does not answer, *ex ante*, the Level 2 question about the shape of the actual contract between A and B, unless either of two situations hold.[13] One situation is when A and B have corresponding individual ideals, both of them recognize this, and there are no obstacles to fruitful bargaining. This promises to be relatively rare. A and B will not have the same ideal contracts if there is a surplus to be divided. In that case, A's ideal solution will give A the bulk of the surplus, with B receiving just a minimal amount over her next best alternative. B's ideal will be the mirror image. The actual contract that A and B strike will depend on how the two bargain over the surplus. This will be a function of bargaining strength (skill and resources) and, quite possibly, normative values, such as a desire for a fair agreement. What is fair or appropriate in the eyes of the two parties could be shaped by a sense of having reached a point of equal bargaining resistance,[14] by preconceptions about property rights and priority of claims, or by some simple focal point, such as even division. Even if A and B have the same ideal contracts, in a world of imperfect information (particularly regarding the preferences of others), they may not recognize this. In this case, they may engage in negotiation tactics (deception, delay, posturing, etc.) that frustrate the achievement of this joint ideal. Accordingly, this first path from the model to an *ex ante* prediction of the actual agreement is a narrow one.

The second situation in which a principal-agent model might be a good indicator of the likely joint solution occurs when the party modeled as the principal has the ability to dictate the terms. In this case, the agent is willing to settle for any contract that beats her next best alternative, as stipulated in the model. Either no surplus is at stake, or she does not recognize the surplus, or she is willing to concede it to the designated principal. The causes could be the agent's ignorance, the agent's desperation, preconceptions about the rights of the principal, or simply recognition of the principal's superior bargaining position.[15] To show that a given contracting negotiation fits these conditions requires some argument beyond the principal-agent analysis itself. In many cases of actual contract negotiations, the individual most logically identified as the principal is in a weak bargaining position. Often the principal either has to take the price set by the agent, or has to negotiate some compromise on her ideal contract. Think of the last time you hired a contractor, a doctor, a lawyer, or a lawn service.

In predicting the shape of actual agreements, it is often necessary to supplement the principal-agent model with additional information about the two parties and their social context. Other theories may be helpful in determining what forces will shape the actual agreement. For instance, Akerlof highlights the potential influence of social customs, such as a "fair" wage,[16] and along similar lines DiMaggio and Powell argue that there are social tendencies toward isomorphism in institutional structures.[17] These factors may well constrain the contractors. No doubt a number of factors play a role in determining the shape of an actual agreement. Quite possibly many of them could be captured in the structure of a principal-agent model by adjusting the agent's reservation utility, but this is typically not done.

For prescriptive purposes, we ultimately want to know the answers to the Level 3 questions. We want to know what sort of contractual arrangements would be best, considering the contract from a social perspective. Desirable contracts should respect rights, promote social welfare, and support (or, at least, not undermine) our shared values about the kind of society we want to maintain. We also want to know how individuals might best be led to the socially preferred arrangements. The actual contract that is struck between two parties may satisfy one relevant condition, namely that at the time of its acceptance it was viewed as mutually advantageous by the parties to it. Yet the agreement may have been the result of deception, desperation, or misconceptions about rights and obligations. Even if we could correct for all this, the contract may still fall short of the ethical or social ideal. It could have undesirable effects on third parties or society as a whole. It could lead to an objectionable distribution of benefits or burdens. It may conflict with other important social values. At least in current Western culture, we are unwilling to accept contracts for indentured servitude. We tend to object to lopsided contracts that may be dictated by a monopolist (or monopsonist). We frown on contracts between Mafia bosses and their hit men. Principal-agent analysis does not speak directly to these issues. It is not designed to. Yet users of this analysis may lose sight of the gap.[18]

One reason that may be offered for ignoring the ethical dimensions of contracting is that such considerations are not amenable to rigorous analytic treatment. While it is true that ethical concepts are often sloppily used, and that no consensus theory of social ethics has yet emerged, the field is not barren. One potential source of insight is the literature surrounding contract law; another is recent work in ethical and social philosophy. Relevant contract law literature covers topics such as duress, unconscionability, voluntary consent, implicit promises, moral limits on promissory obligation, and distributive justice.[19] The most relevant ethical and social philosophy is likely to be found in work on justice and in recent theories related to rational choice and social welfare.[20] This is not the place to defend any one specific theoretical approach to the ethics of contracting. The point is simply that anyone attempting to answer the Level 3 questions must explicitly or implicitly adopt a view on the ethics of contracting. Explicit treatment of the ethical and social issues, guided by recent work in this area, is to be preferred to an implicit casual inference from principal-agent models to social or organizational policies.

We do not need to invoke any controversial ethical concepts to support the point that the principal-agent method of analysis alone cannot answer level 3 questions. We merely need to note that an agent may have multiple principals, each with conflicting interests. For instance, a manager in a publicly held service firm (e.g., a law, accounting, or consulting firm), has at least two principals to consider, the shareholders of the firm and the customers to whom she sells her services. Some would argue that she has other principals (or quasi-principals), such as the bankers who have loaned her firm money, the employees to whom she has promised a safe working environment, and even the governing bodies of the professional association whose designation (CPA, Member of the Bar, etc.) she uses. This is not to mention other relationships (such as familial or community commitments) that officially exist outside of her professional role, but that clearly affect the quantity and quality of effort she can spend satisfying her professional agency obligations. By focusing our attention on only one agency relationship at a time, principal-agent models obscure the fact that other relationships exist and the demands of each must be balanced on a social level. It may be that some invisible hand guarantees this balance, but this has yet to be demonstrated. Such a demonstration is not likely to be a trivial matter.

As a heuristic, principal-agent analysis often transforms the more complex Level 2 and 3 questions into more tractable Level 1 questions. In doing so, it shifts our attention from problems of predicting complex social behavior and developing social policy to a problem of egocentric strategy. Because of the power of the models and because of the way in which the models frame the question to be answered as well as the means for answering it, less sophisticated users might easily lose sight of the fact that the models alone do not get us far beyond Level 1. More work is needed to provide credible answers to the higher level questions. That work should be guided by an understanding of the specific limits and biases inherent in current principal-agent models. It is to those biases that we now turn.

Potentially Harmful Framing Effects

According to my thesis, framing a problem as a principal-agent problem, particularly when using the common assumptions about the preferences of principals and agents, increases the chance of mistakes with regard to the ethical dimensions of contracting. Specifically, I see four major biases that might result from unqualified reliance on this kind of analysis. Model users may tend to:

1. Ignore the principal's obligations to the agent,
2. Develop excessive distrust and disrespect for agents,
3. Overlook ethical constraints, such as fairness, and
4. Miss solution possibilities that include ethical norms.

Each of these effects can lead to descriptive, as well as prescriptive deficiencies.

1. The Principal's Obligations. Principal-agent models focus on the principal's problem, from the principal's point of view. The principal's interests drive the model and determine the shape of the contract that results. The contract must protect the principal from the agent's opportunism. Yet it may fail to adequately protect the agent from the principal's opportunism. This can be a serious problem for prescriptive uses of principal-agent analysis.[21]

Most models neglect the fact that the principal typically enjoys information and resource advantages over the agent. Overall, there seems to be a tendency to ignore the possibility of what Gregory Dow[22] (in a similar critique of transaction cost economics) has called "downward opportunism." As a result, when these models are used prescriptively, they recommend organizational and contractual arrangements that favor and protect the principal, without making a reciprocal effort to protect the agent. Perrow makes the case for reciprocity. He comments that a theory of the firm based on a principal-agent model,

> almost exclusively emphasizes shirking by subordinates (agents) as the only form of egoistic, self-interested behavior that must be guarded against. The possibility that the capitalist (principal) might lie to workers about profit levels or threats of lost business, falsify the records of their outputs, endanger agents' health, all to extract more profit, or simply shirk her

responsibilities is ignored or swept aside by mentioning that a firm will
protect its reputation.[23]

He goes on to argue that reputation is often a weak and ineffective
reason for a principal to curtail abuse. One might add that it seems
odd that the model builders would consider reputation a sufficient
check on abuses by the principal, but not a sufficient check on the
agent. In many cases, for instance when the agent is in a visible position or has a long history in a community, reputational information
may be more readily available on the agent than it is on the principal. The effectiveness of reputation as a check on either the principal or the agent certainly varies from context to context. What is
needed is a careful analysis of reputation asymmetries, rather than
facile generalizations.

A normative bias in favor of the principal is reflected in the language used to introduce and describe this method of analysis. The
very words "principal" and "agent" suggest a strong one-way obligation, the obligation of the agent to work in the principal's interest.
Roberts's teaching note on this subject indicates how the models are
introduced to students at one leading business school. He defines the
notion of an agency relationship by saying that "it refers to a situation where one or more individuals, the agents, are *subordinate to and
supposed to act on behalf of one or more others,* the principals."[24] Roberts
makes no mention of what the principal is *supposed* to do. In a lec-
ture on the general topic of organizations, Arrow talks about the
principal's problem as the difficulty of insuring against the agent's
"failure to do his business *properly.*"[25] Like "supposed," "properly"
has a normative connotation. No parallel concern is expressed about
the principal doing his business *properly.* When agents expend low
levels of effort, they are described as "shirking." This expression
connotes an evasion of duty, not surprisingly labeled a problem of
moral hazard. The agent is violating an obligation to the principal.
No corresponding moral problem is described with regard to the
principal.

The most plausible explanation for this bias rests with the vulnerability of the principal.[26] Because of the information asymmetry and
goal incongruity inherent in the principal-agent relationship, the
principal is especially vulnerable to exploitation by the agent. The
agent may promise one thing and deliver another. This vulnerability
of a principal to an agent makes it reasonable to emphasize the agent's
obligations to the principal. It provides a justification for the principal's seeking a contract that provides reasonable safeguards against
exploitation. This argument parallels Williamson's argument[27] about
the special obligations of corporate management to shareholders. He
argues that because shareholders do not have the same contracting

opportunities as other corporate constituencies (e.g., customers, suppliers, employees, and managers), shareholders are particularly vulnerable to management opportunism. Consequently, they deserve favored treatment.

The argument has some basic moral appeal. The problem with this line of reasoning, however, is that, as Perrow has pointed out, agents are often vulnerable to principals as well. In many cases, it seems only to be a matter of social convention that determines which party is defined as the principal. In those cases, it might make sense to create two different models, alternating which party is treated as principal. For instance, the traditional principal-agent model of the firm could be reversed, treating the employer as the agent of her employees, providing them with several services: accurate reports of their work, safe working conditions, capital to support their efforts, and compensation in the future for work today. This would be a fascinating exercise and, no doubt, a complicated one. To my knowledge, it has been done only in very limited ways.[28]

In any case, it is important to make a distinction between protecting the principal from exploitation by the agent, on the one hand, and maximizing the principal's return, on the other. The two may be the same, but only in circumstances in which perfectly competitive markets require it. Otherwise, one can accept protection against exploitation as a legitimate constraint in the contracting process, without embracing the extreme position of giving the principal's interests unique consideration. Admittedly, this bias is not a problem if we are discussing the principal's individual ideal (Level 1 in the previous section), but it becomes a problem when the analysis is extended beyond that level.

2. Distrust and Disrespect for Agents. Many applications of principal-agent analysis depict agents in a negative light, as individuals who prefer shirking to working, whose promises cannot be trusted, and who will misrepresent information if it is to their benefit. In the extreme, one could easily get the impression that agents are amoral opportunists, out to take advantage of the principal if they can get away with it. While this makes the contracting problem more interesting, it may have some objectionable consequences.

Though this negative depiction of agents is quite common in informal discussions of agency models, it is only fair to note that it is not an essential feature. All that is essential to create a principal-agent scenario is some form of goal incongruity between the two parties. Goal incongruity does not entail that anyone is lazy, greedy, amoral, or opportunistic. Even two altruists can have incongruent goals. One may place her highest priority on saving the whales, and the other may prefer to feed the poor. If the whale-saver wishes to hire the poor-feeder to represent her at the International Altruists Congress, she will face a problem similar to the principal's problem in the classic case. The reason that so few models are built around benevolent or altruistic individuals is probably a function of the historical orientation of economics toward characterizations of human nature as essentially self-interested.

The general weaknesses and limits to the traditional characterizations of rational self-interest have been adequately discussed elsewhere.[29] In any case, the danger here is more specific. It is the danger that students and policymakers may be so impressed with the deductive logic of the common agency models that they uncritically accept the assumptions as accurate, treating people as scheming opportunists, even when such treatment is unjusified. This can lead to contracting and monitoring strategies that are more costly than they need to be and, more importantly, are offensive to the "agents" involved. The intangible costs of excessive monitoring and control are typically neglected by the models. Policies and practices may become unnecessarily coercive and invasive. One major risk is that following the prescriptions of principal-agent models will directly undermine whatever trust might normally exist between two parties in a contracting context. This may be fine when trust is truly unwarranted, but that is not always so. In the worst case, these pessimistic assumptions about human nature could become self-fulfilling.

One might respond that surely intelligent individuals can make assumptions for the sake of conceptual analysis without losing sight of the fact that the assumptions are contrary to fact. Though I know of no direct evidence that individuals exposed to principal-agent models take these assumptions to heart, related studies indicate that concern is justified. Certain social psychology experiments demonstrate that how concepts are introduced in an academic setting can have a significant influence on their use later on. For instance, Langer, Bashner, and Chanowitz show that the way students are introduced to the issue of people with handicaps affects their attitudes towards such people.[30] Promoting more discriminating, creative thinking in the classroom about what handicapped individuals can do tends to reduce prejudice later on. Higgins and McCann show how an academic exercise of writing a description of a person or a group to fit the biases of one's audience can affect one's later impressions of that group.[31] Finally, Kahneman, Knetsch, and Thaler show that business students are more likely than psychologists to make one-sided offers in an ultimatum bargaining game.[32] These experiments occurred in specialized contexts and we must be careful in drawing inferences from them. Yet they make it reasonable to hypothesize that if students in professional schools are not encouraged to think and write *critically* about the assumptions of the principal-agent models, their attitudes and behaviors towards "agents" could be negatively affected.

One might try to minimize this sort of ethical objection by pointing out that as long as she does not engage in force or fraud, the principal is acting within her rights in insisting on a self-protective contract that guards against possible misconduct by the agent. If the agent is offended, she can refuse the contract.

Granted the principal is not violating a specific right of the agent by treating the agent with suspicion. But this misses the point. Even though she is acting within her rights, the principal may be behaving irresponsibly. Her actions may be wasteful of valuable resources (which must be diverted to developing complex contracts and monitoring compliance), and they may contribute to the erosion of the bond of trust that holds a community or an organization together. The ultimate fear is that, if a sufficient number of individual service buyers and governing bodies (public and private) adopt this pessimistic attitude, we could end up with either an offensively controlling environment or economic and social decline. One has images of Montegrano in Banfield's classic study of a backward and distressed Italian community. Banfield concluded that a major factor determining the backwardness of this society was an attitude of "amoral familism" which he defined as acting according to the following rule: "Maximize the material, short-run advantage of the nuclear family; assume that all others do likewise."[33] Banfield's study is certainly open to debate, and principal-agent analysis does not necessarily lead to the same short-term focus. Still there seems to be a legitimate basis for concern.

A defender of principal-agent analysis might argue that its assumptions are sufficiently close to the truth in a wide range of circumstances. Ethicists should not be so naive as to think that everyone keeps their promises, enjoys hard work for its own sake, and is fully trustworthy. A little reflection will provide most of us with sufficient evidence to recognize these idealistic standards as out of step with reality. When did you last use the company or university photocopy machine or the telephone for personal use without offering to compensate your employer? We all yield to temptation now and then. Few of us always provide our best effort. Contracting arrangements and the structures recommended by principal-agent models help agents avoid temptation.

This view is supported by a recent experiment conducted by Baiman and Lewis.[34] Using a principal-agent framework, Baiman and Lewis tested the power of financial incentives to induce misrepresentation. Though they found that their subjects showed some resistance to lying, this resistance (in the context of an experimental exercise) could be easily overcome for a relatively small financial gain.

The Baiman and Lewis experiment is not conclusive on this matter, however. It shows only that in some contexts individuals will
behave dishonestly. Other experiments and our common knowledge
reveal a significant level of honesty and good faith. For instance,
Bohm, in a simulated market test of a television show, found that
subjects apparently gave honest responses about how much they would
be willing to pay for the program, despite incentives to understate
the amount, and Hornstein, et al., found that some 40 percent of
the wallets that they intentionally lost in New York City were re-
turned intact.[35] It would be a mistake to conclude from Baiman and
Lewis that people will be dishonest in all contexts. More work needs
to be done on the extent and limits of such behavior. We need to
know more about settings that are conducive to opportunism, about
types of opportunistic behavior that seem to be the easiest to induce,
and about the sorts of individuals most likely to engage in opportunistic behavior. We need to know the same things about honorable
or trustworthy behavior. Some individual tendencies may be cultur-
ally influenced. It would also be interesting to see whether treating
individuals as if they are likely to cheat will promote more cheating.
It might be the case that people are weak and do cheat, but also that
this behavior would be exacerbated if people are treated as un-
trustworthy. Again more research is called for.

No doubt, in some circumstances, concerns about opportunism are
justified. This is true when the potential cost of opportunism by agents
is great (e.g., with workers in a casino), or when the principal has
reason to believe that the agents are not trustworthy (e.g., when there
is a history of corruption). In such cases, it may be quite reasonable
to engage in self-protection, to suspend trust. Klitgaard uses a very
basic form of principal-agent analysis to diagnose corruption in certain developing countries and to evaluate plans of response.[36] This
exercise does not seem offensive at all. Trust is not called for and
would be unwise in situations involving known corruption. The same
may be true for some arms-length one-shot market transactions.
However, one would hope that these circumstances are the exception rather than the rule. This presents another area for further
research.

A defender of principal-agent analysis might argue that the stark
assumptions of the standard model are justified as "conservative."
But conservative assumptions can be inappropriate and even dangerous. Nichols and Zeckhauser make an analogous point in their
criticism of risk assessment in health and safety regulation.[37] They
propose a realistic expected-value approach to risk assessment to re-
place the plausible-upper-bound approach that is not commonly used.
A realistic (expected behavior) approach to agents may not be as
easy to model, but the limits of an oversimple and skewed approach

need to be factored in. There is nothing wrong with presenting the standard model as a "worst case" scenario, as long as it is clearly labeled as such. Otherwise, the assumptions used in the model could lead to an objectionable bias.

3. Fairness and the Ethical Dimensions of Contracting. As was argued in the earlier discussion of "Level 3" questions, principal-agent models are mute regarding some important ethical dimensions of contracting. As a result, users of these models may be tempted to overlook ethical considerations. Such considerations reintroduce unwanted complications into the decision making process. They may be seen as blocking the path from principal-agent analysis to a conclusion or policy recommendation. Yet omitting an explicit treatment of ethics can lead to descriptive inaccuracies and unacceptable prescriptions.

Many of the ethical questions that can be raised about contractual relationships fall under the general heading of "fairness," and are based on a common concern to limit the extent to which a stronger party might gain at the expense of a weaker party. This is not the place for an extensive analysis of fairness in contracting. However, it may be helpful to outline some of the issues associated with fairness in contracting, as an indication of the extent and complexity of the terrain.

Questions about the fairness of a contractual relationship can be raised in four areas: the process used to reach agreement, the terms of the agreement, the way in which it is implemented, and the outcomes it creates. Fairness in the contracting process is concerned with placing limits on the methods by which one party can gain the agreement of the other. Prohibitions and limitations on the use of such tactics as deception, coercion, manipulation, and exploitation express these limits. These prohibitions are captured by the notions of fraud, duress, and unconscionability in the contract law. With regard to principals and agents, for instance, the question of exploitation may arise when an agent is facing only very unattractive alternatives, and is willing to accept an otherwise unappealing contract.

Fairness with regard to the terms of the contract has at least three elements. In general, the terms should not unduly favor one side; they should be consistent with the terms offered to other parties in similar circumstances; and they should respect the rights of both parties. The first of these was at issue in the above discussion of the principal's obligations to the agent. A contract that does not provide equal protection from opportunism may be unfair. The second element, consistency across contracts, requires that a principal treat agents performing the same service in basically the same way. Differences in treatment need some justification. The third element is aimed at protecting whatever rights each of the parties has, such as rights to certain types of information, to privacy, to due process, to protection from physical harm, and the like. If workers have a right to information about risks in their working environments, the contract should establish a reliable means for the provision of that information. One test that might be helpful in determining fair terms in a contract is to put the principal and agent behind a Rawlsian veil of ignorance. A fair contract is the one that would be created if neither party knows whether she would be the principal or the agent.

Fairness with regard to implementation has to do with good faith and reasonable exercise of discretion *ex post*. It is unfair to break one's agreement without a sound ethical reason. This requirement is complicated by the fact that often some elements of a contract are implicit. One party may be given discretion in interpreting the implicit conditions and in handling unanticipated conditions. (This is an essential feature of hierarchical contracts.) Fairness requires that the party given the discretion exercise it in a way that would have been acceptable *ex ante* to the other party. For instance, a unilateral decision on the part of a principal to institute a mandatory retirement policy for already-employed agents may be unfair.

Fairness with regard to outcomes has to do with the distribution of benefits and burdens affected by the contract. In particular, there is a question about how the surplus is divided and a question about effects on third parties. The concern about distributive justice becomes more pressing when there is a significant disparity in relative wealth positions and bargaining power of the parties. Contracts that enhance that disparity may be objectionable on ethical grounds. The standard principal-agent models, with their bias in favor of the principal, may yield an unfair distribution of benefits and burdens if the standard assumptions are not modified to reflect this concern.

A well developed theory of contractual fairness would provide a specific set of constraints on contractual advantage-taking. It is only fair to note that ethicists and lawyers who have written on this topic exhibit wide differences of opinion with regard to the stringency of fairness requirements in market transactions. At one extreme, libertarian thinkers argue that a contracting process free of fraud and force is sufficient to ensure a fair agreement. Distributive justice concerns are best dealt with *ex post,* through taxation and redistribution (if at all). At the other extreme, Marxists see almost any contract between labor and capital as unfairly exploitative. They would prefer to build distributive justice into the contracting relationship. All sorts of positions have been staked out in between these two extremes. No consensus has developed. The point is only that concern about fairness is legitimate and that questions about exploitation, consistency, rights, relative advantage, and distributional consequences deserve explicit treatment in policy decisions. From the fact that these matters are complex and controversial it does not follow that they should be ignored.

In fact, ignoring concerns about fairness and other ethical constraints on contracting is likely to lead to descriptive inaccuracies. In addition to concern for their own welfare, individuals often have commitments.[38] Some of these commitments have to do with ethical values. These values may affect the contracts people are willing to accept. For instance, most people are committed to some notion of fairness and, in turn, wish to be treated fairly in their transactions with others. This sort of commitment is not explicitly addressed in standard principal-agent models.[39]

This omission can weaken the theory descriptively, because individuals may be willing to pass up a financially attractive opportunity because they view it as unfair. We have some empirical evidence to support this. Kahneman, Knetsch, and Thaler report on some experiments in which the subjects appeared to exhibit a commitment to fairness. In some of these experiments, subjects refused to accept payoffs that they perceived to be unfair, even though this meant sacrificing potential financial gain.[40] It is reasonable to suppose concerns about fairness will come into play in real world contracting settings, as well as in experimental games. In surveying executives about transfer pricing arrangements in large corporations, Eccles found that fairness was an important consideration, along with efficiency, in determining acceptable pricing schemes.[41] This data is modest, but when put alongside our common knowledge, it strongly suggests that principal-agent models that typically exclude preferences for fairness will prove to be descriptively inadequate.

Principal-agent models are also used prescriptively. How can a prescription regarding contractual arrangements not take into account the concerns of fairness? Fairness is one important criterion, along with efficiency, against which contractual arrangements should be measured. Some authors using principal-agent models, when faced with an ethical question, will appeal only to a crude form of utilitarian moral framework that can blind them and (more importantly) their readers to other moral dimensions of the problems they are analyzing.

An example of this occurs in Epstein's use of agency cost arguments to defend at-will employment, as opposed to good-faith employment. He makes some useful points about the costs of good-faith employment arrangements, but when he addresses the central concern about at-will employment, namely the problem of "wrongful" discharge, he presents the following argument in response to the concern.

When one employee is wrongfully discharged, another will typically be hired in his place, so that the personal hardship of one is offset by the benefits that are conferred upon another. The displaced employee may suffer serious emotional or reputational losses, but there are gains along both of these dimensions by the employee hired as a replacement. Thus employees *as a class* may be better off with a rule that facilitates mobility than with one that creates some form of contingent property right in individual employment.[42]

We might grudgingly live with the risk of unjust dismissal, if it could be shown that the social costs of enforcing justice in these matters are exceedingly high. However, Epstein's simple-minded trade-off argument carries no ethical weight. That someone else gets the job of the wronged individual in no way compensates for the offense that has been committed. This sort of argument illustrates the crudest form of utilitarianism.[43] It shows no sense that justice or fairness matter independently of some vague notion of total net utility. It misses the point of concern about wrongful dismissal and completely neglects the moral dimensions of employment relationships. This may be easy to do when speaking in generalities about some anonymous class of (opportunistic) individuals. It is harder to neglect the moral questions when the example is closer to home. For instance, one might wonder how Epstein would react to being unfairly dismissed from his job. Would his moral indignation subside once he heard that someone else (say, the Dean's nephew) was hired into his professorship? How principals use the discretion granted them in their contracts with agents is a legitimate subject for ethical evaluation. The prospect that employer policy or employment law might be influenced by this sort of naive utilitarian thinking is genuinely frightening.

It would be another example of crude reasoning to blame the principal-agent framework for Epstein's insensitivity to issues of fairness. This is one isolated instance. However, we have some indirect empirical support for the belief that exposure to economic frameworks in general may affect one's perceptions of fairness, or one's willingness to engage in unfair behavior. Marwell and Ames report that individuals trained in economics are more likely to engage in free-riding behavior than individuals who do not have such training.[44] This fits with the findings of Kahneman, Knetsch, and Thaler about business students versus psychologists, mentioned in the previous section. It is possible that the systematic exclusion of considerations of fairness in most economic models shapes the way individuals using these models think.

One possible line of defense for the models as they are constructed is to argue that the requirement that an agent's compensation must exceed her next best alternative adequately takes care of the fairness issue. According to this argument, a fair contract may, but need not, provide more than the next best alternative. The market determines fairness both in terms of sharing surplus and in terms of comparable treatment. The models at least guarantee this level of fairness. What happens to the surplus over and above this amount of compensation is not an ethical question. The principal should be free to capture all of it for herself, if she can.

This argument can be contested on two grounds. First, the next best alternative may not set a fair level of compensation. Whether it does or not depends upon a host of considerations, including whether the principal does have a property right to the surplus and whether the alternative available to the agent is a good proxy for the value of the work being done by the agent. The latter might be so when it is set by a large competitive labor market in exactly the same type of work. (Even then some, for instance proponents of comparable worth, might challenge the market's fairness.) When the next best alternative is not determined by a free and open competitive market, there is little reason to treat it as a benchmark of fairness. It is simply an opportunity cost with no ethical implications at all.[45]

Ignoring the concept of fairness affects agency models in other ways as well. For instance, one measure of justice is for the punishment to fit the crime. This may put a constraint on the ways in which principals can punish agents for underperformance. If that underperformance is especially hard to detect, an effective punishment might have to be quite severe to be effective, since the severity will be discounted by the low probability of detection. The efficient contract in such a case might involve punishments so extreme that they are morally unacceptable, such as cutting off a hand if embezzlement is detected. Hand-cutting (ignoring legal complications) could be relatively cheap for the employer and quite a powerful deterrent. However, most of us would find this punishment morally offensive, even if the agent would be willing to accept such terms.[46]

A defender would doubtless object that no agency models even consider corporal punishment as a viable alternative. Usually the only form of punishment discussed is low pay or dismissal. This raises an interesting question. Why not include corporal punishment, or confiscation of property, or forced confinement to quarters by private parties acting as principals? The answer cannot be because it is illegal. Principal-agent analysis is supposed to help us understand and, perhaps, reform the law. The modeler would presumably appeal to reputation effects and morale costs. Yet might there not be circumstances in which some form of extreme and objectionable punishment would be most efficient for the principal, all things considered? I suggest that the model builders do not usually include such options because of an implicit norm against doing so. If model builders are willing to exclude extreme punishment, it indicates that there is some concept of fairness implicit in current practice. This provides a starting point for a critical discussion of where to draw the line.

The point of this section is not to suggest that fairness should always be the final determining factor in contracting. In a discussion of budgeting and compensation in a non-profit organization, Oster points out that some compensation schemes that appear fair can lead to incentive problems.[47] She cites the example of tying department heads' compensation to the size of each department's budget. This may seem fair, but it provides an incentive for budget growth, even though this may not be desirable in every department. She illustrates how a simple principal-agent sort of analysis might help managers recognize and remedy these incentive problems. If the remedy is to be acceptable, however, it cannot lose sight of the manager's concerns for fairness. The optimal compensation scheme is one that provides the right incentives and is recognized as fair.

4. Limited Solution Possibilities. By ignoring the practical importance of ethical values for the participants, principal-agent models also miss out on a potentially important means of solving the principal's problem. The models tend to focus on monetary incentives, because of the way an agent's utility function is typically constructed. Arrow has suggested that ethics may be an important link in understanding how agents can be motivated to honor agreements with their principals when the proper contractual incentives cannot be economically arranged.[48] Internalized, socially reinforced ethical standards may be both an effective and efficient way to check potential opportunism on either side of the agreement. Aoki, in his cooperative analysis of management's role in a firm, likewise argues that some internalization of ethical standards is essential if external controls are to have any chance of success. With regard to inhibiting management opportunism, he says, "Various management-control mechanisms and the enforcement of legal rules governing the conduct of a powerful management tend to be ineffective unless the content of these controls and rules finds approval in the minds and feelings of the management affected thereby. The code of conduct shared by managers may be called the professional ethics of the management and internalization of such a code constitutes one of the most important aspects of the professional training of managers."[49]

Work such as Arrow's and Aoki's suggests that one element in the solution of the principal's problem may be the socialization of both principals and agents, so that they internalize appropriate standards of conduct. To some extent this is done already in child rearing and education. If it were not, contracting would be nearly hopeless.

Principal-agent analysis does not reflect the fact that individuals generally have internal constraints on their behavior and expectations about the behavior of others. It leads us away from socialization, ethics codes, and moral suasion as part of a comprehensive social response to the principal's problem. Instead, it focuses our attention on financial incentives, monitoring, and performance evaluation. Nonpecuniary incentives are typically included in principal-agent analysis only to define the problem. For instance, an agent's preference for leisure is cited to reinforce the risk of shirking. Little attention is paid to the satisfaction that an agent can get from a job well done, or the guilt that an agent might feel for dishonest behavior.

To consider motivation only in terms of monetary incentives may miss important elements and lead to bad policies. Lepper and Greene highlight the possible dysfunctional aspects of reward-based motivation systems when they report on the use of rewards to encourage artistic activity on the part of young children.[50] Children who were taught to draw in order to receive rewards were less likely to engage in the drawing later when no rewards were offered, than were children who were not given external rewards in the first place. Also, work produced by the group initially motivated by external rewards was judged to be less complex and less creative when compared to work of the children who were apparently intrinsically motivated. Again, we must be careful about the inferences that we draw from a specific experimental situation, but this suggests that a narrow focus on external incentives may in fact lead to lower quality of work produced by agents, in addition to blinding us to other possible sources of motivation such as values and norms.

I have tried to make a case that the use of principal-agent analysis has associated risks. Alone it cannot answer the central ethical or social questions about contracting. Even its major virtues, its simplicity and rigor, present certain hazards, because they may draw attention away from important ethical dimensions of the contracting problem and to potential solutions.

WHAT CAN BE DONE?

One way to approach this part of the paper would be to use the subject of what to do as an example of principal-agent analysis in action. The decision makers who ultimately benefit from this development would be defined as the principals and the producers of principal-agent models as the agents. We could then make some assumptions about the utility functions of these agents. How far can they be trusted? Will they shirk? Should they be monitored? How can quality of output be judged? Should agents receive some form of incentive pay to work on problems of pressing practical interest or to address the ethical issues associated with their analysis? Attempts to formalize this problem would provide a useful illustration of the complications involved in using a formal model to solve a real world service delivery problem. However, I choose to eschew this formidable task and instead propose a simple three-pronged strategy that is informed by some of the principal-agent concepts and by plain common sense. Corrective action can be taken on three fronts: by decision makers who may use the models, by academic model builders, and by critics. All must take some responsibility.

Opportunities for Self-Protection

Decision makers who turn to economics for help with problem definition and resolution must take some responsibility for assessing the quality of the help they get. It is irresponsible to use analytic models uncritically. When complex normative issues are at stake, the decision maker must exercise judgment. "The model made me do it" is no excuse. To this end, decision makers should be precise about what question it is they want to answer. If this question differs from the question that the model answers, the decision makers should determine what else is needed to answer the original question and add this to the information provided by the model. It would be appropriate to ask the following questions: What factors beyond the principal's interests should be considered? Are there other "principals" involved? Do the assumptions reasonably approximate the character of the agents? What are the risks of following the model's recommendations? Is there an issue of fairness to be considered? Are there other avenues for resolving the contracting problem that should be explored?

The major difficulty in relying on self-protection is that users are often at a disadvantage with regard to technical aspects of principal-agent models. On many matters they must defer to the expertise of the model builders: Should the model be dynamic rather than static? Should it include multiple agents or a single agent? Has there been recent empirical or theoretical work that should be taken into account? How well does the model capture the economically relevant features of the situation? These questions require some technical expertise. In this instance *caveat emptor* is not the best approach. The situation in some ways parallels that of the medical profession, as Arrow described it.[51] Decision makers must be able to rely on the technical expertise of economists much as patients rely on doctors. This suggests that some code of conduct might help the economists who develop and promote these models.

Voluntary Responses by Producers

Economists are the ones best positioned to equip policy makers to be critical consumers of economic analysis. They should not rest content with teaching a basic level of competence, but also help their clients (students and decision makers) to carefully evaluate whether a principal-agent model is an appropriate tool for analysis, what sort of model would best capture the relevant features of the situation, and what the limits of the model are. They should help their clients develop a critical level of unthinking when it comes to using the analysis. As far as the ethical considerations outlined above are concerned, developers of principal-agent analysis have two acceptable options.

The first is to grant the validity of the ethical concerns, but to suggest that it is not the business of an economist to directly address ethical issues. Rather the policymakers who use economic analysis should see to it that the appropriate values are reflected in the policy process and that any biases and limits of the models are dealt with sensibly. Economists are experts on efficiency and on determining equilibria. This is their distinctive competence. They have no business playing the role of amateur philosopher, moralist, or politician.

This line of response is reasonable, but it resolves the problem only if principal-agent model builders concentrate their work in areas where the concerns are less troublesome, and only if they disclose to policymakers the biases and limits of their models. It is most appropriate in situations in which (1) vulnerability to opportunism is essentially only one-way, (2) there is little legitimate basis for trust of the agents, (3) either fairness is not a major issue or the agent's next best alternative is a plausible guide to fair compensation, and (4) incentives, monitoring, and performance evaluation are likely to be the most effective avenues for resolving the problem. In any case, very serious qualifications must accompany any prescriptive analysis. Many serious researchers in this area, as a matter of course, explicitly note the technical limits of their analysis. Ethical limits and biases should also be noted.

The second option involves an attempt to correct the biases and resolve the concerns by refining and enriching principal-agent models. In some areas this work is already under way, though not always with an explicit ethical justification. Let us examine briefly the ways in which principal-agent models might be ethically improved.

More work should be done on the development of reciprocal principal-agent models to capture situations in which both sides are vulnerable to opportunism. Consideration of two-sided moral hazard no doubt adds mathematical complexity to the models, but, to the extent that this feature of real world relationships can be captured without making the models intractable, the results should prove quite interesting.

Offensive preference characterizations could be eliminated or changed. This has already been done with regard to shirking behavior on the part of agents. Holmstrom and Richart-Costa have constructed an alternative agency model of the firm that does not assume that the agents have a disutility for effort.[52] It explores other possible forms of goal incongruity. Other ideas about how to introduce an appropriate mixture of egoistic and other-regarding motives are to be found in Margolis, Etzioni, and Frank.[53] These authors have not produced formal principal-agent models in their work, but may indicate ways in which new models could be developed. This effort will no doubt have to be handled carefully if it is not to make the models either trivial, or too complex. Leibenstein's[54] work on organizational efficiency and hierarchy may also suggest ways of incorporating different behavioral assumptions. Of special interest is the way he handles some of the cultural differences between Japan and the U.S.

A different way to address the problem of offensive characterization is to make the determination of appropriate levels of trust endogenous to the model. Arrow[55] has stressed the importance of trust to any exchange relationship. No doubt some circumstances justify more trust than others. Those engaged in principal-agent analysis could draw on a growing literature on trust production to find ways to incorporate different levels of trust into their models.[56] This work will likely require dynamic models in order to show how trust might be built up or how it might break down. To some extent work on reputations and the evolution of cooperation is aimed in this direction.

Modelers could also explicitly introduce the notion of fairness into their analyses. This has been done in an informal way by Eccles[57] in his work on transfer pricing, and conceptually by Frank[58] in his discussion of other-regarding motives in the workplace and the role of passions in solving commitment problems. It could be done more formally by developing a specific theory of fairness that is appropriate to principal-agent relationships. Directions for such work may be suggested by Varian's[59] attempts to develop formal concepts of fairness and by Baumol's[60] recent work along the same lines. Another paper that suggests promising directions for further work is Maser and Coleman on three levels of rationality in negotiation.[61]

The argument against including ethical notions such as fairness in principal-agent models is twofold. First, the inclusion would make the models less parsimonious. This argument is not very appealing. A parsimonious and deductively rigorous model might be aesthetically pleasing, but if it is inaccurate descriptively and might lead to ethically unacceptable prescriptions, it is of little scientific or policy-making value. Aesthetics should not be the determining factor. The second defense is that the relevant ethical notions have not been well enough defined to be included in deductively precise models. This may be true, but it simply indicates the need for continued work in this area.

Another approach to some of the ethical concerns would be to alter the basic nature of the relationship between principal and agent from a competitive one to a more cooperative one. This approach is taken by Aoki.[62] He models the firm as a cooperative bargaining problem with management playing the role of a mediator between employees and shareholders. This model may have its own biases and problems, but it avoids many of the ethical concerns that have been raised about principal-agent analysis. Such a model can aim to protect both parties from exploitation while seeking an appropriate division of whatever surplus there may be. I believe that it merits further exploration.

There are countless other ways to modify principal-agent models to respond to the ethical concerns raised in this paper. I hope the avenues I have suggested are sufficient to stimulate the creative capacities of some of those working in this field. The result of this refinement and enrichment process will be an even more diverse range of models than we have now. Some will be so different from the original conception that it will be inaccurate to call them principal-agent models any more: "contracting models" may be a more accurate designation. An analyst could choose the model most suited to her needs. The choice would have to be openly defended as the most appropriate.

Value of Other Voices

Economists may be the ones best equipped to help decision makers avoid some of the risks associated with principal-agent analysis, but they face an incentive problem. Why should they make this extra effort to address ethical issues? Why should they undermine their power and influence by placing warnings on the labels of their models? Why should they take the risks associated with creative, experimental, and interdisciplinary work to address ethical questions? There is also a concern about distinctive competence. Many economists do not feel equipped to grapple with ethical problems beyond those related to notions of economic efficiency. Accordingly, informed critics outside of the discipline can serve a useful purpose. Such critics can address both economists and decision makers in raising concerns about the use of principal-agent models. In the best of all worlds, this criticism may stimulate collaborative work and joint problem solving. It should also keep decision makers on their toes. The challenge is to strike the right balance, to encourage the right amount of model and the right amount of more general ethical reasoning.

WHAT CAN ETHICISTS LEARN FROM ECONOMIC ANALYSIS?

If the dialogue between ethics and the social sciences is to be productive, it cannot simply be a one-way attempt to reform wayward social scientists. Ethicists are also generally reluctant to incorporate insights from other disciplines into their work. Even philosophers working in the field of "applied ethics" often seem to be happily ignorant of how the world works, in particular of how incentives, social institutions, culture, and individual psychology shape behavior. This is not the place to present a sustained argument about why this ignorance should be embarrassing. I will simply note that ethics (theoretical and applied) often makes assumptions about, and has implications regarding, human nature and human behavior in social settings. These assumptions and implications are especially crucial when ethicists attempt to move from theory to specific policy recommendations. It seems only sensible to test these assumptions and implications against the state-of-the-art findings and theories of the social sciences.

Economics provides one perspective on incentives and self-interested behavior. Though its assumptions may occasionally seem morally offensive, in a wide range of circumstances they are close enough to reality to provide some insight into human behavior and its consequences. At the very least, economic analysis can highlight the risks involved in certain policies and actions that otherwise seem ethically acceptable. In order to benefit from this perspective, one need not accept it uncritically nor adopt it as the only worthwhile method of analysis.

Several philosophers have drawn extensively on some methods and insights from economics in their work. Examples include Sen (1981) on poverty and famines, Gauthier (1984) on morality and market failure, Taylor (1987) on cooperation, Hollis (1987) on reason, and Coleman (1985) on the market paradigm. Economic perspectives have also had some influence on such major works as Rawls' *Theory of Justice* and Nozick's *Anarchy, State, and Utopia*. With the exception of Sen, however, most of this work is highly abstract. For some reason ethicists dealing with applied problems have not drawn on economics as effectively as they could.

Most directly, economics can help ethicists think through the consequences of alternative policies or courses of action. Very few ethicists, even those who reject utilitarianism on some level, would deny that consequences are relevant to ethical decisions. Is anyone harmed? Is anyone helped? How are benefits and burdens likely to be distributed? These are all important questions. Too often ethicists are tempted to posit the consequences based on their own common-sense, armchair assumptions about what will happen. Economic models can provide a more systematic way to answer these questions. For instance, charity in any form may seem like a good thing. It pleases the giver and benefits the recipient. However, economic analysis may raise serious questions about the consequences of certain forms of charity. It may harm the recipients by creating incentives for dependence rather than self-sufficiency. Economic analysis can raise considerations that need to be explored in any analysis of the ethics of charity. I am not suggesting that philosophers rely exclusively or uncritically on economic analysis in assessing risk and consequences, simply that they use it as one potentially eye-opening tool.

Specifically, principal-agent analysis can be helpful in this way. For instance, Frank Easterbrook[63] uses a principal-agent perspective to explore the consequences of insider trading. In the face of some who assert that insider trading ought to be allowed because it promotes market efficiency, Easterbrook constructs an argument, using principal-agent analysis, to raise potential concerns about the practice and to make the case that there is insufficient data to assess the economic consequences with any degree of confidence. Ethicists may wish to expand this discussion to include possible objections to the practice that are not captured simply by the consequences, but Easterbrook's analysis provides a useful starting point.

Economic analysis can also be used to help diagnose and remedy ethically objectionable practices. If applied ethics is to have a clear link to policy, it must address the issues of practical implementation. For instance, one might conclude from an ethical analysis that certain forms of bribery are wrong. To an ethicist this is an important result, but with this result a policymaker's work just begins. How can this kind of bribery be stopped? Principal-agent analysis may shed some light. Klitgaard uses just such an approach in his study of corruption in certain developing countries.[64] He shows how the principal-agent model, used in a very general way, can provide a framework for understanding how corruption has been able to thrive, and for developing plans of action to limit it. In most cases that he cites, it seems obvious that presenting rational moral arguments to those taking or paying the bribes would not be a very effective approach. Again, an ethicist may want to go beyond Klitgaard's economic analysis in constructing and assessing plans of action, but his analysis provides a helpful perspective on the problem.

Economic analysis is helpful simply because many of us are morally weak, and often behave so as to serve our own (narrowly defined) self-interest, without paying adequate attention to the effects our behavior has on others. In such a world, we need to balance an ethical level of respect for others with a reasonable level of self-protection. Ethics does not require that we naively trust others in all circumstances. We can also benefit from the analysis of specific contexts that economics permits. For instance, it is important to note that contracting arrangements that are effective in a small community could be completely unworkable in a large market economy, or, similarly, that it is sensible to ask for different contract terms in a one-shot transaction with a stranger than in a long-standing business relationship. Economic analysis can help ethicists balance their ideals and values with a sense of what might be effective in the complex and often impersonal world in which most of us live.

As a final point, I would like to encourage my ethicist colleagues to tolerate, maybe even respect, the tenacity with which some economists approach their work. In the history of science, we find that in may cases tenacity has been a virtue. Persisting in an unpopular approach can lead to new insights. We should not react too strongly when some economists wish to stick to their parsimonious analytic methods, working out new refinements on models and approaches that we find objectionable. Ethics has no more right to exercise disciplinary hegemony than does any other discipline. We should simply make our arguments as forcefully as we can, to the economists and to the decision makers who use economic analysis as a tool. We can only hope this will spur some new lines of research, and will help the decision makers to be more intelligent consumers of academic research.

CONCLUDING REMARKS

At the conclusion of a stimulating essay entitled "Morality and the Social Sciences: A Durable Tension," Albert O. Hirschman sketches his hopes regarding the future of social science:

> Down the road, it is then possible to visualize a kind of social science that would be very different from the one most of us have been practicing: a moral social science where moral considerations are not repressed or kept apart, but are systematically commingled with analytic argument, without guilt feelings over any lack of integration; where the transition from preaching to proving and back again is performed frequently and with ease; and where moral considerations need no longer be smuggled in surreptitiously, nor expressed unconsciously, but are displayed openly and disarmingly.[65]

Alongside Hirschman's moral social science, I hope we also see an informed ethics, one that listens as well as it scolds.

The purpose of this chapter has been to promote an interdisciplinary dialogue between economists and ethicists on the ethical aspects of principal-agent analysis. It has identified ethical concerns with this form of analysis, suggested ways in which the individuals developing and using these models might respond to the concerns, and pointed out some of the lessons ethicists might learn from economic analysis.

It should be clear by now that a number of intellectual entrepreneurs have already made significant efforts to constructively cross these disciplinary boundaries. I have specifically mentioned Arrow, Baumol, Coleman, Etzioni, Frank, Hirschman, Margolis, Sen, and Varian, and there are others. Despite the extensive skills of these individuals, however, much remains to be done. The gap between economic social science and ethics remains substantial.

Work to date has yet to yield a dominant paradigm for the integration of ethics and economics, but progress is being made. I encourage my ethicist and social scientist colleagues to talk with another, to do this open-mindedly and constructively, and to start with the presumption that the other party has something of value to offer. Following this advice would be out of character for most of us contentious, turf-protective academics. It also promises to be frustrating. Risks must be taken and false starts must occur if progress is to continue. Finding common ground and making solid intellectual progress will not be easy, but even if it yields only a small step toward a more ethically reflective social science or toward a more informed and pragmatic ethics, it should be worth the effort.[66]

NOTES

1. The basic ideas behind principal-agent analysis will be explained in more detail in the next section.

2. See Hirschman (1981) for a brief account of this history.

3. Note that this chapter is about applications of principal-agent models, not the use of such models to stimulate more abstract theory. I believe that the legitimate ethical issues lie in the applications. It is also not about the use of economic analysis in general, even though some of the points raised may be indicative of broader concerns. My arguments are intended to be specific to principal-agent analysis. Other applied economic frameworks would need to be considered on a case-by-case basis.

4. These concerns are even reflected in some of the teaching materials used to explain this analysis. For instance, in a teaching note on this subject (see Bibliography) Demski explicitly begins and ends with an acknowledgement of the limits and extreme assumptions implicit in the standard principal-agent model.

5. For a general introduction to this work see Pratt and Zeckhauser (1985), especially the overview chapter by the editors. For a slightly more technical review of the field see Levinthal (1988). The specific influence of these models on contract theory can be found in Hart and Holmstrom (1987) and on the theory of the firm in Holmstrom and Tirole (1987).

6. For ease of exposition I will generally use the singular case (one agent and one principal), except where plural seems more natural.

7. It is not required that an agent have a negative utility for all effort, only that her utility for effort turn negative at some level short of the level of effort desired by the principal.

8. See, for example, Williamson (1985), p. 30.

9. Easterbrook (1985), p. 81.

10. Knight (1921), especially Chapters IX and X.

11. Alchian and Demsetz (1972).

12. Wimsatt (1986), esp. p. 295.

13. In most (if not all) contracting situations, it will be possible *ex post* to construct a principal-agent type model that is consistent with actual contractual arrangements. One way to do this is simply to adjust the agent's reservation utility. This feature of the analysis is not very interesting unless it can be supported by testable predictions. Reliable predictions will require a richer theory of agent's reservation utility than is currently offered, and an account of the likely bargaining process.

14. This sort of notion is developed by Maser and Coleman (1988, pp. 35–39) in their account of "concessional rationality."

15. Interestingly, a Marxist analysis would suggest that in a capitalist society, the principal-agent model does a good job of predicting the actual contractual arrangements between capital and labor. Because labor has no bargaining power, all the surplus goes to the capitalist.

16. Akerlof (1980).

17. DiMaggio and Powell (1983). For an earlier discussion of tendencies toward isomosphism, see Meyer and Rowan (1977).

18. This discussion has focused on the first question on Level 3, the "what" question. Principal-agent analysis with its sensitivity to incentive problems could be useful in answering the second question, the "how." Even there its use needs to be tempered, as will be apparent from the discussion in the rest of the chapter. Nonetheless it could lead to important insights.

19. See for instance, Atiyah (1981), Fried (1981), Kronman (1980), and Posner (1986). Feinberg's (1986 and 1988) observations on voluntary consent and exploitation in criminal law also provide relevant arguments.

20. The most prominent work on justice in recent years has been produced by Rawls, (1971). For alternative views see, for instance, Nozick (1974, esp. Chapter 7) and the essays in Arthur and Shaw (1978). Examples of recent work with a rational choice orientation are Harsanyi (1977), Gauthier (1986), and Hardin (1988).

21. It is only fair to note that some principal-agent work has been sensitive to two-sided moral hazard. For instance, see Carmichael (1983). The existence of such work is encouraging. Yet, at this writing, two-sided models are the exception rather than the rule. Until they gain wider currency, the concerns raised in this section will still be valid.

22. See Dow (1987).

23. Perrow (1986), p. 227.

24. Roberts (n.d.), p. 1, emphasis added.

25. Arrow (1974), p. 36, emphasis added.

26. Goodin (1985) develops a theory of responsibility that is centered on a notion of vulnerability that could be used to support this line of reasoning. He argues that we owe special obligations to those most vulnerable to our actions.

27. Williamson (1985), Chapter 12.

28. See, for instance, Carmichael (1983) and Lazear and Rosen (1981).

29. Sen (1977 and 1986).

30. Langer, Bashner, and Chanowitz (1985).

31. Higgins and McCann (1984).

32. Kahneman, Knetsch, Thaler (1986).

33. Banfield (1958), p. 83.

34. Baiman and Lewis (1987).

35. Bohm (1962), and Hornstein, Masor, Sole, and Heilman (1971), respectively.

36. Klitgaard (1988).

37. Nichols and Zeckhauser (1986).

38. See Sen (1977 and 1986) for discussions of this commitment concept.

39. Below I will discuss the idea that fairness is sufficiently captured by the requirement in principal-agent models that an agent receive compensation in excess of her next best alternative. At this point, I just note that this linkage is not made explicitly in the literature on principal-agent models.

40. Kahneman, Knetsch, and Thaler (1986). It is worth noting that the perceived "fair" payoff in these situations was significantly in excess of the subject's next best alternative, which was no pay-off at all.

41. Eccles (1985).

42. Epstein (1985), p. 140.

43. This argument is crude because it glosses over the costs that are created when the dismissed employee searches for a new job, possibly collects unemployment insurance, possibly moves her family, and when the firm trains a replacement. There is no guarantee that these costs are adequately represented in the utility function of the individual making the dismissal decision. The argument also makes the naive assumption that the reputation gain to the new hire will be commensurate with the reputation loss to the person dismissed.

44. Marwell and Ames (1981).

45. It should be noted that the principal-agent model can be used to determine a fair contract, at least in terms of the division of the surplus, provided that the agent's reservation utility is adjusted to represent some minimum fair level of compensation, rather than just the agent's next best alternative. In such a case, the reservation utility does not necessarily represent the point at which the agent would walk away. Agents may be willing to accept an unfair compensation, if they are in dire circumstances. To some extent, minimum wage laws attempt to legislate this sort of fairness. The idea is that setting a minimum wage prevents certain forms of exploitation.

These laws are highly controversial. I shall not defend from here. I simply mention them as an example related to this discussion.

46. Clark (1985) points out that the law faces this same problem. He sees this as a partial explanation for the existence and value of moral opprobrium.

47. Oster (1988), p. 33.

48. See any of the Arrow references in the Bibliography.

49. Aoki (1984), p. 191.

50. Lepper and Greene (1975).

51. Arrow (1963).

52. Holmstrom and Richart-Costa (1986).

53. Margolis (1982), Etzioni (1988), and Frank (1988a and 1988b).

54. Leibenstein (1987).

55. Arrow (1974).

56. See for instance, Breton and Wintobe (1982), especially pp. 61–88, the essays in Gambetta (1988), and Zucker's (1986) paper.

57. Eccles (1985).

58. Frank (1988a and b).

59. Varian (1975).

60. Baumol (1986).

61. Maser and Coleman (1988). Approaches to fairness in negotiations are implicit in their discussion of the three stages of rationality.

62. Aoki (1984).

63. Easterbrook (1985).

64. Klitgaard (1988).

65. Hirschman (1981), pp. 305–306.

66. I am grateful to Peter Cramton, George Hogenson, Robert Massie, Peter Menell, Margaret Smith, Warren Schwartz, and members of the Georgetown Law Center's Law and Economics Seminar for helpful comments on an earlier draft.

3

Agency Theory and the Ethics of Agency

Richard T. DeGeorge

One of the major attractions of agency theory is its explanatory power. When applied to the theory of the firm it captures in a way no other organizational theory does the relations of shareholders, members of the board of directors, senior managers, junior managers, and workers.[1] As a descriptive technique it is able to handle and make clear some of the tensions between people who occupy each successive pair, and brings to the fore the fact that although people on each lower level act as agents for those on the immediately preceding level, all have their own interests, which they pursue while pursuing the interests of those above them. The managerial problems of control, of efficiency, of the costs and benefits of various monitoring and bonding techniques all become amenable to description, analysis, and then appropriate strategies in game theoretical models. The precision of the latter is as satisfying as the insight into the psychological and other motivations that the theory can both capture and bring into play.

One of the strengths of agency theory is its recognition of and ability to deal with relations. Organizational theory has often been concerned with structures and with roles. Both of these surely have relevance to organizations. But by focusing on relations between people and levels, agency theory captures the dynamic aspects present in actual interactions in organizations and interpersonal relations.

Moreover, this powerful new tool has countless applications. A large number of social relations can be modeled along agency lines. Any hierarchical organization, any instance of authority, many professional relations, and numerous other relations, including those of family and friendship, are amenable to agency analysis. Because of all this, its attraction is understandable and its promise considerable.

As with many powerful theories, however, its proponents sometimes exaggerate its scope, and tend to see everything—all relations, all organizations, all fields—in its terms. Jensen and Meckling, for instance, argue that because they can describe the firm as the nexus of a set of contracting individuals, it follows that the firm is not an individual and so cannot have social responsibility.[2] Those conclusions are not warranted by their analysis. Taking relations seriously does not preclude the existence of structures, roles, and relata. Relations, in fact, can be the glue that turns individuals into larger, identifiable groups of collectives.[3] And a theory that describes a firm in one way does not preclude the possibility of describing it in alternative acceptable ways. Too much weight must not be placed on any particular description, as if it were the only correct one.[4]

Similarly, attempts to encompass and describe ethics in terms of agency have thus far been unsuccessful, and I shall argue that in the long run they are doomed to failure. This does not mean that agency theory has nothing to offer ethical theory, and I shall suggest how both agency theory and ethical theory can enrich each other.

I

Because of its descriptive power agency theory might be thought useful in describing and explaining ethical relations in business or perhaps even in explaining the general ethical enterprise. No one can preclude attempts in this direction. But there are certain inherent limits to any such attempts that it is well to consider.

Agency theory, as the name implies, was originally intended to handle cases in which one party is an agent for another, e.g., a manager is an agent for the owners of a corporation. Agency theory has had the most success in dealing with strategies for efficiency, starting from the psychological assumption of self-interest as the dominant factor motivating both the principal and the principal's agent. It makes no ethical assumption. It claims neither that self-interested action is good nor that it is bad. This is appropriate, for ethically speaking self-interest is neither one nor the other. If a manager who is also the owner of a corporation keeps his perquisites low and works long hours in order to maximize the company's profits, that is ethically acceptable. If a manager who is not the owner keeps his perquisites low and works long hours in order to maximize the company's profits, that is also ethically acceptable. Is it ethically acceptable for the manager to maximize his company perquisites and work much shorter hours than if the company were his?

The answer depends on whether he can still be considered to be doing his job, fulfilling his contract, acting as a responsible agent. Some agents are exceedingly well paid for their work, others get relatively little. As long as they do not do what is unethical—steal, misrepresent, and so on—the better deal they get for themselves, the better off they are. The same is true when a manager hires workers. Self-interested workers want as much pay for as little work as they can get, and the managers (perhaps more accurately the owners) want as much work for as little pay as they can get. We can speak of a just wage and of all parties acting in an ethically responsible manner. But agency theory cannot tell us what these are. Rather the job of agency theory is to help us devise techniques for initially describing the conflict of principal-agent, and then for controlling the situation so that the agent, acting from self-interest, does as little harm as possible to the principal's interests. It helps us devise mechanisms for trading off direct benefits and constraints for the cost of constant supervision. Neither the efficiency of the techniques nor their acceptance by all parties justifies them ethically. Gross exploitation may at times fulfill both conditions and still be unjust.

Since agency theory as such is not interested in ethics, even though it might be applied to that area, it is not surprising that the model does not raise many of the sorts of questions that ethical theorists raise.

At the very start, there are four important differences that distinguish an agency theory approach from ethical theory.

First, ethics is interested primarily in how people ought to act, not in how people do act. If a poll were to determine that most people sometimes lie, that would not make lying ethically justifiable. If an investigation were to determine that most builders in New York pay bribes to get work done, that would not mean that paying bribes is ethically permissible. Now it may be that both truth telling and not paying bribes are more efficient than lying and paying bribes; but that is not what makes the former ethically right and the latter ethically wrong. From the point of view of ethical theory what is required is some explanation of why certain acts are ethically wrong. Description is not enough.

Second, from an ethical point of view efficiency is but one value. It is not ethically overriding. And actions that are inefficient and perhaps unprofitable may be ethically mandatory. It would be nice if there were a perfect fit among actions that are ethical, efficient, and profitable. There is no reason *a priori* to believe that there is such a fit. To the extent that agency theory might attempt to explain ethics in terms of efficiency, it has first to justify the use of that value rather than any number of others. Efficiency may be very important for many firms, for effective competition, and for many organizations. But since it requires justification if it is to serve as an ethical criterion, a theory that starts by assuming efficiency cannot also justify it.

Third, the psychological assumption of self-interest may be descriptively accurate in dealing with many organizations. But it is not the only motivation. Attempts to reduce all motivation to self-interested motivation have a long history in ethical theory, and are usually considered under a position known as psychological hedonism. Psychological hedonism falters on instances of altruism that cannot plausibly be reduced even directly to self-interest.[5] Attempts to reduce all motivation to self-interested motivation stumbles either on the fact that it has to deny first-hand reports of other kinds of motivation, substituting for them an *a priori* certitude that it cannot defend; or it has to reduce altruism, love, friendship, action on principle, and any other non-self-interested motivation to self-interest. If it does so, it still must take into account the differences between these other motivations and what are generally known as self-interested ones. A theory cannot deny general, intelligible, and useful distinctions developed by human society without impoverishing those distinctions and that society. Any attempt to do this requires more justification than any theory so far has yet to produce. Agency theory does not attempt to produce any new reasons here, but simply makes the self-interested motivation a basic assumption.

Fourth, agency theory tends to focus on actions between two parties, principal and agent, and it ignores the effects of those actions—which it possibly calls externalities—on others. But all consequentialist ethical theories, including all versions of utilitarianism, insist that one consider all those affected by an action. To restrict consideration to agent and principal is to artificially restrict one's consideration. This may be necessary and useful for some types of formal analysis, but any such restrictive approach is necessarily very different from an ethical approach.

A possible reply on the part of agency theorists might be that although efficiency and self-interestedness are generally taken as assumptions by those dealing with business organizations, accounting, and other aspects of business, they are not necessary for the theory. Other values may be substituted, and other psychological assumptions made. The theory is flexible enough to accommodate any values or psychological assumptions one wishes. Efficiency and self-interest seem to be appropriate in a business context, but if in another context they are not, then appropriate substitutions can be made. The power of the theory is not lessened thereby, but expanded.

The reply is not without its merit, but the difference between ethical theory and agency theory is revealed in this reply. For although agency theory can be used with any number of different assumptions, ethical theory cannot. The point of ethical theory is to determine and explain which values are ethically acceptable and permissible and which are not. An ethical theory that justifies deception, exploitation, and lack of respect for human rights in business or any other area of life is necessarily defective. The reason is that ethical theory has as its starting point conventional morality, which it may modify, but which it cannot overturn. It cannot be indifferent to which values it chooses or defends or assumes. To the extent that agency theory can be indifferent, it is an essentially different kind of expertise.

If business ethics consisted of norms generated by and in business transactions, agency theory would be extremely helpful in determining appropriate norms. But business ethics is a subset of general ethics, and those in business are no more allowed to establish their own ethical norms than are people in any other sector of life. General ethical norms—truthfulness, honesty, respect for persons—govern all areas of life, including business. To the extent that there are special ethical norms that stem from special relations, situations, and contracts in business, these are not exceptions to general ethical norms but are either specifications of or additions to them. As such they must be consistent with the general norms.

Insofar as ethical considerations come into play before agency theory starts, are appropriate during its application, and continue after agency theory ends, agency theory cannot completely ground or explain ethics and so cannot completely ground or explain business ethics.

Ethical considerations come into play in several ways prior to any application of agency theory. First, they set ethical limits on what both agents and principals are allowed to do. Second, it is always possible to ask whether in a given situation it is ethically allowable and proper to use agency theory. Although agency theorists rightly consider agency theory to be ethically neutral, any tool or theory may be misused or used to achieve an unethical end. Third, the aim and end of the use of agency theory are subject to ethical evaluation.

During its application, ethical constraints constantly hover in the background as they do in all human actions. Unethically justifiable manipulation is both possible and ethically precluded in the application of agency theory. Simply because in itself the theory is ethically neutral does not preclude its unethical application or its prescribing unethical procedures or solutions to problems. Ethical theory cannot supply the best solution to business issues. Business, economic, and agency theory are appropriate here. But ethical theory can preclude the use of certain possible solutions because they are unethical.

After the application of agency theory ethical considerations continue to be applicable as one evaluates the uses to which the theory is put, the results that come from application of the theory, and the net results to all concerned from use of agency theory. As agency theory is discussed, developed, defended, and attacked, agency theorists as well as others should ask not only how effective it is in solving management problems but also, from an ethical point of view, how people are affected by using that tool or by adopting that approach on a large scale. What does the use of agency theory do to the workforce, to business, to society? Does it render it more efficient but less humane? Does it render it both more efficient and more humane? If it adds increased understanding, does it lead to more gross manipulation? Agency theory is still too new for these judgments to be made, but they are appropriate questions to be asked and answered if and when the theory grows in acceptance and is widely used.

Finally, agency is only a part, and a relatively small part, of ethics and of ethical theory. The term "agent" as used in ethical theory is ambiguous. In one sense we speak of ethical agents as any entities that act and are governed by ethical rules. Ethical agents in this sense are distinguished from ethical patients, that is, those who are the recipients of actions. Ethical agents are usually considered the class of rational beings, where "rational" is minimally taken to mean being able to tell right from wrong, and to choose one action rather than another. The stringency of the degree of rationality needed varies somewhat depending on which theory one chooses, but generally normal adult human beings are considered ethical agents in the sense that they are held ethically accountable for their actions. Ethical patients is a broader term, and includes not only normal adult human beings, but also all other entities deserving of ethical considerations as recipients of the effects of the actions of moral agents. Thus infants are moral patients with human rights, even though they are not moral agents. Whether corporations are moral agents, moral patients, or neither, cannot be decided by agency theory.

It should be clear that, in this first sense, an ethical agent is not an agent for anyone or anything else. An ethical agent is a person capable of performing actions or acts that can be evaluated from a moral point of view. The fact that ethical agents in this sense do not act for others is crucial, for it is this independence from others that makes one an end in oneself, someone who is worthy of respect and never to be used only as a means for others. This sense of ethical agency is also crucial for the subjective aspects of ethics—for conscience, will, moral praise and blame, moral responsibility, and the possibility of holding oneself accountable. This independence does not mean that ethical agents are not related to others. They are, and together they form an ethical community that embraces all human beings. Nonetheless, it is because they are ends in themselves and for themselves that they are ethical agents in this first sense.

The second sense of moral agent is the sense used by agency theory. This is the sense in which one person acts for another.

To construe ethics in terms of agency theory is to conceive ethics as based on agency in the second sense of agency, or to reduce the first sense to the second sense. Both approaches necessarily misconstrue ethics. Forcing ethics into an agency theory mold fails to account for many of its aspects.

II

What can ethics say about agency that might be useful to agency theorists?

From an ethical point of view, some fruitful ethical thinking that may be helpful to agency theorists can take place prior to the development or implementation of agency theory. An agent is one who serves in place of another. A worker may be considered an agent for a manager insofar as he does the work the manager wants done and, at least in theory, would do for himself. The manager similarly is an agent for the owners of the firm insofar as he does what the owners want done and, at least in theory, would do for themselves. In more ordinary discourse, a lawyer is an agent for his client and does in a professional manner, using his special knowledge and skills, what he can to achieve the result his client desires.

In an agency relation the person who works for another is the agent and the one for whom the agent acts is the principal. From an ethical point of view both principal and agent are bound by ethical rules. Neither is ethically allowed to do what is unethical. Three general principles apply to all such relations.

First, no agent is ethically allowed to do for a principal what the principal is not ethically allowed to do for himself. Acting for another does not give one ethical license. The fact that the agent acts impersonally does not change the moral character of the act, even though psychologically an agent may feel more detached and less ethically responsible doing certain actions than a principal would. Nor does professional competence allow an agent to do what it is unethical for the principal to do. Professional competence, if anything, gives one more rather than fewer ethical obligations.[6]

Second, from an ethical point of view, agents cannot exonerate themselves of blame for doing what is unethical by claiming they were only acting as an agent for a principal. This is so whether the agents act on their own, using expertise that the principal does have, or whether they act in response to direct commands from the principal to do some specific act. All persons are ethically responsible for their actions, whether performed under command or performed on behalf of another. Managers acting for a corporation cannot justify misrepresentation, overcharging, producing defective goods, under-paying employees, or any other unethical action simply because they do not receive any personal benefit from those actions or simply be-cause they are acting on behalf of the firm or the owners of the firm.

Agency theory typically does not deal with issues of this type, but seeks only to determine how to ensure compliance on the part of the agent at the least cost to the principal. Agents do well to remember that there are certain actions they should not ethically perform, and agency theorists should look for methods to preclude agents being manipulated into doing unethical acts for principals. Agency theory may be ethically neutral, but since it can be put to better or poorer uses, agency theorists informed by ethical theory might benefit by remembering that they too are agents for those who employ them and that there are limits to what they can ethically do for their prin-cipals.

Third, just as acting for another does not relieve the agent of moral responsibility, neither does engaging or employing an agent relieve the principal of moral responsibility. Just as an agent may not do anything unethical simply because commanded or requested or re-quired to do it by a principal, so principals are not relieved of ethical responsibility simply because they have someone else do their bid-ding or act in their name. It is clearly no excuse for someone who hires a hit man to murder his enemy or competitor to claim that he, the principal, did not actually do the shooting. The principal is guilty of murder, just as the hit man is guilty of murder. Principals remain ethically responsible for what they order done. Even more strin-gently, principals are ethically responsible for what is done in their name, even if they did not intend the agent to act as the agent did. A manager who orders an employee to get a job done, and who says, "I don't care how you do it, just get it done" is responsible for what-ever the employee does to get the job done. One cannot exonerate oneself of responsibility simply by saying, "That is not what I in-tended" or "That is not what I would have done" or "I did not know that's what my agent was going to do." Agency may involve the del-egation of authority, or the authority to act in one's name, but it cannot involve complete delegation of responsibility. Otherwise the agent would not be responsible to the principal, and we would no longer have an instance of agency. The initiator of the authority has the responsibility to oversee the way the authority is used and the actions taken to achieve the end desired.

This retention of responsibility by the principal poses problems both in instances involving a long chain of command—typical in large firms—in which the final agent is far removed from the original principal, and in instances in which the agent has and uses technical expertise that the principal does not have the competence to evaluate and so effectively control. In the first kind of case, control must be established at each level. In the second, alternative types of control must be established. Agency theory is especially useful for devising such controls in both kinds of cases.

Once agency theory is in play, especially if one is using a mathematical model, there is a tendency to see situations in terms of game theory, or as abstract puzzles to be solved. Ethics requires that, insofar as any real life applications are made, those who use agency theory always remember that the agents they are dealing with in their theory are human beings who have rights and feelings, and who are deserving of respect. Any attempt at manipulation through incentives, threats, or other kinds of deterrents should pass ethical muster.

Finally, agency theorists would do well to consider how ethical motivation might make certain kinds of control unnecessary. The tendency of agency theorists to assume self-interest seems to be offset only by other agency theorists who see the opposite as altruism. Ethical motivation need be neither. People frequently act on ethical principle and do an action because it is ethically right. To ignore this is to ignore an important fact of business as well as of other areas of life. Firms can promote such action on the part of their employees, and doing so may preclude the need for other types of control. Ethically motivated agents require less supervision than self-interested agents, and exercise effective internal control that no amount of external control can match. A challenge for agency theory is to discover how to utilize, promote, and incorporate such motivation.

III

What can agency theory do for business ethics?

Although agency theory cannot substitute for ethical theory, there are several applications that might throw light on business ethics, perhaps make it more precise, and facilitate its implementation.

Two popular aproaches to ethical theory are utilitarianism and contractarianism. For reasons I have already given, it is unlikely that agency theory can fully account for or develop a model adequate for either a utilitarian or a contractarian ethical theory. But both are amenable to some extent to agency analysis, and may be strengthened thereby.

For example, agency theory may prove helpful in determining proper rules for controlling or directing the actions of agents and principals in a business context. Although questions about the ethics of the actions of someone acting as an agent for another form only a small part of ethical theory, agents may have special obligations to principals because of the principal-agent relationship. We have already noted that any special ethical obligations that such a relationship involves are just that—special ethical obligations. They are added to and cannot lessen one's general moral obligations. But if one chooses to act as an agent for another, then one incurs certain obligations to the principal. Thus if one accepts work for pay from another, one is obliged to do, within the limits of what is ethically acceptable, what one is hired to do. If one chooses to have an agent, one similarly incurs certain obligations thereby. If one agrees to pay a worker for certain kinds of work, one is obliged to pay the stipulated amount.

Agency theory cannot provide the general ethical rules that govern all human actions, but within the parameters of those general ethical rules it might be useful in devising rationally acceptable sets of rules that both sides (agent and principal) would agree to and be willing to bind themselves to. The ethical binding force comes from the general ethical obligation to observe legitimate contracts into which one freely enters, unless there are overriding circumstances that free one from the contract.

Although it is not the case that whatever rules people come up with for their advantage are necessarily ethical rules, or are candidates for ethical rules, agency theory might help devise rules that all involved parties would find mutually advantageous. If those rules were adopted as rules governing their behavior, they would tend to be sustaining in a way that rules that were not to their advantage would not be.

Ethical rules must be universal in the sense that they apply to all and would be seen as reasonable by all—such as the rule not to kill other people. The rule to honor contracts is similarly universal. Specifications of that rule are clearly not universal in the same sense. They are universal only in the senses that they can be acknowledged by all as not violating any other ethical rule and that they would bind all who were similarly placed. This is to say that they are an acceptable instantiation of an ethical rule. Many ethical obligations in business arise through contracts in this way. Hence any theory, agency theory included, that can throw light on such relations and contracts can be helpful not only in clarifying the nature of such contracts, their costs and benefits, but also in helping arrive at workable and hence sustainable contracts and business relationships.

If we follow this line of thought, then there is a sense in which we can—as many people who speak about ethics in business do—talk about the ethical rules of an organization, with the implication that there are different ethical rules for different organizations, and that these ethical rules might be different from the ethical rules for those outside the organization. If in company A each employee agrees not to take any gifts valued at over $50 and in company B each employee agrees to take no gifts at all, then the employees of company A have different ethical obligations with respect to gifts than the employees of company B because of their differing agreements. Both agreements are ethically permissible, and taking gifts in general is not ethically prohibited. But for clarity's sake, we must not confuse such ethical rules, which we call derived or special ethical rules, with those ethical rules that apply to everyone, in and out of any organization.

Special relations can also establish special ethical obligations that one has in addition to one's other ethical obligations. These need not be contractual. Thus parents have special obligations toward their children that are different from the general obligations all adults have toward children, and that are not derived from any contract with one's child. Relations in business can also carry special ethical obligations because of the position one holds with respect to others. To the extent that agency theory helps clarify and specify relations in business and describe the costs and benefits of compliance, control, and coping, it may well throw light on ethical issues in business and suggest both problems to be analyzed and possible solutions.

Nonetheless, we can and should distinguish special ethical obligations of members of a firm from corporate values that a particular firm may choose to emphasize and inculcate in their employees so that, if successfully inculcated, the values will benefit the firm. If these happen to be ethical values, such as honesty and truthfulness, then clearly in addition to having the ethical obligation to inculcate these values, one has a corporate incentive to do so. But not all values are of this type. For instance, loyalty to one's firm may be a value that a firm might wish to inculcate into its employees. Yet from an ethical point of view, corporate loyalty is not strictly required by any general norm, and under normal circumstances is not the sort of norm that can be the result of a contract. It is rather a quality that an employee might develop in response to certain kinds of treatment by her employer. There are many other non-ethically required norms besides loyalty that a firm may wish to inculcate into its employees.

Unless one clearly distinguishes ethical norms in their general, universal application from special ethical obligations, and both of these from other kinds of corporate and social values or norms, one is led to confusing them. The result is either to treat ethical norms as just another set of norms having no overriding or mandatory quality, or to try to infuse corporate or other social norms with the special quality of overriding ethical norms. Both tendencies are mistakes that conceptual clarity can and should help us avoid. Although agency theorists need not indulge in these confusions, the tendency to treat all values on a par for the sake of value neutrality is a temptation agency theorists do well to guard against. If their work is to be helpful in ethical analysis, it is especially crucial that different kinds of values be kept distinct.

Another possibly fruitful union of agency theory and ethical theory arises with respect to incentives and sanctions. Since agency theory is interested in organizational and social control and incentives, and interested in how principals can minimize their costs and residual loss from the impossibility of fully monitoring their agents, work along these lines may help ethical theorists develop a better analysis of incentives and sanctions.

Ethical codes typically carry with them ethical sanctions. Ethical sanctions are either natural, social, or supernatural. A natural sanction, for instance, means that those who do evil must live with the natural consequences of those actions. These might include a nagging conscience, the physical harm that comes from the use of some drugs, or the warped character that one builds and must live with. Social sanctions are of many sorts: from ostracism and tar and feathering at one end to scolding and reproach from others on the other end. In a business context it might involve unwillingness on the part of others to continue to do business with an individual. Supernatural punishment is that meted out by God, usually in the hereafter.

In addition to ethical sanctions, if an unethical action is also made illegal, then one can have legal sanctions—those imposed by law. And we can have corporate sanctions—such as demotion or dismissal—for violations of corporate norms. The prisoner's dilemma, which deals with incentives for certain choices that depend on the choices of others, illustrates how agency theory may help business ethical theory. It is not unethical to suspect your opponent of seeking his greater good at your expense, and the prisoner's dilemma is not set up as a ethical game at all. On utilitarian grounds it would be ethically as well as rationally and self-interestedly right to choose the option that maximizes the good of all involved. Agency theory can help determine which choices those are. The application of incentives and sanctions in the area of business ethics is still little researched and developed. As agency theory develops, its results may be useful to those in business ethics interested in effectively motivating those in business to act ethically.

Agency theory is especially useful in cases of uncertainty and of asymmetric information. These are areas in which too little work in business ethics has been done, not only with respect to sanctions but also with respect to other issues as well. Although from an ethical point of view equal access to information is the ideal, in most situations it is not realized. This makes many contracts unequal. The degrees of inequality that can be tolerated before the contract is void is a moral that is too little discussed.

Similarly, what are called "moral hazard" (perhaps misleadingly) and "adverse selection" in agency theory[7] raise a nest of issues that call for ethical discussion that has yet to take place. Moral hazard arises, for instance, when employers, who cannot observe whether their employees are behaving optimally, institute observable measures as surrogates. The result is that the employees act to achieve the surrogates, whether or not the surrogates help them fulfill their tasks optimally. Or insured persons may find, contrary to the insurance company's desire, that because they are insured they are willing to take more risks than they otherwise would. Adverse selection occurs with respect to a job opening, for instance, as a result of neither employer nor employee being required or able to give complete information about the ability and competence either needed for the job or attained by the job-seeker. Both terms describe a variety of situations. What is ethically appropriate action in these circumstances cannot be determined by agency theory. But agency theorists have highlighted these situations and have suggested strategies for coping with them. Business ethicists would do well to discuss whether working for surrogates is ethically acceptable; how much disclosure on the part of both principals and agents is ethically appropriate in hiring, accounting, and managing; and how much care one must ethically exercise, even if covered by insurance.

Finally, to the extent that agency theory helps develop and determine means of control, it may be helpful in devising techniques by which an ethical principal (e.g., a manager) can control agents' actions in such a way that the agents (e.g., workers) do not act unethically.

Ethical rules, if followed, might promote efficiency. Which rules are ethical would have to be determined by ethical criteria not simply by agency theory. And whether they in fact promote efficiency would have to be determined by research. But if they do, there would be an efficiency argument as well as an ethical argument for acting as ethical rules demand. Acting on ethical rules for reasons of efficiency, even from the point of view of an ethicist, should be better than not acting on ethical rules. If an efficiency argument impels corporations to adopt rules that are in accord with what ethics demands but that they would not otherwise adopt, then so much the better for the efficiency argument.

We should be clear about what we are doing, however. Ethical theorists generally maintain that ethical rules are overriding. They are binding even when they come up against other norms. Hence if following an ethical rule proved to be inefficient, that is a reason a corporation might give for not following it, but that is not an ethically justifying reason. Whether or not following rules that coincide with what ethical rules prescribe promotes efficiency, the ethical rules continue to prescribe and must ethically be obeyed. Since from an ethical point of view efficiency is at best one of the goods to be weighed in any ethical calculation, it is not necessarily the dominant consideration, and frequently will not be.

A further danger is that ethics may tend to become or to be seen as one more way for principals to manipulate agents (or vice-versa). Agency theory does not necessarily advocate this. Yet the use of ethics to improve efficiency runs the risk of making ethics a manipulative tool, unless there is understanding of the nature and content of ethical norms. This makes it all the more important to distinguish clearly between what is demanded by ethics and what is demanded by the corporation's or by the principal's or by the agent's good.

The claim that people in business just as people out of business should behave ethically does not depend on either efficiency or an agency theory. Yet agency theory can contribute to business ethics insofar as it may be a useful pedagogical and motivating tool to develop and help get adopted rules that coincide with ethics. To the extent that it does not get at ethics in the traditional sense but only in a restricted sense, it is a tool that should be used with caution.

Agency theory has entered importantly into finance, accounting, and organizational theory. It is entering management. In each of these areas it has had to be adapted to the field. The same is true with respect to its application to business ethics. Before it can be applied fruitfully, those who do the applying must take seriously the nature of ethics and ethical theory and the limitations these impose on the method of agency theory and on its use within the domain of business ethics.

NOTES

1. See, for example, Jensen and Meckling (1976) pp. 305–60.
2. Ibid., p. 311.
3. See DeGeorge (1983), pp. 3–20.
4. For a development of this argument, see French (1984). For additional discussion of French's view and alternate approach to the ethical status of firms, see *Shame, Responsibility, and the Corporation*, New York: Haven Publishing Company, 1986.
5. For two of the classic refutations of psychological hedonism, see Butler, "Preface" and "Sermon One," *Fifteen Sermons Preached at Rolls College Chapel*, London, 1926; and John Stuart Mill, Chapter IV, *Utilitarianism*, Indianapolis: Bobbs Merrill Library of Liberal Arts, 1957.
6. See, DeGeorge, 1986, pp. 338–44.
7. See, Moe, (1984), pp. 754–58; Radner, (1987); Penno, (1984).

II

HOW GOOD IS
AGENCY THEORY?

4

The Theory of Agency and Organizational Analysis

Barry M. Mitnick

The theory of agency, which seeks to model all relationships of agent and principal in social life, is a very large area of research in accounting, finance, and economics. Though it has always had a significant beachhead in political science, it is only now beginning to invade that discipline, as well as sociology, in a major way. Agency theory has for many years been considered to have something to do with the study of organizations. Indeed, it is considered part of what is called the "economics of organization." But despite expressed concern for the development of organizational theory using this approach (e.g., Jensen, 1983), few researchers have actively applied and extended agency to truly organizational as against formal analytic settings. It is time, to paraphrase Homans, to bring organizations back in.

After offering a brief introduction to agency and its literatures, I shall outline several objections to the content and conduct of agency work in accounting, finance, and economics. I shall then suggest some agency-like literatures in social science whose exploration ought to permit agency to make a substantially greater contribution to our understanding of organizations. Finally, I shall describe some aspects of agency relationships in and among organizations that would be appropriate to explore in order to derive a useful agency-based understanding of organizations. In essence, I would like to pose the practical questions: If, after a decade or so the accountants have failed to reach so much of concern in organizations using agency, what is the problem? And where can help be found?

THE THEORY OF AGENCY AND ITS LITERATURES

The theory of agency has many parents. Like human relatives, some are acknowledged but never spoken to, some are treated as black sheep and tactfully never mentioned, some appear to be unknown to many members of the family, and some are venerated. The objects of veneration can differ, however, depending on who is doing the venerating. This mixed ancestry has a great deal to do with the way in which agency has been applied to organizations.

Agency Theory

The major insight of agency theory is that control loss is inevitable in agent-principal relationships. There will always be costs to the agent and the principal in such relationships and at some point it will not pay the principal to expend the marginal costs of gaining an absolutely perfect agent. The agent and principal are supposed to have potentially differing preferences, so that the principal must expend resources both in trying to instruct the agent what to do and in monitoring and policing the agent's behavior. Thus the theory turns naturally to a consideration of ways in which agents are made to be relatively more efficient performers of the principal's wishes, given the information, effort, skill, and other problems that characterize the relationship. For example, are there particular ways to reward agents that will result in relatively better agent performance? Do different organizational or institutional structures exist and are they better because they handle agency problems more effectively?

At the same time, it must be acknowledged that because control of the agent is never perfect, the agent's behavior will also not be perfect. And thus we are led to explore the ways in which that behavior diverges, and to explain these divergences in terms of different patterns of agency relationship structure and governance. In short, agency theory becomes a study in Murphy's Law.

Literatures of Agency

There are at least three overlapping cohorts in the ancestry of agency theory; indeed, the literature contains different views of what the cohorts have been (for example, see Baiman, 1982; Jensen, 1983; Moe, 1984; Williamson 1985; for a contrasting, ultimately more pessimistic view of agency and organization theory, see Perrow, 1986). I will characterize these three cohorts as the *theory of the firm* or positive theory of agency approach, the *risk and information* or decision theoretic approach, and the *sociological or organizational* or integrative social science approach. There is not space here to adequately survey these approaches; I shall try only to picture them roughly, with an eye to the organization connection at the heart of this chapter.

Theory of the firm approach. It is probably fair to say that, for the theory of agency in general, in the beginning there were Ronald Coase (1937) and Chester Barnard (1938); earlier ancestors such as Frank Knight (1921), George Herbert Mead, Georg Simmel, and others are sometimes also recognized. To later readers, Coase's work crystallized the question of why some economic activity is organized in firms, and other economic activity is left to markets. This may not seem to have much to do with agents or organizations. In fact, it eventually led economists of the firm to explore the features of firms that cause them to be preferable to markets; indeed, it led them to explore the features of firms that made them different from profit-maximizing atoms in the marketplace.

Firms were built of long-term contracts; managers were given control while owners were relegated to the role of residual risk-bearers; managers could seek goals at odds with owners' interests. Core features in the generic agency relation—the divergence of interests and its governance—are thus displayed, and attention is directed to certain simple structures in the firm as organization. The firm is seen as a solution to problems that arise in market transactions.

The theory of the firm saw explorations in the divergence of managerial behavior associated with such names as Papandreou, Penrose, Marris, Baumol, and Williamson. This culminated in Williamson's (1964) theory of managerial discretion, in which managers are assumed to have utility both for self-interested "expense preferences" and for the firm's profit goals.

Williamson generalized this look at the imperfections needed to adjust the classical theory of the firm to more realistic economic institutions. All transactions (inside markets or inside firms) display transaction costs; firms economize on such costs and are thus to be preferred to markets in certain circumstances (see Williamson, 1975, 1985; Williamson, Wachter, and Harris, 1975). Thus a new approach had developed to address the Coasian question. Agency is strongly related to the transaction costs approach; indeed it could be constructed as a subject of that approach. Note that the design issue (i.e., why firms rather than markets), which had been subordinated to concern with the firm's maximand (e.g., does the firm through its managers seek profit, growth, sales, or a trade-off of their own and the firm's interest) persisted as a key focus in this literature.

Alchian and Demsetz (1972) posed the design question again, answering it through reference to the role of managers as contract monitors of joint production on behalf of the risk bearers. Ross's (1973) paper set up the firm's problem explicitly as one of agency, though his work properly belongs more to the risk and information stream (also on agency in a theory of the firm, see Leibenstein, 1976). Jensen and Meckling (1976) seized on the notion of the firm as a nexus of agency contracts and provided extended attention to the consequences of "agency costs" in various issues of relevance in financial economics. The Jensen and Meckling paper, as the first long treatment of the agency conceptualization in the economics literature, has had by far the most impact of any work on agency. Although the Jensen and Meckling paper was clearly cast as another installment in the increasing-imperfections stream of the theory of the firm, its conceptualization of agency costs was general and applicable to any agency setting. Subsequent researchers have made extensive use of this; from being a theory of the firm alone it has evolved into a more general positive theory of firm-like relationships.

This positive theory of agency (see Jensen, 1983) has featured application of the agency costs logic as outlined by Jensen and Meckling (1976) together with the kind of economics reasoning applied to institutions characteristic of the public choice literature. It has perhaps become another way to apply economics to certain behaviors or institutions. The analyses typically do not join the economics with approaches from outside that discipline, however. This can result in an emphasis on issues and methods important in economics, but not necessarily reflective of a more global and, ultimately, more valid approach to explaining the behavior or institution in question.

For example, Fama (1980) points out that markets in managerial talent can act to restrain the potential excesses of managers who control the modern firm where management is separated from ownership. In this context, the separation is actually seen as efficient. In essence, the classical markets logic is used to explain why an important agency problem may *not* develop despite the ownership-management separation. Fama and Jensen (1983a,b) similarly seek to explain how the structure of the firm minimizes agency costs; the firm is seen as an efficient solution to an agency problem. Approaches like this stand the agency logic on its head—rather than an explanation for unavoidable control losses and a focus on the types of losses that occur, we have a focus on how those losses are avoided and efficiency achieved though designs that use in part the efficiency-producing talent of markets. This is an approach that is obviously congenial to economics, and perhaps to economists. In fact, as Williamson (1983) notes, divergences, and losses, do occur; firms are not perfect and the classical theory of the firm is in this sense wrong.

The positive theory of agency is a significant area of research in accounting, where it has been applied to analyze such areas as the role of the auditor and the interaction of accounting or accounting management with government (for example, Zimmerman, 1977; Watts and Zimmerman, 1979, 1983; Evans and Patton, 1983; Wallace, n.d., 1986). Behavioral accountants are beginning to examine social science beyond economics as a way to repair the limitations of the economics-based positive theory. It is not unusual today to find such accountants scanning the political science literature on such topics as municipal management for clues on ways to improve models of municipal fund allocation or the psychology literature for materials on cognitive choice processes.

With the exception of the behavioral accounting research, which is still very much a developing art (but see, for example, the journal *Accounting, Organizations, and Society,* which seems to publish more recognizably "organizational" material each year), the theory-of-the-firm or positive theory of agency literature seems still tied to the methods and norms of economics. Indeed, where efficiency is king, it seems hard to conceive of the development of an adequate model of organization failures.

The risk and information approach. A second stream of research in agency seems to have coalesced around the concepts of risk and information. Indeed, sometimes work in agency is included under the heading the "economics of information." Although grounded in the economics literature, this approach is perhaps most closely associated with finance and some parts of accounting.

Arguments surrounding the concepts of "moral hazard" and "adverse selection" are often cited back to the work of Frank Knight (1921), with modern developments in this area associated closely with the work of Kenneth Arrow and Jacob Marshak, including Marshak's work with Roy Radner on the "theory of teams."

Moral hazard and adverse selection are classical incentives and monitoring problems. In the former, the principal cannot observe the agent's behavior but can judge the optimality of the behavior. The principal thus relies on imperfect surrogate measures, which can lead the agent to displace his behavior toward the surrogates in order to appear to be behaving well. The agent is then rewarded whether or not his behavior is actually what the principal desires. This is the classical insurance problem, in which the insurance will be paid whether or not the property owner handles his goods carefully.

In adverse selection, the principal can observe the agent's behavior but cannot judge the optimality of that behavior. Again, principals may adopt imperfect surrogates for the quality of performance—e.g., does the doctor wear a white coat—and suffer from the deceit of their agents.

As a result of problems like these, this literature has focused on such topics as the supply of information, estimates of its quality, predictions of future reward, i.e., on risk associated with future events, and on incentives that exist for agents to truthfully reveal information to their principals. Indeed, perhaps the major contribution of this approach is its appreciation of the importance of risk preferences in agents and principals. The affinity of finance to this literature is easily understood. Moreover, the multiple ancestry of agency is exemplified well by the situation in the risk and information stream. Besides the foundational work of Knight, Arrow, and Marshak, the immediate parents are sometimes given as Spence and Zeckhauser (1971) as well as Ross (1973). Spence and Zeckhauser (1971) focus on the effects of differing preferences rather than refer explicitly to agents and principals in a general theoretical way. Thus risk (as against many other possible variables in the agent-principal relationship) is raised to the level of a key defining variable.

It has perhaps also been natural that this literature has adopted methods different from those prevailing in the then-existing theory-of-the-firm literature. Rather than using the tools of calculus, the risk and information literature has quite naturally relied on probability and set theoretic approaches; there is a heavy emphasis on formal logical proofs. Indeed, those schooled in traditional microeconomics cannot read this literature with full understanding. Jensen (1983) terms the present version of this literature "principal-agent"; it is the more formally mathematical side of current agency approaches and, possibly because of the demands of logical closure and proof and of the economics formalism, it is the least open to influences from other disciplines (on this literature, see Baiman, 1982).

Because of the extreme demands for closure and proof, and the messy nature of most real world agency problems, much of the work in this area avoids the real problems or addresses what Jensen (1983) terms "sterile 'toy' problems that are mathematically tractable." Despite Jensen's criticism, it is probably true that the results of this literature are valuable in representing the state of our technical competence in formalizing agency problems; in this sense it is not premature to formalize. This is careful and sometimes elegant stuff, even though what is established is usually constrained by unrealistic assumptions. It is important to keep testing the bounds of formalization; at some point the marginal advances may add up or the techniques advance closer to realism.

It is, however, not as yet adequate organization theory. There are usually only two or three parties; multiple agents are similar or are treated in a very simplified way. There is virtually no organization structure. Organization variables are collapsed into decision theoretic variables. Indeed, the models often dwell on a particular choice, e.g., of behavior or reward function. Discussion concerns *ex ante* and *ex post* conditions; the logic of the analysts itself is sometimes displayed in a decision tree-like diagram. The models concern things like choice or existence of particular reward functions under various conditions of preference mismatch, agent effort, state-of-the-world uncertainty, and so on. All of these kinds of variables are depicted mathematically, without any attempt to develop them as indicators for more complex, descriptive organizational variables. Common norms of economics, i.e., efficiency, dominate the analysis. As a result, the risk and information stream appears very far indeed from developing an agency approach to organizations; there is more to organizational life than choice under risk and uncertainty.

The sociological or organizational approach. The third stream is what I have termed sociological or organizational. Barnard's (1938) classic work is its acknowledged parent, though of course the vast cognate literature explicitly on bureaucracy and organizations back to and beyond Max Weber has had much to contribute. Barnard (1938) introduced the notion of an economy of incentives through which a top manager controls subordinates. Herbert Simon's work, which in part developed the grounds laid by Barnard, is often cited by scholars of agency theory. But few actually use his work or the social science work on incentives that followed from it. More ought to.

Three areas are of particular relevance. The first is Simon's extension of Barnard's incentives approach (see the inducements-contributions model of March and Simon, 1958). This led to Clark and Wilson's (1961; see also Wilson, 1973) widely used typology of incentives. Organizations are characterized by their dominant incentives form (e.g., material, solidarity, purposive) and the consequences for member joining and staying are explored. Despite severe logical gaps in its formulation (Mitnick and Backoff, 1984), this typology has seen a great deal of use in such areas as the study of political participation; there is something intuitively appealing and useful about the approach. The popularity of the incentives approaches as a core topic in organizational analysis has certainly faded, however. Until recently, when a few researchers set about repairing the gaps in earlier approaches (Knoke and Wright-Isak, 1982; Mitnick and Backoff, 1984; Kerr, n.d.), the sociological or organizational incentives approaches appeared to have no chance of achieving the recognition and general utility they seemed destined for.

Incentives are obviously a key part of the understanding of any principal-agent relationship; they are among the levers available to the principal to try to control agent behavior. The formal agency literatures recognize this through continual use of the term "incentives," but have never paid any attention to developing a model of incentives or of an incentive relation.

The second area of Simon's work to have relevance here is that on the employment relation (Simon, 1957a). The Barnard conception of superior-subordinate relations is formalized with the employer contracting with the employee to be able to select employee behaviors within a discretionary zone. Transaction cost considerations were introduced in Williamson, Wachter, and Harris (1975) as employees are seen as holders of idiosyncratic knowledge costly to reproduce. Clearly this puts us on the track to an organizational analysis of hierarchy in organizational life.

Juxtapose, for example, the employment relation material with the incentive relation approach of Mitnick and Backoff (1984) in which a sender and a receiver of rewards act through a sender-receiver relation that specifies such aspects as the reward types, incentive messages (what to do to get the reward), contractual structure between sender principal and receiver agent, and so on. Variables in the organizational settings of sender and receiver condition the behavior (e.g., technology, organizational resources, etc.). The Mitnick and Backoff work is presented explicitly as an adjunct to an agent-principal approach to organizations.

The third aspect of Simon's work to concern us here is his writing on behavioral choice (1957b), including "bounded rationality." The term *satisficing* has come into common use to describe the readjustment of goals to achievable levels of performance. A behavioral theory of the firm followed from Simon's colleagues and collaborators (Cyert and March, 1963). Subsequently the field has seen an inventive and quite practical literature develop around the science of realistic human judgment processes (e.g., Nisbett and Ross, 1980; Kahneman, Slovic, and Tversky, 1982), an approach that in a broad sense is seeing applications to organizational modeling (e.g., Kiesler and Sproull, 1982; March and Olsen, 1976). This literature is quite foreign to the practices common in the economics-based positive and information-risk literatures in agency. But its utility to an understanding of agents and principals is transparently clear.

For example, one of the problems that agents face is that of determining their principals and their principals' goals. Will agents choose the first principal encountered, the most cognitively salient one, the easiest to perceive or understand, and so on? Will the agents choose goals that are standardized, or simplified, or the ones most like their own? (For a discussion, see Mitnick, 1974; Moe, 1984, also notes the desirability of linking behavioral concerns with the otherwise more formal aspects of agent-principal research.) Indeed, it would be surprising if even the formal risk-information approach, with its explicitly decision theoretic focus, did not begin eventually to incorporate these elements; with a little thought, it is obvious to see how at least some of the concerns reflected in behavioral decision theory can be included in the formal modeling that characterizes the area. As mentioned earlier, the behavioral accountants have begun to be concerned with such things.

I have strayed from a review of materials dealing explicitly with the agency approach in order to better explicate the nature of a sociological or organizational perspective on agency. Agency is both a social relationship and a component of organizational structure. We are concerned with complex individual and organizational goal sets, with some goals endogenously determined (e.g., preferences for salary) and others exogenously set (e.g., social norms of helping; the fiduciary norm). We are concerned with the complex structure of agent-principal relationships, including how they evolve and are managed over time. The contract by itself is important, but so is its management. Indeed, in agency we are concerned with the problematic behaviors that occur. Mechanisms for coping with agency problems may be studied descriptively and prescriptively, but we do not presume a bias toward efficiency (though efficiency may be one along with other norms).

Not only is bounded rationality assumed, it is also disaggregated and incorporated. It is insufficient, for example, to specify that opportunism is at work; we would also be interested in the particular forms of cognitive or preferential failure (or creativity) that occur. Agency occurs within a social or organizational setting; the variables traditionally found relevant in the vast literature on organizations largely ignored by the economists should also be relevant here. Classic sociological questions find relevance as well. Consider, for example, norms and social control; collective action (agency turns out to be a major way in which collective action dilemmas are resolved); authority and bureaucracy (agency occurs in authority relations). Although far better grounded in natural phenomena, the sociological or organizational approach to agency is also obviously more messy and less certain of its logical achievements.

Arrow, whose work has contributed so much to the risk and information stream, has been sensitive to many of these issues for a long time (see Arrow, 1963, 1970); he has written on the role of fiduciary-like norms and ethics in the market system. But despite the creative use of the agency approach by some institutionally-oriented economists such as Victor Goldberg (1976; see also Tirole (1986) on agency and collusion in hierarchies), the disciplines have remained remarkably disjunct in their treatment of agency. Ironically, the recent surge of interest in agency applications in political science has apparently come from the influence of work in economics rather than from the work of those relatively few researchers already in political science who have pursued a more organizational approach.

To my knowledge, the theory of agency as an explicit approach to a wide range of social phenomena was introduced, independently, by Ross (1973) in economics and by myself (1973, 1974, 1975b). I generalized from my reading of Simon, Williamson's work on managerial discretion (1964), the law of agency, and other works on the firm and on incentives and exchange. I called it the "theory of agency" because of common usage of the term "agent" and because of the existence of the law of agency. The law of agency seemed to be a potentially fecund source for the study of social relationships but was unreasonably tied to narrow and idiosyncratic issues in the law. An important factor was a point made by Alchian (1965) in a review of developments in the theory of the firm. Alchian observed, in essence, that divergence between the owner's and manager's interests was maintained because it did not pay the owners to exert full control. I generalized this into what I consider to be the key maguffin of agency analysis, the inevitability of control loss (cf. also the work by Williamson on control loss).

I have applied the agency approach in a variety of sociological and organizational settings, scattered through a number of published and unpublished papers and a book. The topics addressed include certain basic conceptual and theoretical issues in agency, such as the creation of agency, the structure of agency relations, the norms that inhabit those relations, the policing of agency, and so on. The work also includes a number of applications to such areas as advisers and policy analysts, regulatory behavior, boards of directors, boundary-spanning personnel in organizations, implementation, collective action, the concept of the public interest, bureaucrats as agents, public affairs managers, control systems and fleet management, and several other contexts.

Other researchers who have taken agency approaches anchored more in social science generally than in economics include, but are not limited to, Banfield (1975) and Moe (1984) on corruption and private versus public organizations, Stinchcombe (1975) on norms of exchange, Marsden (1982) and Galaskiewicz (1985) on brokerage behavior in networks, Emerson (1981) on agency and exchange theory, and Eisenhardt (1985) and White (1985) on agency and organizational and systemic control. There are now a number of works in the political science literature using the agency approach, though most use formal approaches derived from the economics literature rather than more broadly-based sociological or organizational perspectives. There are a few works, like Rose-Ackerman (1978) on corruption, that rely on the positive theory approach seen in economics, but consider a variety of institutional aspects. In additional, there is a large literature in social science that uses agency concepts but not as part of a general theory of agency (for a review of agency in political and some areas of social science see Mitnick, 1984). Examples relevant to the topic of this paper include Jelinek (1981) on agency and organization structure; Azumi (1972) on actors in organization environments as agents; Milgram (1974) on agency and obedience to authority; Swanson (1971), Eckstein and Gurr (1975, p. 15), and Coleman (1974, 1982) on agents for collectivities, "collective individuals," or "corporate actors"; Howton (1969) on organizational "functionaries," and several works conceptualizing boundary-spanning personnel as agents (see Mitnick, 1982, for citations).

The existence of this corpus of social science work using agency concepts is not generally known; only a relatively few researchers have actually made use of what they saw a a general theory of agency as distinct, say, from a concept involving agents. The extent of the social science literature using some aspect of agency is impressive, however, and suggests that there is something intuitively useful about the idea of modeling agents and principals.

SOME CRITICISMS OF THE ECONOMICS-BASED APPROACHES TO AGENCY

Despite the expectations of some of the leading scholars in the area (e.g., Jensen, 1983), an adequate organization theory is very far from achievement in the agency approaches common in accounting, finance, and economics (hereafter "AFE"). This is especially so for the risk and information stream but obtains also for the positive theory developed to date. In this section, I shall outline what I perceived to be some of the major impediments.

1. Reliance on prediction as the primary criterion of a good theory. AFE approaches typically follow Milton Friedman in using good prediction as the criterion of a good theory. This permits researchers with a preference for certain forms of mathematical rigor and closure to construct agency models with extraordinarily restrictive—and unrealistic—assumptions. But even if such an agency theory may prove to yield good predictions about behavior, would we really *understand* that social behavior so much better? To achieve a certain quality of understanding, we must aim at naturalistic theories with reasonable simplifications. These simplifications should occur, of course, so that the major features of the behavior are retained or reflected in the model.

Following Mario Bunge and certain other philosophers of science, I would insist that the simplification necessary in the construction of scientific theories need not, for a good theory, involve grossly false representations about the way the world works. I can predict with absolutely perfect certainty (at least with certainty better than that in any social science theory I know of) that it is morning when our seven-year-old daughter comes into our bedroom to watch early-morning cartoons; I do not require an astronomical theory about the sun and the planet's rotation—I require only my "daughter theory." But I am not sure I understand the daily cycle of light any better. Further, note that although Ptolemy's theory might actually continue to serve the layman's (though not the astronomer's) day-to-day needs quite well, no one uses it—as a simplification, it is held to be wrong. If agency theory is to have any hope of contributing an adequate theory it must pay attention to real organizations.

2. Ignorance of the wider social science literature. Approaches in the AFE area seem unaware of the immense literature in social science that concerns matters relevant to agency. They also ignore the quite sizable literature that at least uses agency language (e.g., references to things like "the agent role") if not the theory of agency per se (for many examples in the segment of the literature especially relevant to political science, see Mitnick, 1984). To some extent reference to other literature is not necessary if the concepts of agency are kept very few in number and very abstract, with few exact parallels elsewhere in the "messier" and generally less formal social science literature at large; as noted below, this tends to be the case in much of the AFE literature, particularly the risk and information component. Here models are constructed through formal representations of concepts like reward function, effort, risk averseness, state of uncertainty, etc.

But of course there *are* things in that large relevant social science literature that are helpful in understanding agency. Consider an example from the theory-of-the-firm segment of agency theory. Using agency arguments, Fama and Jensen (1983a) attempt to explain the appearance of the corporate form, with a controlling board of directors separate from management. They explain the use of boards by arguing that their multi-member form makes collusion between the managers and the controllers (on the board) difficult. But there are many ways to separate management and control; use of the board form is not the only means available. What alternative means of control exist? What about boards that seem to exist only for symbolic or legitimacy reasons? What explains the failures to exert control even where the corporate form described by Fama and Jensen (1983a,b) exists? Do the literatures on organization design, organization control, the symbolic functions of leadership, and the legitimacy of human institutions tell us anything about this? Even if the Fama and Jensen argument is more powerful and more compelling, it is never compared with its perhaps disjointed competitor. More than this, could Fama and Jensen be improved by incorporation of the insights of decades of work in organization theory?

3. Limited targets of explanation: limited problem focus. For example, the risk and information stream emphasizes decision making, with a particular concern, of course, for the effects of different distributions of information and perceived risk. But agency problems are not all exercises in insurance. Indeed, the difficulties in the AFE area relate to more than what Jensen called "toy problems." The whole approach—not the particular models—is limited. This is not to say that results of interest and elegance cannot be obtained using the risk and information approach; they can. But there is so much social behavior of agency that escapes attention. For example, what about the types of characteristic agency failures? How are they characteristically coped with? Perhaps the trade of mathematical rigor for wider understandings would be worth it. Indeed, there is no need for a trade; there is of course great value in continuing to do formal theory in this area. But there has yet been so little done on the study of the incredibly pervasive and theoretically productive social behaviors of agency.

From a wider social science perspective, AFE approaches suffer unit-of-analysis and level-of-analysis problems. Despite the expressed attempt to be organizational, the approaches focus on the individual-level decision making. The sociologists (and, indeed, economists like Thomas Schelling) have made much of the unintended consequences that attend collective behavior. Where is the place of "emergent" behaviors? What about organizational boundary-spanning and inter-organizational behavior? The units of study should expand beyond corporations and managers; Fama and Jensen (1983a,b) and a few others have made an effort to extend the analysis to nonprofit organizations and non-corporate organizations like partnerships. But this still leaves uncovered a huge selection of social agents.

4. Limited concept and explanation space. By largely excluding the literature of the other social sciences, the AFE literature has lost the opportunity to enrich the utility of the concepts employed and the explanations derived. The concepts tend to be collapsed in that many aspects social scientists have considered important in the past are collapsed or subsumed under an abstract concept. It is not that social scientists have necessarily been looking at the wrong variables to date (though surely this could conceivably be the case); it is that the AFE literature simply assumes away many of the key explanatory problems by using collapsed and simplified concepts and structures of explanation.

For example, Jensen (1983, p. 325) in his article advocating an organization theory based on the agency approach, offers the following "three-part taxonomy to characterize organizations":

a. the performance and evaluation system,
b. the reward and punishment system,
c. the system for partitioning and assigning decision rights among participants in the organization.

As a way to *begin* to consider control hierarchies in organizations, this seems very promising. As a taxonomy to characterize organizations it might well serve to distinguish them along some lines of differences important in explaining some key behaviors. As a taxonomy adequate to build a theory of organizations it might elicit disbelief from organization theorists who hang their hats in the Academy of Management or the American Sociological Association. Jensen never suggests that this typology may capture only the decisional aspects of organizational control; there is an enormous amount of organizational behavior apparently untouched by this, and a host of contextual organizational variables that create contingencies.

To take another example, consider the treatment of agency costs in Jensen and Meckling (1976). In this now classic article, agency costs are defined to include monitoring expenditures by the principal (including all costs in attempting to control the agent, not just costs of *ex post* feedback on agency behavior), bonding expenditures by the agent (the costs of activities to guarantee that the principal's interest will in fact be served), and a residual loss (due to the failure of the principal to get exactly what she wants) (Jensen and Meckling, 1976, p. 308). Elsewhere Jensen indicates agency costs include a separate "structuring" cost for contracts between agent and principal (Jensen, 1983, p. 331).

The Jensen and Meckling (1976) agency cost definition tells us very little about organizational relationships. To give content to these cost categories we must do a great deal of conceptual work. Mitnick (1974, 1976) uses a different, perhaps a bit more organizationally relevant, yet still simplified (perhaps too simplified) cost language, distinguishing a variety of "specification" costs (to tell the agent what to do), "monitoring" costs (to measure the agent's performance), and "policing" costs (to constrain and correct the agent's behavior). These are further subdivided to reflect the organizational decision and control structure. Furthermore, the agency approach can structure a complex incentive systems approach that does include common organizational variables, though still at a relatively simple level (Mitnick and Backoff, 1984). Certainly the agency approach is adaptable to organizations, but we need to face up to the fact that we are dealing with organizations, not superior-subordinate dyads.

5. Conceptual analysis can be weak from the perspective of careful work done elsewhere in the social sciences. There is a tendency to ignore the need for precise definitions. Although mathematical applications can clearly substitute in removing potential ambiguities, we sometimes do not really understand the researcher's exact intended meaning in all applications.

Consider, for example, Jensen and Meckling's (1976, p. 308) definition of an "agency relationship as a contract under which one or more persons (the principal(s)) engage another person (the agent) to perform some service on their behalf which involves delegating some decision making authority to the agent." What is "delegation"? What is "decision making"? What is "authority"? Must it always occur under contract (are altruists not agents)? It *is* possible to work out the definition of agency a bit more carefully, using carefully defined versions of common sociological concepts.

6. Driven by the discipline not by the explanatory problem. Agency approaches in the AFE area tend to be driven by the methods and traditional foci of those disciplines, rather than by the central analytic problems of social agency. I have already noted the limited problem and conceptual focus. It is significant to add that these limitations appear to be perhaps too responsive to existing disciplinary concerns and orthodoxies.

For example, Fama and Jensen (1983a,b) focus on the reasons why certain forms of governance in organizations exist. They discuss, in particular, how these forms apparently solve agency cost problems. Thus the institutions are seen as efficient coping mechanisms; the analysis, like other analysis in economics, seeks to show how efficiency, the key criterion, is achieved. Note also that Fama and Jensen (1983a,b) concentrate on issues ("residual claims") that are posed in a way perhaps more of interest to a scholar in finance than to a social scientist seeking to explain societal relationship of agency.

Now, this is undoubtedly useful and produces some valuable insights on organization form. But it turns the key driving idea behind using the agency approach on its head. The important thing about agency is that the residual losses persist; it ordinarily does not pay principals to achieve perfect agency because the marginal benefits do not exceed the marginal costs. Of course we want to know how institutions *cope* with and *constrain* agency losses. We don't *control*, we *cope* and *constrain*. What explains why coping mechanisms fail? What are the types of failures and their consequences? The agency approach tells us the donut always has a hole; therefore we need to study both the donut and its hole. Absent the hole, however, we do not really need the exercise (for an argument that also criticizes the assumption that efficient results occur, see Williamson, 1983).

7. Static bias. The typical AFE analysis ignores true process aspects. Though scholars do pay some attention to sequencing of decisions and, indeed, are quite careful in specifying decision trees and *ex ante* and *ex post* conditions, they are far from incorporating true dynamic considerations. For example, implementation of public policy (as well as of organization programs) can be modeled using agency and related incentives concepts (Mitnick and Backoff, 1984). If there is anything the implementation literature has taught us, it is that the decision to implement is quite different from the process and subsequent outcomes of implementation. What comes to be administered by local governmental agents is usually quite different from what we would predict based on a statue passed by Congressional agents. Agency as it exists in the AFE area gives us no mechanisms for handling such complex systems. Indeed, if anything, it is intra-organizational and intra-hierarchical; it provides no organizational theory to deal with changing systems of inter-organizational relations. I think agency can do this, but present AFE approaches do not seem well designed for it.

SOME LITERATURES RELEVANT TO AGENCY ANALYSIS

In this section I shall briefly outline a number of partially overlapping literatures that ought to be of significant interest to anybody intent on developing an agency-based theory of organizations. This is by no means an exhaustive list; if anything, it is merely suggestive. I have of course omitted particular social applications areas, though certain literatures, such as that on the behavior of professionals, ought to tell us much that is generalizable about agents.

Although what follows is an example of the "laundry list," it should be emphasized that the literature as it stands now seems generally ignorant of the relevance of most of these materials. Although a few scholars have stretched their work to embrace cognate ideas in other disciplines, we have proceeded for well over a decade now without really exploiting the obvious ties. It is time to shake the disciplinary trees to find apples for a common sauce.

1. Human judgment theory. Work in this area seeks to determine how real individuals with "bounded rationality" actually make decisions. Typically, their decision making is biased and suffers from cognitive limits on perception and assessment (see, e.g., Kahneman, Slovic, and Tversky, 1982; Kiesler and Sproull, 1982; Nisbett and Ross, 1980). Certainly this literature ought to contribute to our understanding of how agency problems and agency costs are produced, as remarked upon earlier in this paper.

2. The sociological literature on norms. Many norms are relevant to agency; most are ignored by writers in the AFE tradition. Examples of such norms include reciprocity, helping, giving, the valid-agreements-should-be-kept norm, and the fiduciary norm (see, e.g., Mitnick, 1974, 1975a, 1976, for a review and some application; see also Stinchcombe, 1975). The fiduciary norm, which instructs the agent to act solely for the principal, is one of the coping mechanisms mentioned earlier; it is a way for the principal to economize on specification and policing costs.

An area related to the study of norms, especially the fiduciary norm, is the study of trust in social relationships. It could be argued that systems of agency function reliable and efficiently primarily due to trust (on such systems, see several works by Janet Landa (e.g., 1981) on ethnically homogeneous middlemen as well as the related work of several anthropologists; see also, for example, Banfield, 1958; Breton and Wintrobe, 1982; Barber, 1983; Eisenstadt and Roniger 1984; Ouchi, 1980, on "clans"; and Shapiro 1987, which appeared after the present chapter was written). Thus the study of the origins, forms, and consequences of trust can contribute to the understanding of agency.

3. Organizational control. Any literature concerned with control (e.g., influence attempts, persuasion, power, manipulation, compliance, social control, and so on) is relevant to the study of agency. Agency is of course centrally concerned with failures of control, i.e., the failure of the agent to act perfectly in accord with the principal's wishes. In addition to some of the original works in this area, a few works have recently linked agency and control explicitly (e.g., Eisenhardt, 1985; White, 1985). The literature on organizational control is very large (examples of the kinds of works that are relevant include Kaufman, 1973; Dornbusch and Scott, 1975; Dunsire, 1978; Vaughan, 1983; Mintzberg, 1983; Thompson and Jones, 1986; for a bibliography see Stout, 1980) and much of it is relevant.

4. Social control. There is a large literature in sociology on social control (for one example using agency-like language, see Zald, 1978; on social control, see also e.g., Willer and Anderson, 1981; Gibbs, 1981, 1982; Davis and Anderson, 1983; Black, 1984). Agency analysis should be informed by reviewing existing work on systems of social control. Who are the control agents? Who do they act for? How are their control means designed, and how does each means perform? (On regulation and agency, see Mitnick, 1980.)

5. Authority relations. There is a substantial literature in sociology and organization theory on authority relations. Besides a great deal of

normative material, there are substantial works that proceed with a
respectable amount of qualitative formalism (see, e.g., Eckstein and
Gurr, 1975; Stinchcombe, 1975; Dornbusch and Scott, 1975; Mitnick, 1974, 1976). Authority relations differ in the amount of discretion permitted the agent and on a number of other dimensions. Their
study ought to inform the modeling of hierarchical relations of agency.

6. *Exchange theory.* It is incredible that so few scholars outside of sociology have as yet made use of the exchange theory literature. There
are obvious links to the transaction costs literature. Agents and principals may be viewed as participants in exchange systems. The major
scholars in this area are very well known and include Homans, Blau,
Emerson, Coleman, and others. Recent work on *brokers* in exchange
systems has many similarities to work in agency, and some of its has
explicitly acknowledged the relevance of agency to work in the area
(see, e.g., Emerson, 1981; Willer and Anderson, 1981; Marsden, 1982;
Cook, 1982; Galaskiewicz, 1985).

7. *Transaction costs.* The relevance of Williamson's transaction costs
approach (Williamson, 1975, 1985) has already been noted; indeed
Williamson (1985) himself offers a view of the relationship. In his
earlier work, Williamson considered the concept of "control loss";
Williamson and Ouchi (1981) have discussed the relevance of the
transaction costs approach to organization theory. An organizational
approach to agency should not, however, be seen to be purely a theoretical subset or adjunct to an orthodox transaction costs perspective. While the transaction costs perspective focuses on the frictions
of exchange, the agency approach is concerned with the problems
and costs of control. In addition, in taking an organizational approach, we are admitting a broader range of sociological and organizational variables, i.e., a greater range of social science. The close
relationship of the central logics of each approach, however, is obvious.

8. *Incentive systems.* In my discussion of the literature earlier, I indicated the ancestral dependence of agency on earlier research on incentive systems (e.g., Barnard, 1938; March and Simon, 1958; Clark
and Wilson, 1961; Wilson, 1973) and its continuing relevance (e.g.,
Mitnick and Backoff, 1984). Incentives, viewed from a sociological
or organizational perspective, are an essential component of explanations of control in agency relationships.

9. *Networks.* Modern work on sociological networks as headquar-
tered in the work of scholars associated with the International Network for Social Network Analysis is often of great relevance to agency

studies. Many of the scholars in exchange theory who worry about such things as brokers cast their work in network terms (e.g., Willer and Anderson, 1981; Cook, 1982; Marsden, 1982; Galaskiewicz, 1985). Many important social relationships of agency occur in networks. An example is the study of boards of directors and interlocking patterns.

10. Boundary-spanning and interorganizational relations. To escape its existing intraorganizational (indeed, its dyadic) bias, agency work might well examine the literature on agents at organizational boundaries (for a summary, see Mitnick, 1982). There are some particularly interesting questions surrounding the creation of interorganizational units (e.g., the United Way), which often act to resolve agency problems for member (constituent) organizations. Boundary-spanners face classic agency problems in mediating between organizational principals and environmental actors whose views they must often represent.

11. Compliance and implementation. These literatures, which are focused in political science and management science, identify important issues relevant to the response of agents to attempts at control (for an application of agency to implementation and extensive references, see Mitnick and Backoff, 1984; on compliance, see, e.g., Etzioni, 1961; Krislov et al., 1972; Coombs, 1980; Diver, 1980; DiMento, 1986).

12. The law of agency. An entire body of law grew up to handle questions of agency; surely the experience of the law in particular agency dilemmas ought to be suggestive for a social science of agency. Yet relatively few agency scholars have drawn on those materials (see Mitnick, 1974, 1975a; Clark in Pratt and Zeckhauser, 1985).

Again, I would emphasize this is only a short and suggestive list of relevant literatures.

SOME TOPICS TO ADDRESS IN AN AGENCY-BASED APPROACH TO ORGANIZATIONS

To conclude my analysis, I shall offer a quick outline of some organizational topics that certainly should be addressed in future work on agency and organizations. Again, the list is hardly exhaustive.

Agency is fundamentally *relational* and *systemic,* and approaches that attempt to bring it to truly organizational contexts must respect this. Many of the topics that should prove most relevant, and many of the ways in which research will cumulate or focus should concern relationships and relational variables. For example, variables like discretion or authority must be defined relationally, i.e., as conditions between agent and principal, rather than as isolated quantities. Thus, discretion can be seen as the existence of agent choice that makes a difference to a principal, rather than merely as the existence of agent choice.

Agency theory when applied to organizational contexts need not display the formal, deductive structure of the risk and information perspective. The theoretical and empirical characteristics need not be different in important ways from what is commonly seen in, say, the resource dependence literature. But agency brings a distinctly different explanatory mechanism centered in the often unavoidable problems of control.

There is, of course, a very substantial literature on organizational control which, as noted above, should certainly inform work on agency. But agency ought to be a particularly valuable approach because it is so general and, thus, potentially so integrative. Agency is not merely a narrow approach to understanding principal-agent relations like those of shareholder-manager; agency applies to all relations that are analytically concerned with acting-for and control. Thus it can both explain and serve as an organizing umbrella for related concepts and theoretical approaches.

Furthermore, agency is particularly suited to bridge the gap between theory and application. Concerned with control, agency focuses our attention on the analysis of incentive systems. It revives the stream of research from Chester Barnard, potentially helping us distinguish what is or is not manipulable, what techniques of coping reduce the agent's sphere of undesirable discretion, what designs of organization or institution can function most effectively under different contingencies.

In general, future work on agency and organizations will need to respect the systemic structure of agency. We need to know about the dynamics of agency, from creation to termination; the management of agency relationships and the monitoring and policing methods and processes that guard against deviations; the behavior and dynamics of systems of agents. For prescription as well as to generate basic understandings we need to understand the characteristic agent, principal, and system problems of agency as well as the coping mechanisms that address these problems. Indeed, the management of agency relationships is likely to be a study in the management, or containment, of agency problems.

1. Why and how are agency relations created? How do they evolve over time? Why and how are agency relations terminated? It is somehow insufficient to rely only on an efficiency argument (they reduce agency costs) allied with a natural selection argument (they survive) (see Jensen, 1983; Fama and Jensen, 1983a,b). Surely this is

part of it. But there are perhaps more direct answers. Agents perform tasks principals are incapable of doing; agents perform tasks it does not pay principals to do even if they are capable; agents solve collective action dilemmas; agents serve in symbolic roles. We are far from truly understanding the origins, evolution, and termination of agency.

2. What are the characteristic problems of agency? Agency problems have been spoken about as far back as Ross (1973). Until recently, however, there have been no attempts to lay out the kinds of problems that do occur (see Mitnick, 1984). Agency problems exist on the principal "side" (agency control problems, including information acquisition, preference mismatch (including risk issues), effort, and capability or skill problems), and at the system level (e.g., emergent problems). Surely if the key tension here is irreducible control loss, we should try to be systematic about the kinds and consequences of the losses that occur.

3. What are the coping mechanisms of agency? As mentioned earlier, Fama and Jensen (1983a,b), among others, have indeed been concerned with aspects of this question. But we need to examine the question systematically, for all agency relationships, including looking both at institutional and micro-tactical solutions. Ideally, we should aim for a theory of agency problem remediation in which particular coping strategies are linked to particular agency problems.

4. How are agency relationships managed or controlled? Related to the previous question, we are interested in the governance of agency relationships. How are they structured? How do they operate? What is the nature of the relationship between agent and principal? Relevant here are both structural issues, such as the design of authority relations, and management issues, such as the design and operation of incentive systems. Indeed, we may ask, what are the basic types of agency relationship?

5. How are agents monitored and policed? Besides the general question of coping methods (and institutions), we may focus on particular methods of information acquisition on agent behavior and policing or enforcement means. What are the dynamics of policing? If the structuring of agency relations fails to limit agent behavior sufficiently, what are the forms of and prospects for various corrective interventions?

6. How do agents behave in systems, how do agency relationships interact, and how do systems of agents behave and evolve? For example, it can be argued that agents bargaining with one another are less likely to reach agreement than principals bargaining for themselves (e.g., Mitnick, 1974). Are certain agency systems more stable or more productive or more efficient than others? Organizations and, indeed, all collectivities tend to be governed by collectives of agents

(not individuals, symbols, physical referents, etc., alone) (Mitnick, 1985). Is governance by a collective of agents more stable, effective, and legitimate than other forms of governance? If so, why?

CONCLUSION

The theory of agency is an extraordinarily promising approach to the study of an enormous variety of social relationships. Lest it suffer the premature fate of such earlier and related approaches as organizational incentive theory, we need to work to make it more systematic, more organizational, and more powerfully general. Existing approaches in the AFE area, while extremely useful within certain contexts, do not now promise the general organization theory that some in the area say is potential. Indeed, we need to "bring organizations back in."

NOTES

I would like to thank Ellen Baar, Marshall W. Meyer, Andrew Van de Ven and participants at a seminar at the University of Minnesota, and two discussants at a meeting at which an earlier version of this chapter was presented, John A. C. Conybeare and Mathew D. McCubbins, for their comments or suggestions. I also gratefully acknowledge the partial support of the General Electric Foundation for the research on which this chapter is based. This chapter was written originally for presentation at the 1986 Annual Meeting of the American Political Science Association, Washington, D.C., and revised for the Agency Theory Conference, Center for the Study of Values, University of Delaware, Virden Conference Center, Lewes, Del., June 9–11, 1987. The last substantive revision of this paper was in September 1987.

5

Agents for the Truly Greedy

Lisa Newton

Agency theory assumes that the corporation is no more than an aggregate of individuals contracted to serve the owners as agents of their economic interest.

But the established tradition of political philosophy, from Aristotle to Jefferson, updated by French, has it that the corporation can be much more than that. As social animals, it is as natural for us to create new, collective beings—beings that then take on character, personality, rights, and duties of their own—as it is for us to eat and sleep. Indeed, without membership—a concept more complex than it may seem—in such beings, the human is radically incomplete.

To judge between the two accounts of "the corporation," we must recognize that neither account is self-evidently true in itself, nor entailed by any self-evident laws. Indeed, current consensus and case law support *both* accounts, with schizophrenic effect. To judge between them, we must examine the implications of each. The endeavor yields contrasting accounts of the nature of the moral human life an of the good society. The writer opts for one of these accounts, the account that follows from the assumption that the corporation is a moral person, while acknowledging the virtues of the other account.

THE THEORY AND ITS QUESTIONS

Agency theory has apparently assumed an important place in the literatures of accounting, finance, and economics;[1] this paper will explore it only as a theory of the nature and function of the corporation, an attempt to account for what does go on in the corpora-

tion and to assert what should go on. The fundamental effort of
agency theory is to understand all inner relationships of the organization as relationships of principal and agent, where the principal
decides the appropriate course of action and the agent's job is to
carry it out. To the extent that the agent does exactly what the principal wants, without supervision, the relationship is "efficient"; but
of course, since the interests of principal and agent do not ordinarily
coincide, and since their goals in the relationship are to that extent
incongruous, such compliance is next to impossible, and the principal must incur the cost of "monitoring" the agent to keep him in
line, while the agent must incur the cost of "bonding" himself, or
guaranteeing that he will in fact perform as directed. No matter how
much monitoring and bonding takes place, control loss is inevitable,
and there will be agency, or transaction, costs in trying to get anything done.

On this theory, then, an organization is best understood as a set
of internal contracts, where each functionary "contracts," with the
party whose agent he is, to perform the function desired by the principal. At the top of the chain of agency obligation is the owner of
the organization—in the case of the corporation, the shareholders,
or risk-bearers—for whose ultimate benefit everyone else is hired.
Directly responsible to the owner are the directors, whose job it is to
arrange for management; management does the rest of the hiring,
and monitors all contracts to make sure that they serve the interests
of the investors.[2] The keynote article for this analysis was apparently
Michael Jensen and William Meckling's "Theory of the Firm," published in 1976 but still universally quoted; it was the first to present
the firm as a nexus of agency contracts, and to pose the questions of
the means to make those contracts more efficient.[3] On this theory's
reading of the corporation, the interests of the principal (the investors, owners, risk-bearers) rule the series of agreements of factors of
production, each of which is to carry out specific action to serve that
interest; after that, the end given, all questions turn on means: How
shall we optimize the monitoring of those factors for that service—
obtain maximum compliance at minimum monitoring cost? What is
the most efficient ordering of those contracts? And the like. Once
the answers are found, they should be valid for any organizations at
all, e.g., those in the not-for-profit sphere, and should provide a
general understanding of human behavior in organizations.

From the perspective of a philosophical analysis, these would not
be the first questions that would occur. The account as given is value-
laden to an extent unusual even in the highly moralistic field of economics, and the first job of philosophy must be to unpack at least a
few of the normative assumptions built into that model. A first set
of questions, for instance, might turn on the identification of prin-

cipal and agent. On what criteria do we decide which is which? And what if the agent inevitably serves several principals? It may turn out to 'be very difficult to reduce any interesting relationship to the "principal-agent" structure posited, and completely impossible to reduce a complex social accomplishment like the corporation to any combination of such relationships. For a second set of questions, it may be worthwhile to pose to agency theory some of the traditional political questions; for instance, where are the interests of everyone else and the world at large in that dyadic model? Where is the responsibility to all the people outside of the shareholders whose intersts must, now in law as well as in morals, be taken into consideration by the modern corporation? Or, more pointedly, granted that we have no intention of letting "the firm" go off and make its own rules in derogation of the public good, how can the contracts internal to the firm be monitored to make sure that they serve the public good? A third set of questions might be more psychological or sociological in nature; social science is not our field, but the situation as posited is bizarrely at odds with ordinary observation and causes unavoidable puzzlement. Is that the way, for instance, that businessmen really live their days—sullenly carrying out contracts to be the "agents" of the shadowy "risk-bearers" out there, while deviating from their contracts to serve their own selfish interests as much as the monitoring devices will allow? It is not clear that people really work that way, and if the theory entails a sociology that is fundamentally false, does not some of that falsehood leak back into the theory?

OF POTTERS, POTS, AND PRINCIPALS

We may begin with the first assumption: that it is obvious in any formal human relationship who is the principal and who is the agent (and that obligations will naturally flow from the specification of that relation). In fact, the identification of the appropriate principal, and relationship, often runs afoul of the same difficulties that complicate attempts in philosophy of science to identify "the cause" of an event. An event may be simply specified: a bullet fired from a firearm passes through the outer layer of a bulletproof vest and is slowed as it passes into the fabric. But whether shot is to count as cause and penetration as effect, or vest construction to count as cause and retardation as effect, depends on the purpose of observing the event: whether we are investigating firearms for vest-penetration capabilities or investigating vests for bullet-retardation capabilities. (Note that change in focus of investigation does not change the truth of any statement made from the initial perspective. Norms and obligations, however, will surely change with change of purpose.)

Even when the effect is clearly identifiable, we must appeal to the purposes of the investigation to select among the multiple causes of a normally complex event. The automobile skids off the rain slicked road at night and hits a tree. The cause of the accident was: the slick road, the distracted (or, if relevant, impaired) driver, the bad curve, the poor signage, the badly designed car, or the presence of the tree, depending on what participant in the situation you intend to blame, rebuild, fine, sue, or cut down. (A conclusion that the darkness of the night was to blame would result in a no-blame situation, which is always an option in such causal explanations.)

Similar difficulties in identifying the principal in a principal-agent relationship have been documented in the literature of business and professional ethics. Our attempt some years ago to specify the lines of accountabilty for a floor nurse in a hospital addressed some of those difficulties;[4] we found that on well accepted principles of agency theory, the nurse was "the agent," simultaneously, for the physician, the hospital, the patient, the profession, and the state—not necessarily in that order or, indeed, any order at all. Nor may we assume that the corporation presents a much simpler picture. The law has been that the management, under the Directors, has a fiduciary relationship to the owners, to preserve and increase their wealth; that reading would lead to the assumption above, that the owners are principal and everyone else agent. But in providing loan guarantees for the Chrysler Corporation, to rescue it from bankruptcy, our lawmakers seemed to be operating on a very different assumption: that the corporation is at least as much an agent for the interests of the workers and the community at large. Surely the Chrysler bailout was not sold to the Congress on grounds that it would enrich the investors.

The possiblity that Congress might have so acted—or rather, that according to the assumption presented platitudinously in the theory, that of course all effort must be for the sake of the principal, i.e., the owners—points to the ugly side of agency theory. The theory does not claim, nor does it exhibit, any neutrality among persons when it comes to identifying the principal. The wealthiest participant gets to play principal every time. It is always the wealthy—the investor, the director, the manager, the employer, the patron, the well-heeled in general—who has to incur the monitoring costs to make sure that the agent—the invested in, the directed, the managed, the employee, the patronized—does what the principal wants him to do. The entirety of corporate enterprise seems, from the theory, to be dedicated to the enrichment of the rich, to satisfy the greed of the truly greedy. There is no need at this point of the argument to start evaluating the moral consequences of plugging this theory into human endeavor—the moral risks, as it were, of thinking in terms of moral hazard—but we may take note that the theory seems to have been concocted for those of wealth by their loyal defenders. This may come back to haunt us.

The question of Potter and Pot, to put the matter theologically, replicates itself on several levels of philosophical analysis; it should not surprise us in this new guise.[5] We never do know, in any typically variegated human relationship, for whose sake the relationship exists; in our efforts to direct it toward its proper ends, we often do not know what those ends are. This fact does not make all analysis of relationships in terms of agency inappropriate. But it certainly suggests that any attribution of agency is open to doubt and reinterpretation, and correspondingly that all normative or evaluative judgments based on such attribution (for instance, that the relation between A and B is "inefficient" because B is not doing just what A wants B to do) must be tentative at best.

OF CORPORATE RESPONSIBILITY

To approach the second set of questions, it may be worthwhile to ask why this theory is so familiar. Clearly it follows for agency theory that there can be no such thing as corporate responsibility for community welfare, for the community figures nowhere in the principal-agent relationships. It is this theory-compelled irresponsibility that provides the link—indeed, we have seen this theory before. Once upon a time, it was the only description of the corporation in any literature at all. The corporation was then described as a legal fiction, the creation of law and answerable only to law. It was presumed to consist of the law's permission to individuals to carry on certain enterprises in ways that would advance their own interests, making the prospect of investing in such enterprises more attractive by limiting the risk of investment to the amount invested. As the investors, or stockholders, were the owners of the company, it was for their benefit that the business was carried on. The enterprise might entail the hiring of labor, the purchase of supplies, establishment of factories in various places, but these entailments conferred no rights on the laborers, suppliers, or community, and were incidental to the main purpose: the return to the stockholder of the profit from his investment. The account of the corporation is from the 19th century; its most familiar recent defender is Milton Friedman.[6]

There is a spectacular arrogance in that naive conception of the corporation. Underlying the structure is the claim that those who put up the initial funding for any enterprise have an unlimited right to the product of the thought and labor of indefinitely large numbers of people, generation upon generation, and an indefinitely large amount of the scarce and limited natural resources of their country. We are presented with a vision of huge factories, thousands of human cogs toiling and suffering in the clanking and steaming machinery, thousands of tons of coal and iron yanked from the ground, its waste destroying the countryside, all to feed the gaping maw of capitalist greed. The vision is familiar: it is best captured in Charles Dickens' *Hard Times*[7] (although the Stahlstadt of Jules Verne's *The Begum's Fortune* does a decent job of it),[8] every man of letters in the nineteenth century was appalled by it, and we all know that it is wrong. Why is it wrong?

Why is it wrong? For starters, we might, by chance, need no argument beyond the bare presentation of the theory itself to see its ethical flaws. We might be in agreement that greed is immoral and an unworthy motive for humans, destructive of the character of the citizen and therefore dangerous for the commonwealth; we might agree, therefore, that it should not be encouraged or even sanctioned as a motive force for industry. (We certainly don't need it as an "incentive for investment," which can be supplied in other ways, public and private.) We might, even more likely, agree that it is morally outrageous that the truly greedy should inherit the earth, its resources, and all the human effort that is needed to transform those resources into marketable goods and services. But such agreement cannot be presupposed, and even outrage profits from precision in reasoning. What follows may help to put our objections to the vision in some usable order.

With some reluctance, I am putting the moral objections to the naive conception of the corporation (other than those above, which appeal to moral outrage and the notion of the virtuous human being) in the language of rights and conflicts of rights. I am not convinced that rights theory is the best approach to any ethical problem, nor that rights talk clarifies all moral matters. But rights language does permit a certain economy of argument, when we are attempting to place moral claims in parallel. For the sake of economy, then, we may sum up the ways that the naive conception of the corporation is wrong as a series of rights claims. The naive conception is violative, or condones violations, of:

A. The right of the individual, always to be treated as an end in himself and never as a means merely.
B. The right of the association, to function according to a set of structured expectations that constitute internal justice, and not to be subjected to arbitrary demands from without; the right of the community, to have all associations within it function for the interest of the whole.

C. The right of the land and environment, to have its limited resources conserved and its ecosystems protected from damage. (If
this "right" seems to implausible, it can be recast as the right of
future generations to maximum resources and an undamaged
environment.)

We may take these on in order.

The Individual Approach

The derivation of the ethical impermissibility of the naive conception from the rights of the individual is persuasively presented in
Evan and Freeman's "A Stakeholder Theory of the Modern Corporation: Kantian Capitalism."[9] As the title suggests, the starting point
for the authors' reasoning is Immanuel Kant's injunction to "Treat
humanity, whether in yourself or in another, as an end withal, and
never as a means merely"—the second formulation of the Categori-
cal Imperative.[10] The evil of the naive conception, then, is that it
sees the people employed by the enterprise as no more than partial
tools toward the accomplishment of projects that serve no ends of
theirs, but only those of others. Therefore each person must live,
and be regarded, only as a tool, or object, for purposes that must
remain forever outside him. For the nineteenth century writers, the
person most obviously excluded from full personhood by this warped
perception was the worker in the mill. Thus Dickens characterizes
"the multitude of Coketown, generically called 'the Hands,'—a race
who would have found more favour with some people, if Providence
had seen fit to make them only hands, or, like the lower creatures of
the seashore, only hands and stomachs . . ."[11] Evan and Freeman
extend the analysis to include suppliers, customers, and the local
community as "stakeholders" in the business, along with owners,
management, and employees. ". . . [E]ach of these stakeholder groups
has a right not to be treated as a means to some end, and therefore
must participate in determining the future direction of the firm in
which they have a stake."[12] The basic principle of respect for human
dignity requires that no enterprise that affects me shall be carried
on in derogation of my rights (Evan and Freeman's Principle of Corporate Rights, oddly named but entirely clear in application), or in
immunity to liability for its effects upon my interests (Evan and
Freeman's Principle of Corporate Effects.)

In this prong of the attack, the stakeholder is viewed as individual;
only individual interests are taken into account, even if the individuals have banded together, as in a labor union, to press those interests, or even though they are affected by virtue of their location in
a community in which the enterprise is carried on. The corporation's

customers, the company workers, and the residents of the company's locations may be taken as typical of the stakeholders; "suppliers," widely scattered, are harder to account for. All of these categories have successfully pressed their rights against the corporation within the framework of American law, with all the limitations entailed by that choice of medium; we shall take them in order.

As the corporation is no more than a creature of the law, only the law, the traditional defender of individual rights, can limit the original "right" of the shareholders to run the company for their own benefit alone. And indeed the law has done just that. Waves of legislation early in the century limited the "right" of the company to make exploitative contracts, legitimized unions, and formalized ways to force collective bargaining. The original "wages and hours" laws were supplemented by the National Labor Relations Act in the 1930s, and broadened to anti-discriminatory powers by Title VII of the Civil Rights Act. The stockholders' agents are now strictly constrained to hire, pay, treat, and fire workers according to rule of justice.

The 1960s saw new waves of legislation, this time oriented toward the consumer. Evan and Freeman supply evidence that "Caveat emptor has been replaced, in large part, with caveat venditor. The Consumer Product Safety Commission," for example, "has the power to enact product recalls, and in 1980 one U.S. automobile company recalled more cars than it built." [13] At this point in the process, "Let the buyer be protected" sometimes reaches beyond the buyer's ability to cooperate, as with the information provided to consumers on the ingredients and side effects of any pharmaceutical product, in detail and in volume quite beyond the power of the consumer to digest or evaluate. Yet the message of the whole is stronger, and more effective, than the impact of the individual regulation: from now on, the protection of the consumer shall be the responsibility of the corporation, and that protection shall precede return on investment as a motive for managerial provision.

The most recent wave of protection from corporate action is aimed at the community. Recent and pending legislation may require such diverse performances to protect workers and community, as issuing a 60-day warning before a plant can be closed, disclosing intentions to attempt a "hostile takeover," cleaning up any toxic materials on company property, and disclosing to employees and the community the presence of any toxic substances or other dangerous conditions in the manufacturing process.

Law gives, and the law very easily takes away. Private property was never an absolute right in our law. It was always *one* way, and a very powerful way, of asserting individual rights. But there are other individual rights claims to stand against it, and the law has limited the free use of private property as often as it became bothersome to the public good. So the moral of this story of the stakeholders is very simple. The first principle of our law is that you shall not conduct an enterprise that affects the lives of others without those others having a right to limit it at the point where their interests are affected. It may take a while, and some social empowerment, to get the interests of all the stakeholders legitimized, but in our law they have a right to legitimate consideration, and given time, they will obtain it.

The only trouble with this optimistic conclusion is that these stakeholders are protected only as individuals. As we have seen in this section, the traditions of the Common Law, which recognize only (real or fictive) individuals, join with legislation in protecting the rights of identifiable workers and customers. These are affected by corporate action as individuals, although they may have to unite into a group in order to have their individual cases recognized. The Common Law cannot act to protect corporations or the communities in which they operate; very recent legislation has just begun to extend such protection. The law can protect individuals, but not individuals-in-association; it does not know how to protect the inner order of an association. There is at least one tradition that claims priority for that order, and to that tradition we now turn.

The Political Approach

The understanding of moral and social theory as a matter of individual rights is, as we know, relatively recent, most conveniently dated from Thomas Hobbes' transformation of Natural Law theory into a Natural Rights theory in the seventeenth century.[14] Prior to that point, emphasis on the individual had seemed almost perverse; the point of Ethics was to guide the individual most successfully into the community, the science of which was Politics. Aristotle's *Politics* provides the theory behind this social focus in perhaps the clearest form: the individual simply is not a complete moral person, worthy of moral consideration. The person is worthy of protection as a part of the community, as the hand is worthy of protection as part of a living body. Alone, the individual is not human, but is no more than a beast (or possibly, Aristotle piously allows, a god), as the amputated hand is no more than meat.[15] It is not the human alone, but the human-in-association, that is morally considerable. It is the association that has the rights, including the right to rule the individual as the organism rules its parts, with a bond so close and strong that no "conflict of interest" between them can be articulated.

Conflicts of rights, on this theory, arise not among individuals, or between individuals and their associations, but among the associations themselves. Every association, like every human activity, aims at some good, which defines its function and provides the standard by which we evaluate its functioning. Of several associations, the one that takes precedence shall be the most inclusive in its aims, the one whose objects is the general good of all the people; that association is the *polis,* or political association.[16] It follows that every association shall have the right to pursue its objectives, as given at its inception, without hindrance, save that these objectives shall be subordinated to the overreaching objectives of the state, or community, which has the care of all the people as its charge.

It is difficult to make a simple translation of that conception into language acceptable to a generation used to focusing on individual rights. Probably the best approximation would go something like this: It is acknowledged (from Plato, Hobbes, or whatever source we choose in political philosophy) that humans must associate together and work together in order to get anything done; that is, that while joining any particular association may well be voluntary (the individual chose that association), joining in association in general is not optional. But the creation of an association demands much more of an individual than any contract for a piece of work could demand. Thus, for instance, when I agreed to write this paper, I agreed to a specific, limited piece of work, to be performed by myself, at my own pace, on my own time, in my own way; such an agreement could be taken as paradigmatic of the kind of work for which I could "contract." But when I agree to join with many others to work over the long term, as when I sign on to work for a corporation, I commit much more of myself than that. I commit my time and schedule, typically (at very minimum) the daylight hours of 5/7 of my life; I commit my creativity, my capacity to work, since the expenditure of that time will not leave me with much energy to expend elsewhere; I commit to accept and work with a variety of strangers, to adjust to their needs and to support their endeavors, thus tying up my ability to form relationships with others; and I commit, as a result of and means to all of the above, my loyalty to the corporation. In a sense, I have agreed to subordinate my own ends, during those hours, to the ends of the corporation; I have agreed to become an organic part of the larger corporate organism; I have freely agreed to become a means to corporate ends. (Even in Kantian terms, this is not a violation of my right to be treated as an end withal, since the commitment is voluntary.) When I join on with a company, *a fortiori* when I join in the creation of a company, or any association, I do not have "a contract" to perform little bits of work for it, easily detachable from the rest of my life as lived; on the contrary, that association comes to define a large part of what shall count as living my life. We are time-binding creatures; we live much more in the significant memories of the past and the significant expectations of the future than we do in the instantaneous present. If I have a commitment to an association, especially one entrenched by years of work with it, you do much more than attack my paycheck when you attack my association: you attack me, in that you attack much of what I take to be significant about myself. It is for this reason that the highest of the associations, the political association, acts with my authorization when it calls upon me to lay down my life for it if it is attacked; it is for this reason that I will obey that call. The partial associations within the political association—church, neighborhood, corporation, or family—rarely call upon me to die for them (although I might be willing to); but they certainly absorb my life as much as and more than the state does, and I see no reason why I should not demand that the state protect them for me if they are attacked, with threat of dissolution, by some other association or individual.

That argument is a long way around to a corporate right to exist, and to maintain itself in the form to which it has committed itself. But that right is all we need to protect it from "its own" shareholders, if the possessive is the appropriate form for the institutional fund managers and arbitragers who know no more about a company than the current prices of its stock. And that right, exercised, is all we need to establish the responsible personhood of the corporation, to make it socially responsible. When an association is created, whether it is a mutual stock enterprise or any other type of collective endeavor, all of those who will be caught up in its life must associate their lives with its, and by that necessity obtain the right to continue that association as long as their objectives and functioning mesh with the objectives and functioning of the corporation as a whole. (Lack of mesh is the occasion of resignation and firing.) It can legitimately be brought to a halt from the inside by the agreement of all its participants, when it is seen to be incapable of seeking its objectives and fulfilling its functions, and from the outside by the public at large, when its objectives are seen to clash with the public good. But private external attacks are another matter. Against these it has a right to defend itself, its members have a right and obligation to defend it, and the state has an ultimate duty to defend it, against those who would destroy it for personal profit. The hostile takeover, and the naive conception of the corporation that justified it, do not float over that reef.

The naive conception of the corporation is wrong, then, not only because it ignores the individual rights of the individuals drafted into its service and otherwise into participation in its life, but because it ignores the social nature of the human being and the enormous, but necessary, commitment of life and energy needed to create an association capable of getting any work done at all. If all those individuals took seriously, for one minute, the naive conception's assumption that they were putting in just as little effort each day as could yield a day's pay, and that they held themselves ready, each day, to abandon the corporation and go do something marginally more profitable for them as individuals, the corporation as we know it would never have produced its first widget. (The fate of our other associations—church and family, for instance—on such assumptions, can only be imagined.)

Rights, corporate or individual, are not self-enforcing. As the remedy for the individuals is in the courts of the Common Law, custodian of individual rights—even if legislation is sometimes necessary to empower the individuals to bring their suits—so the legislature, custodian of the public good, is the appropriate body to protect the association. It follows that the economic means of extending such protection are in the power of that same body. This fact has long been recognized when it came to advancing funds (as in public projects too risky to tempt private investors), guaranteeing funds (as in the loan guarantees that saved Chrysler Corporation), levying taxes, and reforming financial practices that seem to be contrary to the public interest (as in the Securities and Exchange Acts). It is less well recognized that the whole system of private property on which such undesirable practices depend is equally a product of public decision. If the financial community turns out to be irretrievably dangerous to the preservation of useful associations, and if it is concluded that there is no remedy short of the abolition of all private property beyond that reserved for personal use, then private property, too, can be abolished. That conclusion would have to be demonstrated, of course, and the institution of private ownership of industrial enterprises would surely have its defenders. But no economic doctrines, or practices, are written in stone; what the public has permitted, the public can, for good reason, proscribe.

In sum to this point: if the society is viewed as a nexus of individual rights, the naive conception of the corporation falls to the assertion of stakeholder rights contrary to those of the stockholder; if the society is seen as a nexus of associations, the view I find more true to human nature as observed, that conception falls to the right of the association to resist the unlimited claims of any individuals, even among its own stakeholders, and any external associations except the political. In the last section, ownership, or private property, was eventually seen to be one, but only one, way of having or asserting individual rights; in this section, private property is seen to be only one means of organizing economic distributions among the associations of the society, and by no means a necessary means.

Another set of considerations limits the naive conception of the corporation, having to do with the use of the world's resources and the disposal of humanity's wastes. We shall consider these only briefly, for they have, apparently, no solution and very little tradition.

The Environmental Approach

Managerial theory handles environmental objections under the categories of "externalities" or "moral hazard." "Moral hazard" exists wherever, for whatever reason, it seems to be possible to reap the benefits of industrial enterprise without paying the true costs of it, so there is no incentive to economize.[17] There are two aspects to the environmental objections: we may call these "input" and "output" problems.

The input problems stem from the use of limited natural resources in the industrial process. The "value" of fuel oil, for instance, for the corporation that burns it in the process of doing whatever they do, is precisely the lowest price that is offered on the market when they go to buy. The value of the beef that the corporation buys to make its fast-food hamburgers is, again, the lowest price obtainable from the market. The corporation, under its naive conception, is not even allowed to calculate into its costs the value of oil averaged over time, from (say) 1900 to 2050—let alone from 1900 to 2250. We have only been consuming oil from the ground for a century and a half (or so). We have increased consumption, at geometrically increasing rates, ever since. We know that the supply is limited. Yet we have no way to price oil to reflect the supply and demand factors in 50 or 100 years, let alone 500. We draw checks on the future—"by then we'll have solar energy"—we hide heads in the sand and continue to buy at the lowest price available and use carelessly. In the case of the hamburger, there is no way to calculate the real cost of supplying the South or Central American beef, that will include the price of the equatorial rainforest destroyed to provide two or three years of pastureland for the beef that will bring in the cherished foreign exchange. The rainforest balances the carbon cycle in the global atmosphere, keeping carbon dioxide down and oxygen up, giving us breathable air and counteracting the "greenhouse effect."[18] The cost of tearing down the rainforest is likely to be astronomical; but the price of the Central American beef on the market right now is lower than competing North American sources, which are yard-fattened, with very little environmental effect, here or elsewhere. The corporation has never been able, under the naive conception or any corrected conception suggested in the last sections, to figure these real costs into the price of its raw material.

More familiar is the output problem, the problem of pollution. Notoriously, "No one has an incentive to incur the cost of clean-up or the cost of nonpollution, since the marginal gain of one firm's action is small. Every firm reasons this way, and the result is pollution of water and air."[19] We seem to have granted, on this subject, that Federal legislation is necessary to protect the environment from wastes, to eliminate the competitive pressure to cut costs by dumping wastes in the nearest stream—or up the nearest chimney. (There is no such admission on the input side of the question.) Yet even here we have no way of calculating the average cost, to the public, of waste disposal averaged over (say) the 300-year period from 1850 to 2150. We know that in 1850 you could dump anything almost anywhere at almost no cost to the global environment (although local effects of smoke and soot in a factory town could be nothing short of spectacular). We know that in 2150 the cost of any pollution will be astronomical. But how high, and how fast? And how can we force companies now to internalize that cost, at any level, when just a generation ago no one thought to put that cost on the corporation at all?

These environmental costs, surely not new but just as surely newly recognized, are not measurable on any scale we have available to us. They are not unique to the naive conception of the corporation, therefore not unique to agency theory's recreation of that theory, and therefore not essential to any consideration of agency theory's adequacy as a theory of the corporation. But any adequate theory, now or in the future, must find some way to calculate these costs, and assign to each enterprise its fair share of its true costs of operation.

THE AGENTS OF THE GREEDY

In the preceding sections, we have set forth the naive (nineteenth century) theory of the corporation, the corrections to that theory from the background of individual rights, further (and much more drastic) corrections to that theory from the perspective of associational integrity, and final, if somewhat indigestible, corrections from the perspective of environmental crisis. We felt that this background was essential to understanding the relatively recent blip in corporate theory, "agency theory." We have referred, very briefly, to this theory in the preceding sections, after its brief exposition in the opening paragraph, but have postponed its evaluation to the present section in order to see how much was left to be done. In very brief, it seems that there is little left to be done.

Agency theory seems to be no more than a restatement of the naive conception of the corporation, the only modern touches being the starting point in accounting, and the insistent posing of the question, how *shall* we (and at what cost) get the agent (the firm's manager) to carry out the desires and serve the interests of the principal (the shareholders or owners)? The effect is to beg any questions we might have had about whose right is it to tell whom what to do (Evan and Freeman are eloquent on this point) by the simple devise of designating one party as "principal" and one party as "agent." As those are legal terms, and built into our law is the fiduciary responsibility held by the latter to serve the former, the theory consists of an attempt to bury a whole normative theory in its name.

The answers to the third set of questions suggested at the beginning, questions of psychology, sociology, and the nature of work, may perhaps be sketched from the materials above.

1. Agency theory asks: How shall we best, and at lowest cost, monitor the agent to make sure he serves the interest of the principal? Answer: We shall not; the cost of monitoring would be much too high, high enough to consume any profits from the operation, *if* the managerial agents were bound to serve the company only by individual contracts, each motivated by self-interest. As a matter of fact, they are very often motivated by trust, and loyalty, and joy in their work, and habit, and by the dependence of their co-workers on the work that they are doing; and these motivations are both stronger and more reliable (within limits) than self-interest.

2. Of what value is the notion that the corporation is to be seen as a nexus of agency contracts among all factors (individuals)? Not very much. Negotiating a self-interested contract is not only a wearing enterprise, not to be engaged in often if emotional health is of any concern, but one that totally destroys the spirit of teamwork that is essential for day-to-day operations. Typically, self-interest functions as a limit, rather than as a motivation, for work for the corporation: I will not join the corporation at the beginning unless I can be persuaded that it is in my long-term best interest to do so, and if, in the course of my work, it intrudes upon my notice that I am being exploited—that I could be doing considerably better for myself elsewhere, for the same effort—I will reconsider all the (noncontractual) relationships that actually govern my work, and look to change employment. But while things are going well, the demands of the job and the expectations of the co-workers push "self-interest" into the background.

3. And finally, what light is thrown upon corporate enterprise, either for profit or (see Wanda Wallace's explorations on the subject)[20] not for profit, by the division of the factors of production into "principal" and "agent"? Alas, not very much. The corporation makes sense, in its initial or naive form, if we postulate that the owners are the principals and the managers are the agents. It makes just as much sense if we postulate, after Evan and Freeman's analysis, that the

community of stakeholders is the principal and the corporation itself, especially management, is the agent. But it continues to make
sense if we assume the position of the 1950s–1970s Boardroom, and
take management to be the principal and all the other stakeholders—labor, stockholders as represented by the Board of Directors
(all friends of the CEO), quiescent customers, prospering suppliers,
adoring community, flattering professors of management and economics—as the agents of the purposes of the Board. Those days are
gone forever. As things stand now, *all* those days are gone forever,
as the corporations merge and spin off, and the financial institutions
that used to rule them go into a state of collapse. By the time this
article reaches print, government may be the principal of every public firm; but that speculation needs further research and awaits another paper.

And then, ultimately, what is gained by the application of agency
theory to the attempt to understand the corporation? About the only
candidate for gain is the shareholder, who must always appreciate a
theory that *defines* him into the most favorably positions in the distribution: If I am the shareholder, whenever it is asked, who shall
reap the benefits of corporate activity, and who has the right to
whatever surplus there may be from corporate operation, the answer is, me! And the other claimants are ruled out, not by fair comparison of desert, but by the way the terms are defined. Then the
theorists, traditional flatterers of those of great wealth, pressing the
claims of the truly greedy, themselves become their agents. Whatever the merits of analysis according to this theory in its home fields
of accounting and finance, attempts to apply it in management theory can only be mischievous.

NOTES

1. Barry M. Mitnick (1987).
2. Armen Alchian and Harold Demsetz (1972) pp. 777–795.
3. Michael C. Jensen and William H. Meckling (1976), pp. 305–60.
4. Newton (1979).
5. "Listen again. One evening, at the close/ Of Ramadan, ere the better
moon arose,/ In that old potter's shop I stood alone,/ With all the clay population round in rows./ And strange to say, among that earthen lot,/ Some
could articulate, and some could not./ And suddenly one, more impatient,
cried,/ 'Who is Potter, pray, and who the Pot?' " From the *Rubaiyyat* of Omar
Khayyam, Edward Fitzgerald's translation.
6. See, for the classic exposition, Milton Friedman (1970) pp. 32–33.
7. Charles Dickens, *Hard Times for These Times* (1868). See especially the
description of Coketown (Chapter V; p. 19).

8. Jules Verne, *The Begum's Fortune* (1958). See especially the description of Stahlstadt, (Chapter V; p. 56).

9. William M. Evan and R. Edward Freeman (1988).

10. Immanuel Kant, *Foundations of the Metaphysics of Morals,* translated by Lewis White Beck. Indianapolis: Bobbs-Merrill, 1959.

11. Dickens, op. cit., p. 56.

12. Evan and Freeman, op. cit., p. 97.

13. Id. at 98.

14. Thomas Hobbes, *Leviathan,* 1621.

15. Aristotle, *Politics,* Book I, Chapter 2.

16. Aristotle, *Nicomachean Ethics,* Book I, Chapter 1.

17. See Evan and Freeman, p. 99. No one has ever given me a satisfactory explanation as to why the pass-along possibility is called a "moral hazard."

18. Rose, Miller, and Agnew (1984).

19. Evan and Freeman, op. cit., p. 99.

20. Wanda Wallace (1986).

III

IS EGOISM A NECESSARY
ASSUMPTION OF
AGENCY THEORY?

6
Ethics and the New Game Theory

Gary Miller

While economics has its origins in the ethical inquires of the moral philosophers, the relationship between ethics and economics has become attenuated in the twentieth century. This chapter attempts to analyze some of the reasons for this, and to argue that recent developments in game theory provide the basis for a renewed foundation for the ethical study of economic behavior.

WELFARE ECONOMICS AND THE INDIVIDUAL

Ethics is the study of the moral responsibility of the individual. Welfare economics, on the other hand, makes no statements about the moral responsibility of any individual. Welfare economics allows a series of policy prescriptions that carry no moral responsibility for the individual economic actor at all. This derives from the fact that welfare economics, like all of neoclassical economics, takes as its basic behavioral premise that individuals must pursue their own self-interest. The policy prescriptions of welfare economics are not directed at that level, but at the level of government in general.

For example, welfare economists recognize the potential for pollution externalities to create market failure. Market failure occurs when the rational actions of economic actors lead to inefficient equilibria. From these equilibria, it is possible to imagine gains that could be distributed in such a way as to make all the actors better off. In the case of pollution, a reduction in pollution would create net societal gains. However, given the incentive system the actors are working under, the individuals involved face a disincentive to take the actions necessary to realize these gains. From a game theoretic standpoint, the economic actors are trapped in a "prisoners' dilemma," or, more generally, a "social dilemma" game.

Welfare economists do not advocate the direct solution to the problem—requiring individuals to take those individually costly actions that would lead to social gains. On the contrary, welfare economists never consider the possibility that individuals might take such an action. Rather, their policy prescriptions require the government to tax pollution in such a way that firms find it in their self-interest not to pollute. In welfare economics, unlike ethics, the trick is to imagine a set of incentives that align individual self-interest and group well-being, and then call for the creation of that set of incentives. In some sense, welfare economics is inimical to ethics, normally understood, in that its goal is to place individuals in the position of never having to make difficult ethical choices.

We could provide numerous examples of the intention of welfare economists to absolve individuals from moral responsibility. When market conditions are right for a natural monopoly, the welfare economist does not prescribe self-denial on the part of the monopolist. Rather the prescription is for the correct tax and pricing policies that align the monopolist's interests with those of the public. When information asymmetry creates the potential for market failure, as in the investment industry of the Depression Era, the welfare economist does not prescribe honesty on the part of the investment company. Rather, the prescription is for a disbursal of information that allows for the correction of market failure automatically.

For welfare economists, the possibility of market failure due to monopoly, externalities, or information asymmetry is the challenge to be met, not individual ethical weakness. We can tell if that challenge is met by asking if the welfare economists' prescriptions would create an "Invisible Hand" world, in which individual self-interest is the engine for social well-being.

Ethics, on the other hand, seems to be about the clarification of individual obligation to transcend narrow self-interest. To take an obvious example, in a recent issue of the *Journal of Business Ethics*, two ethicists promoted a series of moral rules (coincidentally ten in number) including *Don't cause pain, Keep your promise,* and *Don't cheat.* An economist must necessarily regard these as unrealistic, or even threatening. Do individual economic actors have a moral responsibility to follow these rules even if competitive practices in their industry are such that they would be driven out of business by doing so? Do they have a moral responsibility to follow these rules even if breaking the rules would allow them a competitive edge that would drive their competitors out of business? Economic theories allow predictions based on profit-maximizing behavior; their success allows economists some confidence in regarding these moral rules as being irrelevant. If ethicists were successful in getting economic actors to follow economic rules at whatever cost, then it would require the abandonment of the discipline of economics as we know it. Neoclassical economists have invested a great deal of human capital that ethics is in some sense putting at risk.

WELFARE ECONOMICS AND DETERMINISM

DeGeorge, in his book *Business Ethics* quite correctly points out that "We are excused from moral responsibility if (a) the action in question is an impossible one to perform; (b) we do not have the ability required in the given case."

This precept seems to make a great deal of sense, and I certainly do not intend to challenge it. However, it creates a certain inevitable tension between the entire field of ethics and the field of social science, because a great deal of social science, including all of neoclassical economics, is dedicated to the discovery of interrelated predictability of social actions. Just as the field of psychology has supported the plea of insanity to absolve individuals of moral responsibility, economists can support the claim of any price-taker in a competitive market to non-responsibility for any given instance of market failure or economic injustice. There was a great deal of moral outrage in Los Angeles about the growing problem of smog after World War II, until it became obvious that smog was caused by everybody and nobody as they drove their car from their new suburban house to work in the new mall twenty miles away. For neoclassical economics, the workings of the competitive market are an anonymous and inexorable machine, a machine that any one individual is powerless to change.

The economists in our midst specifically assume individual self-interested maximizing behavior, in the context of competitive markets, as the starting place for our theories. Thus we explain the amount of worker safety in a particular firm in terms of the profit-maximizing behavior of managers, shareholders, employees, suppliers, and customers in a firm. Some firms are driven to invest heavily in worker safety by competitive market forces that make such investments worthwhile in terms of low employee turnover, etc. Other firms in other industries are driven to invest little in worker safety by the competitive forces in their industries, which make such investment unprofitable. The firms in the more dangerous industry have to balance the cost of investing in worker safety against the premium necessary to hire workers for more risky jobs, but that balancing at the margin is done, in the "ideal" neoclassical world, in terms of profit maximization, and profit maximization alone.

Furthermore, since the labor market supplies a mix of safe jobs with no risk premium and risky jobs with higher wages, employees can select either kind of job. Thus, people who are particularly upset at the possibility of on-the-job risk are efficiently sorted into and out of the appropriate jobs.

How do ethical concerns on the part of managers, stockholders, or others enter the picture? They appear simply as patterns of preferences that can be satisfied as consumption items, at a cost. Thus, if a particular manager were driven by his or her conscience to spend more than the profit-maximizing amount on worker safety, that would be an instance of managerial discretionary spending that would by definition lower profits. In a competitive industry, that firm could pay for the manager's non-profit-maximizing indiscretion by being driven out of the marketplace. Or the action might simply lower the value of the firm's shares in the capital market, and in the "ideal" competitive market for capital and managers, lead to a disciplining action such as a takeover bid by a manager who promises a more efficient, profit-maximizing use of the firm's resources.

The individuals involved respond to incentives in ways that they must respond, disciplined by market competition. If a particular employee doesn't want to work at a dangerous job, even with the risk premium on wage, then he can quit. By definition, there are other potential employees willing to take over at that equilibrium wage level. If a manager doesn't want to supervise employees who are taking this risk, then she too can quit. The competitive labor market becomes a selection device by which risk-acceptant employees are sorted into high-risk jobs (like skyscraper construction) paying a risk premium and risk-averse employees are sorted into low-risk, low salary jobs. A manager whose sense of ethics makes it difficult for him to supervise people who are going to be dying of cancer as a result of a task he set for them, will very likely leave that job for another, perhaps lower-paying job. To the extent that a significant number of managers find it ethically appalling to supervise employees who are at risk from accidents, or toxic chemicals, then the managerial labor market sorts out those ethically concerned managers into jobs where they do not have to pay this ethical price, while paying an ethical risk-premium to managers who are willing to supervise employees who are falling from skyscrapers or dying of cancer. Competition in the managerial labor market not only efficiently sorts out those managers with commitments from those jobs at which they will be ethically at risk, it also guarantees that the ethics premium that must be paid to managers who are willing to stomach the more unpleasant managerial tasks is kept to a profit-maximizing minimum.

Similarly, market forces guarantee that shareholders who don't want to participate in the exploitation of South African labor can easily sell their shares in the wrong stock. This keeps them individually pure, but guarantees that the ownership of these firms will be held by people without such ethical qualms.

Driven by the engine of self-interested maximizing behavior, the firm is seen as a great deterministic machine. Who is responsible when an employee gets injured, or gets cancer due to exposure to a dangerous chemical in the workplace? Market competition absolves everyone from ethical responsibility. Since there is competition in the labor, managerial, and capital markets, every individual participant can convince himself that the only option he has—exit—is pointless, because someone else will necessarily fill his role if he leaves. Thus, market competition is a means for (1) guaranteeing that the people who are least concerned about ethical implications of their tasks will be filling the most ethically sensitive roles, (2) and absolving those individuals who are in the ethically risky roles of responsibility by pointing out the pointlessness of exit.

An economist with this neoclassical view of the world is constrained from making very strong or pointed statements to individuals in the roles of economic actors. You don't find economists telling shareholders they have an ethical responsibility to divest themselves of stock in companies that place workers at risk, because economists necessarily see that behavior as inefficacious on two grounds: (1) it tells people to behave in ways that are exactly in opposition to the economists's view of their decision-making process—if shareholders were to take this ethical advice, then economists would have to abandon their own theories of how the world works; and (2) such advice is inefficacious because the economist knows very well that if some portion of the population does divest themselves of the stock, someone else will simply buy it at something of a discount. The same is true for any other individual-level ethical advice that the neoclassical economist can give.

Because a certain amount of efficient worker risk is seen as the efficient and equilibrium outcome of a quite mechanical, competitive market process, no single actor has the power to do anything about it. Thus, by DeGeorge's precept that moral responsibility can only occur for crimes that an individual has any power to do something about, no individual in an economic system has moral responsibility for pollution, or other market failures, or other ethical failures.

THE ETHICAL BASIS OF MODERN GAME THEORY

On the other hand, the ethical foundations for economics become completely transformed by the recent advances in game theory.

The "Gang of Four"—Kreps, Wilson, Milgram and Roberts—put

economics on an altogether different footing with regard to ethics and the individual. These people have, of course, been studying non-cooperative games with inefficient equilibria—prisoners' dilemma games, and games of asymmetric information such as principal-agent games. These are related, of course, since principal-agent games typically involve some efficiency loss. They have pointed out that there are strategies available when these games are played repeatedly that are not available when they are played only once; and they also point out that these strategies support many more equilibrium outcomes.

In his paper, "Corporate Culture and Economic Theory," Kreps analyzes some of the implications of this for the study of the firm. These implications have immediate application to the ethical problem of worker safety in the firm. He points out that the hierarchical relationship in the firm is one in which there are likely to be unforeseen contingencies. It is hierarchical because the employee (agent) grants the firm "much more authority in saying what adaptation will take place" to these future contingencies. He presents a simplification of the game being played by agents and employers in the firm in Figure 6–1. The analysis of this game is that, once agent A has decided to give trust to B, B is certainly better off abusing the trust. Player A must anticipate this, so that the predicted outcome is for A not to give trust. The outcome is unique and deterministic. Because the one-shot game has a unique equilibrium, once again, the economist is without the basis for making any ethical recommendations. He can't tell A that he has an ethical responsibility to trust B; furthermore, he can't tell B he has an ethical responsibility to honor the trust; if B follows the advice, the economist has to give up being an economist and become a psychologist, to figure out why.

What happens when this game is played repeatedly? The most important thing is that the range of possible outcomes is greatly increased. Kreps refers to the folk theorem of noncooperative game theory, which "states that we can sustain as a noncooperative equilibrium payoff any feasible vector of expected payoffs for players that

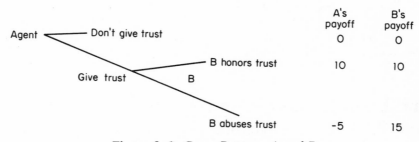

Figure 6–1. Game Between A and B

are sufficiently above the worst that others can inflict upon them." The term *feasible* means that there must be some way to play the game and get those expected payoffs.

Now the folk theorem is a problem for the scientific goal of economists, who want to have nice precise predictions. Unfortunately, nice precise predictions are rarely possible in repeated game theory. There are too many sustainable outcomes, and the actual outcome from along the very large feasible set seems to be determined by psychological, social, and political kinds of factors. In the games being analyzed here, the anonymous, inevitable machine of neoclassical economics is replaced with a very nearly formless mass of social possibilities. But this very indeterminacy means that a discussion of ethical alternatives at the individual level is now much more meaningful. As Kreps points out, the actual outcome selected among the very large set of outcomes feasible in a repeated game theory is affected by mutually reinforced expectations about what is normal, feasible, and yes, even ethical. Ethics, rather than being totally outside the system as with neoclassical economics, is built right into the analysis of the firm as repeated game. At the positive level, we *must* know something of the mutually created expectations and norms about what is right and wrong in the principal-agent relationship.

As an example, let us go to Kreps's "trust-honor" example. Kreps points out two equally feasible equilibrium outcomes. One of them is for B to announce his intention to be trustworthy as long as A trusts him, live up to this expectation, and for A to trust him as long as B in fact honors the trust. The key to achieving Pareto-preferred outcomes is in the firm's creating a reputation of honor, and maintaining that reputation.

A second, equally feasible outcome is for B to say, "I intend to honor your trust two out of three times, and to abuse it once every three, as long as you continue to trust me. But if ever you choose not to trust me then I will abuse your trust forever more, every time I get the opportunity." A's best response is to trust B and take his lumps every third round, because that is still better than taking the short-run alternative of just not trusting B.

Both of these outcomes are equally feasible, from an economic standpoint. But the second alternative raises interesting questions at both the positive and normative level. If getting to the first outcome depends on mutually reinforcing expectations and cooperation, is it not possible that building up what Kreps calls a corporate culture of trust and trustworthiness is psychologically and politically more sustainable when it does not involve violating a trust every third time? In other words, when might player A rebel against the building of norms that involve what are perceived as asymmetric sacrifices? We can all understand what it takes to maintain a reputation of being "trustworthy." Is it possible to maintain a reputation of being "trustworthy two-thirds of the time"? The two scenarios, although equally likely from the standpoint of economics, are much different from the standpoint of the psychology of reputation-building. And arguably, one scenario is much more ethical than another.

The interesting thing is that theoretically, the problem that has been bedeviling repeated game theorists is the indeterminacy of the game. This theoretical indeterminacy allows us to talk about "right" and "wrong" choices when one is in repeated prisoners' dilemma games; and most temptingly, the possibility is raised that ethics will have a predictive usefulness; that is, we do not expect some outcomes that are theoretically feasible to occur because they are ethically indefensible.

The applications of the Kreps analysis of trust and trustworthiness to the ethics of worker safety are obvious. When an employee goes to work for a firm, he is accepting a relatively open-ended contract that accepts the right of the firm to specify his behavior in a rather large, ambiguous number of unforeseen contingencies. The firm must establish a reputation of "trustworthiness" in order for an employee to be willing to do so. And one of the dimensions in which the employee must trust the firm is that of personal safety.

Every firm establishes a reputation with its own employees, and that reputation determines the degree of productivity, morale, flexibility, and honesty that the employees bring to the job. A firm that "skims" on worker safety has to pay the consequence that its employees are going to have an untrusting attitude, which will be reflected in ways that the managers can hardly imagine. Unless a firm is willing to have an employee workforce with the morale of a slave labor camp, it has to prove itself honorable with regard to worker safety.

REPEATED GAME THEORY AND ROLE UTILITARIANISM

I would like to point out in closing that the perspective of repeated game theory and reputation building seems to capture the concerns that many philosophers seem to have with benefit-cost analysis and other forms of "economic" analysis. Harsanyi, for instance, criticized "act utilitarianism" in favor of "role utilitarianism." For example, Harsanyi asks about whether one person has a right to break a promise when breaking the promise imposes low costs on others and gives one's self very large benefits. From the standpoint of act utilitarianism, Harsanyi points out that it is justified. From the standpoint of role utilitarianism, it may well not be justified because of "the disutility to society as a result of decreased public confidence in future promises when people learn about this breach of promise." It hardly needs to be said that this kind of analysis flows quite clearly from repeated game theory and reputation effects. While viewed as a one-shot game, breaking a promise may be worthwhile; but the implications, for society and future plays of the game, of allowing contracts to be broken for short-term economic gain are immensely negative.

A distinction analogous to that between act and rule utilitarianism is suggested by some objections to the economics of cost-benefit analysis. For instance, Kelman objects to the practice of even trying to put a cash value on lives, in benefit-cost exercises. At one level, Kelman's objection is rather foolish quibbling. On the other hand, suppose the ability to sustain a "trust-honor" outcome in the Kreps game depends on the ability of the two sides to establish what Kreps calls a "culture" of cooperation and commitment. What does it do to this culture of commitment if actor A knows that actor B is actively figuring out how many profits it would take for it to make it worth his while to send actor A to his death? You don't have to be too much of a soft-hearted liberal to expect that such a realization on actor A's part would throw a great deal of cold water on his willingness to trust and cooperate with B. And given that the manifestation of his culture of mutual commitment is the repeated willingness of each player to ignore short-term incentives to screw the other person to the wall, this cold water bath could eventually lead to a complete breakdown in this fragile, psychological spiderweb of mutual commitment. In other words, I am suggesting that a complete behavioral understanding of the psychology of culture-building in repeated games could lead to ethical and policy implications that are a great deal more surprising than Kelman's.

CONCLUSION: ETHICS OF
PRINCIPAL-AGENCY RELATIONSHIPS

The applications of all of this to principal-agency relationships must be clear. Normal market relationships are anonymous and short-term, in which an auctioneer or similar mechanism mediates the transferral of items at market-driven exchange rates. In the classical market model, there is little opportunity of motivation for coalition formation. On the other hand, principal-agent relationships are generally long-term and personal. They are much less determinate, and the advantages of socially mediated cooperation are obvious. While the classical market usefully abstracts from the socio-biological basis for developing cooperation, such cooperation is eminently efficient in principal-agent relationships. As Arrow has pointed out on page 50 in his 1985 review of principal-agency theory, "there is a whole world of rewards and penalties that take social rather than monetary forms.

Professional responsibility is clearly enforced in good measure by systems of ethics, internalized during the education process and enforced in some measure by formal punishments and more broadly by reputations."

Thus, in repeated game theory, economics might well have bumped its nose on the natural limits of its original assumptions. Applying self-interest assumptions and monetary incentives yields no determinacy; the folk theorem establishes the infinite degrees facing self-interested individuals in such a setting. The study of the evolution and usefulness of ethical norms constraining individual choices becomes, in this perspective, not a superficial afterthought, but a necessary broadening of the economic enterprise as we seek closure in repeated, personal relationships.

7

Accounting, Principal-Agent Theory, and Self-Interested Behavior

Kenneth Koford
Mark Penno

A common research tool used to study the economic aspects of accounting systems is mathematical modeling. A major assumption made in these mathematical models is that economic agents display self-interested behavior. In a broad sense the notion of self-interested behavior is appropriate in that most accountants attribute self-interested behavior to individuals who are controlled by accounting systems. However, the assumption made by mathematical economic models is rather severe in that it imputes behaviors that are totally described by self-interest. A purely self-interested individual, for example, would prefer one decision over another decision even when the marginal personal consumption associated with the preferred decisions becomes quite small, while the damage done to other individuals remains large.

A common mathematical model in accounting research is the principal-agent model. The principal-agent model views the economic organization (the firm) as an association of individuals, one of whom (the principal) represents the owners, with the rest (the agents) representing the employees. The objective of the principal is to maximize his or her expected utility by providing incentive schemes (contracts) that direct the agents' self-interested behavior toward the principal's interests (e.g., profit maximization). Accounting systems enter into the principal's decisions in that they are typically an integral part of the set of controls instituted by the principal to put bounds on the set of feasible actions that agents can take. The typical cost-benefit tradeoff consists of balancing the increased costs of more elaborate accounting against the benefits of more efficiently directing self-interested behavior.

We suggest that when the assumption of self-interested behavior is relaxed, some results of principal-agent models change. The different results, however, may more accurately reflect accounting institutions and concerns. In particular, detailed control systems that are cost-justified when all agents are self-interested may not be justified when agents display some ethical behavior. Also, informal social control mechanisms may be alternatives to formal accounting mechanisms. Finally, since agents have some underlying ethical standards, accounting control systems will be more effective if they reinforce and utilize those standards.

AN ECONOMIC DEFINITION OF
SELF-INTERESTED BEHAVIOR

In most economic literature (principal-agent theory in particular) a person (agent) is viewed as making decisions to maximize a utility function, which depends only on the individual's consumption. Such an agent is described as being rational. That is, he or she can compute utilities properly (or consistently) and this computation is unaffected by any consequence decisions have on other agents' utilities (unless of course if other agents' consequent behavior affects the decision-maker's consumption in some way).

Sen (1987: 80) defines three features of self-interested behavior:

- *Self-centered welfare.* A person's welfare depends only on his or her own consumption (and in particular it does not involve any sympathy or antipathy toward others).
- *Self-welfare goals.* A person's goal is to maximize his or her own welfare, and—given uncertainty—the probability-weighted expected value of welfare (and in particular, it does not directly attach value to the welfare of others).
- *Self-goal choice.* Each act of a person is guided immediately by the pursuit of one's own goal (and in particular, it is not affected by the recognition of mutual interdependence of respective successes given other people's pursuit of their goals).

Thus if agents care for other agents' utilities or uphold an abstract value such as "I shall not lie, cheat, etc.," agents are engaging in non-self-interested behavior or displaying what might be referred to as ethical behavior. Such behavior can have a variety of sources. It could be inborn, or genetic: a basic personality trait. More likely, it could be the result of childhood and school socialization, and other learning prior to the current job.[1]

Principal-Agent Theory and Self-Interested Behavior

Principal-agent theory is a branch of economics that models firms as a collection of contracts among agents. Agents are assumed to be self-interested and contracts are designed to provide incentives for self-interested agents to cooperate. An important ingredient in these contracts is publicly available information about the agents' decisions. For example, a principal-agent formulation of a firm might be a principal (investors) who hires an agent (manager) to provide effort that is unobservable by investors and causes disutility for the agent. In the absence of public information the agent will shirk because this maximizes utility and the principal is unable to prove that the agent did not work. Hence such mechanisms based on publicly available information such as reported profit become useful for motivating effort, for if the agent shirks under a profit-sharing arrangement, he or she may not be maximizing expected utility. Hence, not only is publicly available information important for contracting, institutions like financial accounting take on a significant economic role.

SELF-INTERESTED BEHAVIOR AND ACCOUNTING

We do not attempt to survey the accounting literature; rather, we use three accounting issues to illustrate how accountants have viewed human behavior.

Internal Control

To ensure against losses caused by fraudulent conversion of assets or inappropriate management policies, firms institute internal controls. Checks on agents' actions facilitate internal control.[2]

For example, consider a newsstand operated by its owner (Johnson and Jaenicke, 1980). While books and records are necessary for tax purposes, the accounting system can be very simple. The owner doesn't even need a cash register. However, the owner's (principal's) risk increases if an employee (agent) collects the revenue. The high convertibility of cash indicates a high risk worthy of internal controls such as overall reconciliations of daily deposits with deliveries and returns of newspapers and magazines. As the business grows and ownership grows more remote from operators, more expensive controls may be required.

Internal control is thus of interest to accountants because good internal controls allow outsiders to put more faith in the statements prepared by the firm since agents may attempt to cover up cheating or poor performance or the information system may produce unintentional errors. As a result, auditors typically study a firm's internal controls before making a judgment on the financial statements prepared by management.

In determining the extent of internal controls, the auditor or accountant designing the system must presume the possibility of self-interested behavior by agents.[3]

Uniformity Versus Flexibility

There has been a long debate in the accounting literature as to whether different firms should account for a given transaction in an identical way (uniformity) or to grant different firms the discretion to interpret the relevance of that transaction to the firm's overall economic position and modify its report accordingly (flexibility).[4] The reasons for and against uniformity might preclude useful information while flexibility might permit manipulation (e.g., firms might choose an allowable interpretation that maximizes investors' perception of the value of the firm). In practice, accounting allows for some flexibility—but not as much as firms would choose, reflecting the attribution of self-interest to the preparers of the financial statements.

Conservatism

An interesting feature of accounting rules is that to a large degree they allow for voluntary negative restatements of assets but not voluntary positive restatements of assets.[5] Thus, if a machine or inventory becomes obsolete, it can be "written down" by expensing the remaining book value of the item but it cannot be "written up" to recognize a market value in excess of the book value. Again, because such actions are to some extent discretionary (the firm can shop around for favorable asset appraisals), the asymmetric treatment of unfavorable and favorable news reflects an implicit assumption that managers are self-interested (since compensation rises with favorable news).

THE RISE OF PRINCIPAL-AGENT THEORY IN ACCOUNTING

By the mid-1970s many academic accountants felt that while the issues just discussed were interesting and intuitive, they did not lend themselves readily to the formulation of well articulated hypotheses.

While principal-agent theory consists of very sterile, simple game-theoretic formulations such as the two-agent scenario, it assumes the self-interested behavior present in the above examples. As a result, principal-agent theory has become a vehicle for studying a diverse array of accounting issues, from auditing to budgeting. In particular, it analyzes how accounting procedures can harness self-interested behavior and direct it in ways beneficial to investors and society as a whole. Some of the implications of these models also correspond well to current practice.[6]

While principal-agent theory assumes that all agents are self-interested, in reality only some agents may be self-interested, or the degree of self-interested behavior may vary. Principal-agent models typically assure honesty and obedience from self-interested agents by imposing risk on risk-averse agents. For example, by compensating an agent on the basis of the firms' net income the principal might obtain obedience (hard work) from that agent, even though the agent's effort cannot be observed. However, imposing risk on risk-averse agents is an added cost to society. In a world where some agents are to some degree naturally honest and obedient (in the absence of incentives imposed by the principal) it may be possible to reduce the risk imposed on each agent, if a priori we could determine the degree of an agent's self-interested behavior. Thus the notion that human beings are to some degree ethical or interested in others' welfare allows a potential refinement of accounting theory.

ALTERNATIVE WAYS OF MODELING ETHICAL BEHAVIOR

Casual empiricism could suggest that people exhibit varying degrees of ethical behavior. That is, individuals may not always choose alternatives that maximize self-interest if other ethical considerations are involved. We propose two different approaches to modeling this phenomenon: (1) Assume that some people are ethical and others are not ethical (purely self-interested); or (2) assume that a given individual's behavior will appear to be ethical in some situations and unethical in other situations. Whether a person behaves ethically depends to some extent upon balancing self-interests against the interests of others or balancing self-interest against some sort of moral standard. We discuss aspects of both approaches.

Agents Endowed with Either Self-Interested or Ethical Behavior

There are many ways of relaxing the assumption that all agents are self-interested. One way is to simply assume that some agents are

Table 7–1. Choices and Payoffs to the Principal

	Agent's Choices	
Principal's Choices	Cheat	Don't Cheat
Install system	$-F-C, G-pZ$	$-F, 0$
Don't install system	$-C, G$	$0, 0$

self-interested and others are non-self-interested or "ethical," where ethical agents *always* tell the truth, regardless of the cost. They cannot shirk or steal, either, since they can be asked their effort level or whether they are stealing.[7]

If the firm and the auditors cannot distinguish the two types of agents, standard results of principal-agent theory change. Essentially, the value of monitoring of given internal control systems is reduced as the proportion e of ethical agents increases. We illustrate with an example showing the value of internal control systems.

Assume that the principal has only two choices:[8] install an internal control system or do without such a system. The internal control system has a fixed cost of F. The agent has two choices: to cheat (e.g., shirk) or not to cheat. Cheating provides a gain to the self-interested agent of G. The system has a fixed probability p of discovering cheating given that it has occurred; an agent discovered cheating pays a penalty (being fired?) of Z. If an agent cheats, the firm incurs a loss of C. The internal control system is installed at the beginning of the accounting period so the agent knows the principal's choice before deciding whether to cheat.[9]

The choices and payoffs to the principal are displayed in Table 7–1. Suppose initially, that $e = 0$. Clearly, if the principal does not install the system, the self-interested agent will always cheat and cover it up with a lie, and the principal will incur a loss of C. If the principal installs the system, the self-interested agent will cheat if and only if $G - pZ > 0$. Thus, if every agent is self-interested, the system is not profitable as long as $G - pZ > 0$, since the agent will still cheat and the principal will incur the additional cost of the system. Z may be large, for example, if there are criminal penalties for cheating. If $G - pZ \leq 0$, the principal must decide if the costs of the system are greater than the gains from deterring cheating. Having the system costs the principal F, while not having it leads to a loss of C; so if $C > F$, the principal will install the system and the agent will not cheat. This is shown in Figure 7–1. A standard principal-agent analysis assumes $e = 0$ and would claim that the system should be installed whenever $C > F$, but that would not be correct if $e \neq 0$. If $e > 0$, the expected payoff structure to the principal will change, as illustrated

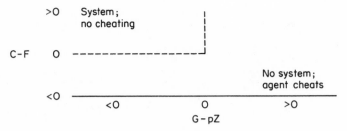

Figure 7-1. Comparison of the Costs of the System and the Gains from Deterring Cheating

in Table 7–2. Now, the self-interested agents will still cheat if there is no internal control system, but since the ethical ones will not, the expected losses decline. The principal will still not audit if $G - pZ > 0$, since the unethical agents will cheat. But if $G - pZ \leq 0$, the principal will audit if $(1 - e)C > F$. As e rises, the system is not installed for C close to F; if e were 0.9, audits would only be undertaken if $C \geq 10$ F. Thus, the horizontal boundary in Figure 7–1 rises as e increases.

Self-Selection The results of the preceding section presume that ethical agents are distributed evenly throughout the organization. However, if organizations have a variety of tasks with different incentives, agents may be able to choose their tasks. For example, if internal controls are difficult to implement in a finance department and the other department is a manufacturing unit where all activities are fully known, then self-interested agents may benefit from transferring to the finance department. Depending on the difficulty in self-selecting, the equilibrium could unravel if the principal can anticipate such behavior. Therefore, this subsection considers an example of internal control (or more generally, monitoring) given the assumption that agents can self-select.

Our example requires some additional structure. Suppose the utility for all agents in the manufacturing unit is m, a small positive amount, and that the gain to self-interested agents from cheating is

Table 7–2. Payoff Structure When $e > 0$

Principal's Choices	Self-Interested Agent's Choices	
	Cheat	*Don't Cheat*
System	$(1 - 3)(-F - C), G - pZ$	$-F, 0$
No system	$(1 - e)(-C), G$	$0, 0$

Table 7–3. Returns to Agents

	Opportunistic	Ethical
Other sector	G	0
This organization	0 (or m)	0 (or m)

G. (We will show that m must be between 0 and G for an equilibrium to exist between the two units). But, in the finance unit, when the system is absent, utility for cheaters is $G(G>m)$ and for ethical agents it is 0. So ethical agents will prefer positions in manufacturing, and opportunistic agents will choose finance.

Consider what would happen if there existed another organization external to this one. If there is some external unit or sector that gives ethical and opportunistic workers the same return, the self-interested workers must obtain either the same or a better return in the unit we are examining, since they can always imitate the behavior of ethical workers. If, however, there are profitable opportunities for self-interested agents outside the organization, they will take advantage of these opportunities. Specifically, take the opportunities of the other sector to be those of the example in Figure 7–1, with values that lead to the No System-Cheat equilibrium as shown in Table 7–3. The self-interested agents cheat and obtain G, while the ethical agents don't cheat and obtain 0 in the other sector. Now, this organization will respond by installing an internal control system with a sufficiently higher probability of detecting cheating, p' $(p'>p)$, so that its optimum is now in the System No-Cheat quadrant in Figure 7–1. Self-interested agents will find their best strategy within the organization is not to cheat, just like the ethical agents. However, they can choose whether to be in this organization (obtaining 0 or m) or in the other sector (obtaining G), and so they all migrate to the other sector. (If their migration leads to a disequilibrium in the number of agents, this unit may be required to provide a small additional compensation m to assure that enough (ethical) workers will choose it.)[10]

Complexities of Self-Selection. Note that the previous notions of self-interested and non-self-interested agents presumes a structure that (in the absence of costs) makes firms desire non-self-interested or ethical agents to select their firms. In some instances firms may desire to *screen out* ethical agents.[11] For example,[12] certain trucking firms under competitive pressure from deregulation may encourage employees to cheat the government by carrying false logbooks in an attempt to violate regulations specifying the number of hours employees can drive. Certain trucking companies have fired employees for speaking out against these practices.

Similar cases may exist in firms doing business abroad or with some local officials. The law bans bribery to obtain business, and firms claim to order their sales agents to carry out this policy. However, these agents appear to find it profitable to engage in bribery. And the firms must find it desirable to avoid ethical agents, those who will not violate federal and state law and the firm's written policy.

Suppose we assume the same definition of "ethical" as the previous subsections and also suppose that firms wish to attract ethical agents. What means are available to firms to obtain ethical agents? More careful monitoring is a clear method, as it reduces the gain from being self-interested. Interestingly, this model never eliminates that gain, suggesting certain absolute advantages to being a self-interested agent. Note, however, that if we change the model slightly it is possible to change these incentives drastically. Suppose ethical agents gain utility from telling the truth, and self-interested agents are indifferent between lying or telling the truth. Then it may be possible to screen out self-interested agents costlessly and there may be certain absolute advantages to being an ethical agent. Such alternative approaches depend on relatively complex utility functions. For example, suppose that "ethical" agents gain positive pleasure from specific ethical actions, such as honest students who sometimes enjoy the feeling of trust and responsibility that comes from acting honestly under an honor code. (Alternatively, deviations from norms may result in sanctions; see Akerlof, 1980.) Thus, an "honor code" type of organization might provide enough utility to attract ethical agents.[13] A comparable case in corporations is the trust that comes with "management by objectives," in contrast to "management by detail." Workers who gain utility from being trusted will select the former. Of course, organizations that offer autonomy are likely to attract "unethical" agents, who wish to avoid observation. In a similar vein, similar agents may gain from being in the same organization (Stiglitz, 1986, or more generally Schelling, 1978). It may be that ethical agents gain utility as the number of other ethical agents in the organization increases. Encouraging social customs that screen desired individuals may be viewed as establishing internal controls. Hence emphasis is shifted from mechanical controls (e.g., physical counts of inventory) to an assessment of the "corporate culture" (or social norms). Thus, this "corporate culture" (social custom) technique could provide incentives that facilitate desired self-selection.[14] As such, "corporate culture" must be considered when designing accounting control systems.

But this line of analysis seems inconsistent with the usual principal-agent approach of detecting and deterring opportunistic behavior:

that is, it is inconsistent with detailed checking of agent actions. Thus, the principal-agent assumption that all agents are self-interested may undermine alternative ways of obtaining honest and obedient behavior.

Agents with Situation-Specific Ethical Behavior

In the previous section we relaxed the assumption of self-interested behavior in a special way. We assumed that we could separate agents as either self-interested or ethical (truthtellers). In this section we relax the assumption of self-interested behavior somewhat differently. We assume that while all economic agents may be generally motivated by self-interest, certain decisions that they make are determined by ethical considerations. In particular, if a decision involves two alternatives that provide approximately the same consumption, the decision may be motivated by ethical considerations. For example, if two decisions provide an agent with approximately the same compensation, but one hurts other individuals in the organization, the agent may choose the decision that does not hurt other individuals even though this may lead to lower compensation.

The notion above is made precise by Radner (1981), who introduces the notion of epsilon equilibrium. A decision is said to be an epsilon equilibrium choice if the difference, in terms of expected utility, between the decision and alternative decisions is less than the number epsilon. Radner points out that when the expected utility difference between cooperating and not cooperating is sufficiently small (epsilon) and agents choose to cooperate, they may make themselves worse off in the short-term (by epsilon) but better off in the long-term (losses due to not cooperating are eliminated).

In this chapter, we assume that if the utility difference between self-interested behavior and non-self-interested behavior is sufficiently small, (1) agents will choose non-self-interested behavior if that behavior is associated with a higher moral value (e.g., honesty, cooperation, making others better off) [15] and (2) accounting systems may help to direct the agent in choosing alternatives to the self-interested choice.

Thus this section views agents as behaving ethically only on "the margin." Note, however, that this margin could be quite large or quite small, for very ethical and mildly ethical agents. While agents have different attitudes toward ethical behavior (that is, they are different types), there may be some common elements. In particular, we might think of general ethical standards as a public good that (weakly) facilitates overall economic efficiency. The "ethical component" of utility functions may be reinforced by sound accounting practices. Here we suggest some ways in which utilities might be modeled, and how that might affect accounting principal-agency theory. We believe (by introspection and casual observation, along with some careful experimental evidence) that most people have attitudes toward telling the truth and putting out "fair" amounts of effort; [16] these are not currently included in principal-agent models, and so may neglect a significant element of reality. People's attitudes toward the "truth" or "fairness" depend upon whether it is clear to them and to others what is true or false, fair or unfair. Accounting systems can reinforce or dissipate these perceptions.

There are two natural approaches to deviations from "truth" or honest effort. One indicates a "best" point or range; deviations from it lead to a loss of utility that increases continuously with the deviation, and quite likely rises more than proportionally to the size of the deviation (at least over some range), as shown in Figure 7–2(a). [17] Thus, a modest amount of unethical behavior leads to slight losses of utility. There might also be a maximum loss of utility or self-esteem from unethical behavior, such that the loss of utility would reach a maximum, as in Figure 7–2(b). The other possibility is that, like mortal sins, an act either is or is not ethical. This case, which has a distinct focal point (Schelling, 1960) or "bright line" that clearly distinguishes ethical from unethical behavior, is illustrated in Figure 7–3; the agent has a large loss of utility from any behavior in the unethical range. Which approach best represents the agent's utility depends on many things including the agent's characteristics and characteristics of the setting in which the agent must make a decision.

Both of these approaches raise problems for the dominant "first-order" approach to agency modeling. The discontinuous model requires that one examine boundaries as well as first-order conditions. Utility losses like those in Figure 7–2(b) imply that there can be two local maxima, one highly unethical, and one in the "little white lie" region.

These utility questions suggest approaches for designers of accounting control systems. Are there ways of setting up clear ethical boundaries that will be respected? Assembly lines, quotas, and precise accounting systems establish clear boundaries between conformity and violation. For example, the boundary between appropriate and improper business expenses can be quite unclear. Yet an accounting system can establish clear rules as to ethical conduct that reinforce people's ethical standards. If the agent in the earlier newsstand scenario commonly made change from his own pocket, it would be easy to (mistakenly) misstate receipts, while a cash register creates a clear standard for receipts. [18]

When clear ethical boundaries cannot be established, is it possible to make clear distinctions between ethical and unethical behavior, so

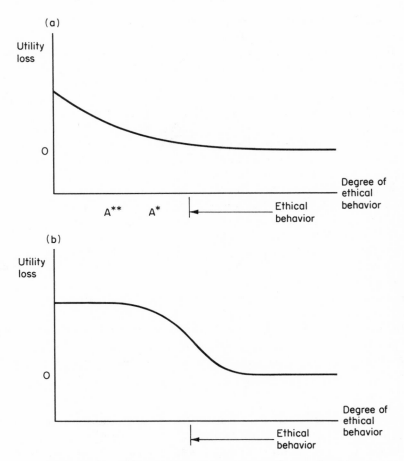

Figure 7–2. The Relationship Between Utility and Ethics

as to maintain the continuous form of disutility of Figure 7–2? What can keep these distinctions from unraveling, if people usually end up near the borderline? The problem is that agents will be drawn to the area around A* in Figure 7–2(a)—where behavior is slightly unethical. The "mildly unethical" behavior will be redefined, perhaps to A**, and so on. Casual observation suggests that something like this occurs in activities like marketing and advertising. One solution is to develop systems that reward people for ethical behavior (and that do not impress less ethical people who happen to be acting ethically), systems that include awards and praise. With such a system, more ethical "types" could self-select into the organization, and would reinforce the social norm that A** really is quite unethical behavior.

A different modeling approach to ethical behavior attempts to de-

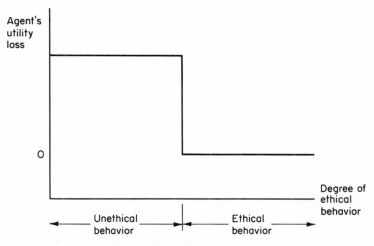

Figure 7–3. The Relationship Between Utility and Ethics

velop the agent's utility explicitly as a function of societal moral standards. This can be done by considering multiple principles—the organization, society, government, or religions. For accountants, The American Institute of Certified Public Accountants, the Financial Accounting Standards Board, the Securities and Exchange Commission, and other accounting (or accounting-related) organizations may act as principals. For example, the American Institute of Certified Public Accountants has a "Code of Professional Ethics" that governs the conduct of its members. Many of these societal schemes seem to create clean boundaries: one lies or does not, acts morally or immorally. Sometimes certain specific acts are considered unethical. These broader views of organization are highly relevant to accountants' work, and they may give firms tools to use in setting up their own schemes. We conclude with an example that shows two principals.

An Example

Agents are considered to be utility maximizers who are largely self-interested but lose some utility from unethical actions, and also face the outside principal's ethical standards. The inside principal and the agent have a straightforward conflict over income. The inside principal can, however, create an accounting distinction between actions—those that are legitimate and those that are not; that distinction makes the agent "ethically concerned." We assume that the agent's utility is the sum of three components: the monetary return, an effect attributable to an outside principal, and an effect attributable to the accounting system. The inside principal's utility is solely a function of monetary return.

Table 7–4 gives the basic data for the problem. There are six actions available to the agent, listed 1 through 6. According to the outside principal's ethical valuation, actions 4 through 6 are clearly ethical, while actions 3 through 1 become more and more unethical. The dollar returns for the principal and agent respectively are shown next—indicating a simple divide-the-dollar conflict of interest.

The remaining lines show the agent's sum of utilities from the agent's dollar return and alternative divisions by the inside principal between proper and improper activities. The line ΣU for agent, Case 1, is the agent's utility from money given the outside principal's effect, without any intervention from the inside principal. The agent will lose some utility for unethical actions but will still choose action 1, as he did without the intervention of the outside principal.

Suppose that the inside principal can create a distinction between "ethical" and "unethical" acts. The principal has no power to "enforce" the rule; rather the system creates an accounting "focal point" or clear division between ethical and unethical acts. The agent sums dollar return, the outside principal's value, and the marginal effect of the accounting system to determine his utility for all acts in each category. The accounting system implicitly (from the inside principal's perspective) defines act 1 as unethical and acts 2 through 6 as ethical. The utility of act 1 decreases to 2.5, making act 2 the agent's best. Hence the principal gains from drawing a line discouraging the "highly unethical" act 1.

Clearly, anything that strengthens the outside principal's sanctions can give additional force to the accounting rules. At some level of the outside principal's value, the accounting system can prevent *all* unethical acts (from the outside principal's perspective) and ensure act 4. However, if the outside agent's sanctions have only limited power, the accounting system *cannot* prevent all unethical acts and it may not be wise to attempt to do so. In the previous example, if the

Table 7–4. Inside and Outside Principals

		Agent Actions					
		1	2	3	4	5	6
Outside principal's value		−1.5	−1	−.5	0	0	0
Dollar returns		1, 5	2, 4	3, 3	4, 2	5, 1	6, 0
Marginal effect of accounting system		−1	0	0	0	0	0
ΣU for agent	case 1	3.5	3	2.5	2	1	0
	case 2	2.5	3	2.5	2	1	0

accounting system were to define all unethical actions, actions 1 through 3, as improper, the agent would still choose the "highly unethical" act 1.

CONCLUSION

An important role of accounting is to provide control for complex organizations. Research efforts include various disciplines with varying methodologies, one of which is the principal-agent framework employing mathematical modeling as the primary research method. The major assumption of the principal-agent framework is that individual behavior is self-interested. This chapter had discussed various ways of retaining mathematical modeling as the primary research method while relaxing the assumption that all agents are self-interested. Our results indicate that such an approach may better reflect how individuals behave and may have implications for managers and designers of information systems.

NOTES

1. See Stigler and Becker (1977) for a model of habituation of a different type, Milgram, (1963) for striking experimental evidence of differences in ethical behavior.

2. For an overview of internal control, see Johnson and Jaenicke (1980), pp. 1–17.

3. Now, the principal's risk of fraudulent conversion of assets is a "business" risk subject to the same (expected) cost-benefit analysis as other business decisions. Thus a principal generally prefers a system that "almost always" prevents fraud to one that always prevents fraud when the latter system is much more expensive.

4. See Chatfield (1974), pp. 297–298, for a discussion of uniformity versus flexibility. For a more thorough treatment, see Mautz (1972).

5. For an example of conservatism, see Parker (1965).

6. For an introduction to principal-agent theory applications to accounting, see Namazi (1985).

7. Thus the world is sufficiently simple that the principal knows what questions to ask.

8. This model is similar to a model found in Scott (1988). Also see Penno (1988).

9. An example of the problem is seen in Green and Laffont (1986); it is discussed in broader terms in Hart (1983) and Hart and Holstrom (1987). The latter discusses briefly (p. 105) the analysis of honest buyers.

10. This organization is assumed to be small enough that it does not need more workers than all of the available ethical workers.

11. The desire to attract self-interested types would appear to be partic-

ularly relevant when the owner (principal) is responsible to other principals (such as the government) and, in turn, may have an incentive to cheat. Furthermore, the market itself may screen out ethical owners (leaving only self-interested ones) because in a market where some competitors cheat and other competitors do not cheat, those who do not cheat might not be able to make a non-negative return.

12. See Royko (1987), p. 3.

13. See Alchian and Demsetz (1972, Section 5, "Team Spirit and Loyalty").

14. Kreps (1984) has analyzed the importance of corporate culture in the context of game theory. See also Miller (1987).

15. One example of concern for others' welfare is (potentially) the affection family members have for each other. Family-run businesses have potentially fewer incentive problems than other types of business.

16. See Eavey and Miller (1984) and Kahneman, Knetch, and Thaler (1986) for experimental evidence on the importance of fairness. Moore (1978, Ch. 1) describes moral codes, and emphasizes the importance of justified authority in moral codes.

17. Consumers appear to have this utility form for goods (Lancaster, 1979).

18. Why do some accounting systems create derision and evasion, rather than a desire to comply? We suggest that agents have underlying senses of reasonable standards that the accounting rules can make more precise. Arbitrary or unreasonable standards create a kind of moral disregard, even rejection of the ethical validity of the standards. (This situation could be modeled with "multiple principals" as explained in the following paragraphs.)

8

Why Be a Loyal Agent?
A Systemic Ethical Analysis

Ronald F. Duska

The question guiding this chapter is a rather simple one. "In a free market economic system, driven by motives of self-interest, why should one be a loyal agent and act in another's (the principal's) interest, if it does not benefit the agent?"

Suppose a stock broker who is your agent, having promised to service your account, was approached by a wealthier, more prosperous client. Given time constraints he could not immediately service both. Delay in servicing your account would cost you money, but you would not know it. In such circumstances, if the point of being a stockbroker is to make money, why should your broker concern himself with your interests first, if that would cost him? This question is an example of the perennial ethical problem, "Why keep a promise when it is inconvenient, in a society where the rules encourage everyone to do only what is convenient?" This is the general form of the ethical problem of agency in a market system.

There is an obvious answer to the problem. "Don't keep such promises. To do something for another in a system geared to maximizing self-interest is foolish." Such an answer, though, points out an inconsistency at the heart of such a system, for a system that has rules requiring agents to look out for others, while encouraging individuals to look out only for themselves, destroys the practice of looking out for others, i.e., it destroys agency. This is structurally identical to the inconsistency Kant points out in his ethical theory. A society that has rules governing promise keeping, which begins to encourage keeping promises only when convenient, wills the disintegration of the practice of promise keeping.

Along these lines, this chapter will highlight the paradox of agency in the market system by showing first, that the system needs agents who act on behalf of other's interests, and second, that the system (as promoted by neoclassical economists such as Milton Friedman) encourages self-interested behavior, which is antithetical to the self-sacrificing behavior necessary for agency. Consequently the system, if is not modified, encourages the destruction of any meaningful notion of the agency-principal relationship. We will suggest a modification of the system using the loyal agent as a model.

A word about methodology: The paper utilizes ethical analysis, which I take to involve two operations, first the analysis, and second the evaluation of either beliefs, practices, or systems having moral import. Economic systems have moral import since they do things for and to people. Hence they are subject to ethical analysis. Unlike some of my colleagues,[1] I do not think that agency theory as construed by economists "makes no ethical assumptions," nor do I think that the concept of the self-interested rational maximizer is "neither good nor bad."

Many economists simply assume the ethical legitimacy of the free market system and the ethical neutrality of the self-interested rational maximizer model. But, paraphrasing Aristotle, any system like any activity aims at some good. It has a *telos,* i.e., it is created for some purpose, which is its raison d'etre, which legitimates it for the society within which it exists. To analyze the ethical acceptability of these purposes is the task of ethical analysis. The agency relationship provides a fruitful area for investigating the legitimating purposes of the market system and business.

We begin then with the assumption that any human system has a purpose, which defines and legitimates it. Adopting Wittgenstein's concept, we will treat these systems as "forms of life." "Forms of life" are conventional systems developed for some use, systems that develop rules implicitly agreed upon by those who share in that form of life. Following Wittgenstein's clue, ethical analysis begins by looking for agreement in forms of life, not explicitly contractual (deliberate) agreements, but learned agreements. The agreements are found in the language we use and concepts we share, which reflect the rules governing our societal living together. Our economic system (form of life) has rules we all agree on—rules about what's fair, or deserved, or just, or right. These rules are so much a part of our society, such basic principles, that we may not be conscious of holding them. But while a society's adoption of these rules implicitly legitimates them for the society, the task of the philosopher is to discover these rules, demonstrate their presence, and evaluate their worth.

In our society, the neoclassical theory of the social responsibility of business best articulates the rules of the economic system we live by. But when we philosophically analyze that form of life we see a built-in paradox, for the basic rule is the rule of the market to maximize self-interest, but it is a rule legitimated by suggesting that such self-interest fulfills the utilitarian goal of producing the greatest good for the greatest number. Our form of life, in a sense, begins with Adam Smith's invisible hand, the guarantee that exclusively self-interested pursuit will benefit the whole of society. This classical ethical justification of the market system is adopted by neoclassical economic theorists such as Milton Friedman, and functions as an ethical justification of the economic system.[2]

Hence, our society defines and legitimates business's purpose, so that the goal of making a profit makes some behavior acceptable that ordinarily would be condemned. For example, we condone (justify) the firing of a loyal employee to cut costs under the rubric of "that's business," for we believe or agree with Friedman and the neoclassical theorists that "business's primary and only responsibility is to make a profit."[3] We agree on rules of fairness that dictate who "deserves" what and for what. The system has its own principles of distributive justice, and the economist does not just engage in descriptive tasks, for to the extent that he accepts the standards of the system, such as efficiencies at all costs, he accepts the justice of the system. "Profit" may descriptively mean value over costs, while "wages" are what are paid to workers, but we have generally agreed upon rules about who gets the profit and who "deserves" the profit, and why they deserve it. The answer to the *why?* is the ethical reason. Anyone who has taught a course in business ethics and has asked students, *Who* is entitled to the profit? must be impressed by the unanimity of students in thinking it goes to the owner of the means of production. At any rate, how profit and wages get distributed and the reasons legitimating that distribution are prescriptive considerations dictated by the purposes of the system. In short, the economy does things to people, and defenders of economic systems necessarily become defenders of ethical systems.

Adopting this as our task, we will attempt to analyze and evaluate the market system and its relationship to the concept of agency. We will attempt to show that a system that recommends egoism, but justifies that egoism by a utilitarianism, is in conflict with any use of a concept of agency that implies loyalty. This will become clearer as we turn to an analysis of the principal-agent relationship.

AGENCY AND THE PROBLEM OF AGENCY

The agency relationship that concerns us is a business (economic) relationship modeled after other principal-agent relationships in which an agent is a person who acts on behalf of another person, the principal. The doctor-patient or lawyer-client relationships are clear examples of agent-principal relationships. The doctor as agent is expected to do what is best for the patient, the principal, and the lawyer as agent is expected to do what is best for the client. It is also expected, and this point is crucial, that, if necessary, the doctor or lawyer will set aside their own interests for the sake of the patient or client. Today a question has arisen about a doctor's responsibility to care for a patient with AIDS even if it means the doctor is risking his own health. The fact that the burden of proof is on those who argue against the doctor's being altruistic shows that the ordinarily accepted notion of an agent is one who acts for another, even at a cost to himself.

The principal-agent relationship arose in business because modern commercial relations needed people who could act on behalf of others. As Metzger says:

> . . . It is difficult to imagine how modern commercial relations could continue without the legal institution of agency. If agency law did not exist, an individual proprietor's ability to engage in trade would be restricted by the need to make each contract for purchase or sale in person. Because they are artificial persons that can act only through their agents, corporations could not function without agency law. Agency makes it possible for such actors to expand the range of their economic activities by increasing the number of transactions that they can complete within a given time.[4]

So agents are necessary for business. While there may be cases where the entrepreneur is the sole owner, makes all the purchases, runs the entire business, and acts as his own agent, as soon as a business expands, the owner or entrepreneur needs agents to act on her behalf.

The original concept of agency used in business was a legal concept that defined agency as "A two party relationship in which one party (the agent) is authorized to act on behalf of, and under the control of the other party (the principal)."[5] The laws of agency imposed a specific duty of loyalty on the agent. Robert Clark identifies this as a "fiduciary duty of loyalty" contained within the law's concept of agency, a duty conceived in order to "help deter abuse of managerial discretion."[6]

Such a duty of loyalty means the agent cannot always put himself first. Clark, in support of the claim that the agent has a duty to put the interests of the principal before his own, quotes Justice Douglas's "Seven Commandments of the Fiduciary Relationship." The first commandment clearly requires periodic self-sacrifice on the part of an agent. "He who is in such a fiduciary position cannot serve himself first and his cestius second."[7] Further, Clark asserts that in the law, almost by definition, the manager's job, as agent, is to act on behalf of others in carrying out corporate business activities.[8]

Since the first application of the agency-principal relationship to commercial ventures required loyalty, the concept of agency logically implied loyalty. However, as economists began to address the concept of agency they dropped the notion of loyalty. Our contention is that it was necessary for them to drop the notion of loyalty because the view of human nature that they adopted was the view of the self-interested rational maximizer, a view incompatible with any notion of a loyal agent. In order to see this, we look at how the problem of agency arose for economists.

THE ECONOMISTS' PROBLEM OF AGENCY

Jensen and Meckling[9] note that the problem of agency is raised by Adam Smith in the following passage.

> The directors of such (joint-stock) companies, however, being the managers rather of other people's money than of their own, it cannot well be expected, that they should watch over it with the same anxious vigilance with which the partners in a private copartnery frequently watch over their own. Like the stewards of a rich man, they are apt to consider attention to small matters as not for their master's honour, and very easily give themselves a dispensation from having it. Negligence and profusion, therefore, must always prevail, more or less, in the management of the affairs of such a company.[10] (Adam Smith *The Wealth of Nations*, 1776, Modern Library, 1937, p. 700)

Pratt and Zeckhauser state the problem for twentieth century readers.

> A predominant concern for an economy, discussed since the time of Adam Smith, is to assure that production is conducted in the most efficient manner. . . . But even if we could figure out, or were willing to let the market figure out, the most efficient way to produce goods, there would be the problem of ensuring that each individual perform his or her agreed-on task.[11]

Economists, then, seek ways "to structure an agreement that will induce agents to serve the principals interest,"[12] and what was a solution for lawyers becomes a problem for economists. For lawyers, agents are, by definition, individuals committed to being loyal, individuals bound by their word or their fiduciary bond. For economists, agents need inducement to fulfill their agency obligations because economists view human beings as self-interested rational maximizers, self-interested in the sense of selfish. We define selfish behavior as self-interested behavior at the expense of others. That means that given a conflict of interest, the individual will always put herself first. (Any other view of self-interested becomes vacuous, for there is nothing wrong with putting oneself first, if no one else suffers. But do humans invariably put themselves first, i.e., are they selfish? The crucial situations in life are those where the pursuit of one's own interest will hurt another. If there are times when humans put their interests aside, we need to be able to explain this altruistic behavior and factor it into our predictions. If there are not these times, then the view of self-interested maximizers is equivalent to the view of selfish maximizers. The failure to make the distinction between self-interested and selfish is crucial and leads to several of the difficulties we will address in this chapter.)

Hence, for economists, inducing the agent to do the principal's bidding is a problem because they adopt the paradigm of the self-interested rational human. This view of economic man expects no altruistic behavior, and hence no loyalty. From such a perspective, no predictions are made that would assume loyal non-self-interested behavior.

As we saw, Smith wrote that we could not expect "that (managers) should watch over other people's money than their own." While fiduciary responsibility requires just that, the economist's view of a human being does not expect adherence to altruistic fiduciary responsibility.

Clearly, there is an extent to which Smith and the economists are right. Human beings are self-interested and will not always look out for the interests of others. But there are times they will set aside their interests to act on behalf of others. Agency situations were presumably set up to guarantee those times. But agency, then, assumes the possibility of other-directed behavior. If, like the economists, we assume no altruistic behavior possible we radically alter the concept of agency, and skew the problem of agency costs.

But do economists make such an assumption of exclusively self-interested behavior? I think so. To show that, we will look at two attempts to set up the problem of agency costs, beginning with the attempt by Terry Moe. According to Moe, "The agent has his own interests at heart, and is induced to pursue the principal's objectives only to the extent that the incentive structure imposed in their contract renders such behavior advantageous."[13]

This implies that agents act exclusively out of self-interest, for it claims that the agent will be induced to pursue the principal's objectives, "only to the extent" that such behavior is advantageous to the agent. But an agent who acts for another only when it benefits the agency is not really an agent. This way of setting up the problem destroys the very concept of an agent, because it assumes altruistic agents are impossible.

But such an assumption has serious consequences. As we already saw, it destroys the original concept of agency. Secondly, to the extent that it is wrong and does not factor in altruistic behavior, it skews predictions of behavior. But more, as it gets accepted as a legitimating reason for certain behavior in our form of life, it becomes subtly self-fulfilling. In short, if I think humans are always going to be selfish, and cannot help but be so, it becomes the height of foolishness to sacrifice myself, or to predict their behavior on any other than selfish grounds. This is a classic example of self-fulfilling prophecy. Finally, such a prediction disintegrates the very concept of agency. After all, *ought* implies *can,* and if I cannot go against my nature, and my nature is exclusively self-interested, I would be foolish to expect I could act otherwise, and expect others to act otherwise. But this makes the agency relationship foolish.

But not only does the assumption have bad consequences, it is mistaken. As we said, it is true that people act in their own interest most of the time, but there are clearly times when they don't—when they act in the interest of others. Factoring in those times when behavior is not exclusively self-interested would seem to be important for any scientific explanations or predictions.

Of course defenders of psychological egoism, the theory that all human behavior is always self-interested, would deny the above. But enough has been written about the tautological or trivial nature of that claim, which makes behavior self-interested by definition. Ironically, though, some of the best evidence against psychological egoism is found in the operation of agents. That is, when we look at people acting on behalf of others, as their agents, we see people who set aside their own interest for the sake of others. To show the falsity of Moe's claim we need only substitute the word "doctor," for the word "agent." Remember that Moe cites the doctor as a prime example of an agent. So, substituting "doctor" for "agent" in Moe's quote, we get the following assertion: "The doctor has his own interests at heart, and is induced to pursue the principal's (the patient's) objectives (health) *only to the extent* that the incentive structure imposed in their contract renders such behavior advantageous."

But is this not patently false? Do doctor's really only pursue the patient's health to the extent that that pursuit is advantageous to the doctor? Hence, the manner in which Moe characterizes agents is not always true of doctors (hopefully it is rarely true), and doctors are a prime example of agents.

Perhaps, though, Moe's characterization of agents is true in systems where "the incentive structures" make self-interested behavior the norm, e.g., in a business structure. If that is the case there is a real difference in the notion of an agent as ordinarily used and the notion of the agent as it is used in systems having self-interested incentive structures like the business structure. Thus, Moe could restrict the self-interested assumption to business practices, so that only in the context of business does the agent act opportunistically. Human beings in the business structures then would be viewed as acting in a thoroughly self-interested manner, and Moe's passage could read, "In business the agent has only his own interests at heart." This sounds very much like Adam Smith's view and the latter day view of neo-classical economists such as Milton Friedman.

But there is a problem with this view, for Moe does not intend to restrict his claim to business structures. Rather he thinks that the economic analysis of the problem of agency can cover organizations of all kinds. He cites with approval the following passage of Jensen and Meckling's seminal work on agency.

> The problem of inducing an "agent" to behave as if he were maximizing the "principal's" welfare is quite general. It exists in all organizations and in all cooperative efforts. . . . The development of theories to explain the form which agency costs take . . . and how and why they are born (sic) will lead to a rich theory of organizations which is now lacking in economics and the social sciences generally.[14]

A theory of organizations, pervading the social sciences, which is used to make policy decisions based on the patently false rational maximizer paradigm, is enough to give one pause, for two reasons. First, predictions will be based on false assumptions of human behavior, and second, as is shown in the prisoner's dilemma, if we use those false assumptions about others in calculating our responses to them, they become self-fulfilling prophecies.

But let us return to the claim that economists assume exclusively self-interested behavior. We find that assumption also made in Jensen and Meckling. They do not categorically assert psychological egoism, but they use it as a working hypothesis. "If both parties to the relationship are utility maximizers, there is good reason to believe that the agent will not always act in the best interests of the principal ."[15]

But why assume that both parties in an agency relationship are always utility maximizers? Rather, is it not the very nature of an agency relationship to require the agent to set aside his own utility? For example, a student engages me to write a letter of recommendation for her. But the student doesn't assume I am a self-interested utility maximizer, so the student doesn't assume a problem of agency.

From the student's point of view I am a professor, and part of my job, one that is tedious and hardly to my advantage, is to write a certain amount of letters of recommendation. The student assumes that is done because most teachers are supposed to do that.

But let's return to Jensen and Meckling's quote. "There is good reason to believe that the agent will not always act in the best interests of the principal." But what are those good reasons? When won't the agent act in the best interests of the principal? Only when it is detrimental to the agent? But that is precisely the time when agency is needed. And to say that agents act on their own behalf when their interest would suffer if they don't, is to aquiesce in psychological egoism and make agency impossible. If there are factors other than self-interest motivating the agent, it would behoove the economist to discover them and modify the assumption. Economists who use the rational maximizer paradigm exclusively turn agency on its head, for if human beings are exclusively rational maximizers, agency on behalf of others is impossible.

Now the implications of this are arresting. We can expect the original concept of agency, which contained notions of loyalty, fidelity, stewardship, trust, and concern for others, and hence implied a view of human nature that was at times altruistic, to be changed, in the hands of the economists, into a concept of purely contractual relationships, made between rational maximizers, such that every human relationship is an agency relationship, and the notion of agency loses any special force. But this is exactly what happened in recent work on agency.

Note how Pratt and Zeckhauser described the agency relationship. "Whenever one individual depends on the action of another, an *agency relationship* arises. The individual taking the action is called *the agency*. The affected party is the *principal*."[16] But relationships where one individual depends on another are pervasive. Thus Pratt and Zeckhauser see the relationship as "pervasive in business. Recognizing this recurrent pattern, which underlies a variety of surface forms, helps explain a great deal about how business is organized. That is, business' relationships are structured so as to enable principals to exert an appropriate influence on the actions of agents."[17]

Of course, the agency relationship viewed this way is pervasive. But it is not only pervasive in business, it is pervasive everywhere. If an agency relationship exists, *"whenever* one individual depends on the actions of another," then every relationship is an agency relationship. But such a description distorts the meaning of agency. Slaves depend on masters, and as Hegel showed, masters depend on slaves, but is the master-slave relationship an agency-principal relationship? In one sense every person can be shown to depend on every other person's actions. But if all agency involves is a dependence relationship with no further specification, then the "agency relationship" is simply a relationship, and nothing is gained by adding the qualifier "agency" to it. But such a pervasive concept is not rich and can hardly explain a great deal about how business is organized. The agency relationship can be pervasive in business then only at the cost of the concept's becoming vacuous. An employer is not the agent of the employee, even though the employee *depends* on the employer. But the employee may be the agent of the employer.

Thus far we have seen that "agency" at one time meant a relationship requiring loyalty and fidelity in the service of another, and was a solution to a limited number of situations in business. An agent who lived up to her moral commitment of loyalty was an efficient solution to Smith's problem of getting one person in business to act for the sake of another. In most cases, even today, as a matter of fact, a loyal agent will be the most efficient solution to the problem of agency costs, but then only where agency is limited in its applicability.

AGENCY COSTS

How does the above impact on the problem of agency costs? We wish to suggest that the reason the agency literature has become so popular is that agency presents a solution to some costs rather than a problem. That is, if we have loyal agents, some agency costs are reduced. But what are these costs?

In agency theory there is talk of transaction costs, i.e., what it costs to get the agent to do the principal's bidding. Since an agent is to do what is in the best interests of the client or principal, and since the agent is a different person with his own perceptions and interests, at least three types of costs arise: (1) because the agent needs to learn what the principal needs or wants, there are the information costs required to instruct the agent; (2) there is the cost of checking or auditing the agent's behavior to see if it is done right—the monitoring costs; and (3) since the agent has her own desires, which may conflict with the principal's, some costs will be required to get the agent to do the will of the principal—motivating or policing costs. These monitoring, motivating, or policing costs are the costs that are of concern to us in this chapter. There is no way to avoid information and mistake correction. But at times the agent's loyalty could eliminate motivating and policing costs. So we need to ask what incentives or motivations are likely to bend the agent's will to the will of the principal.

There seem to be four possible types of motivation usually recommended. The first two are the obvious modes of motivating, re-

warding and punishing. A principal can engage in positive rein-
forcement with the use of money or other incentives, (the carrot) or
penalties (the stick) to encourage the agent. Besides these motiva-
tors, the principal has the law as a prod in the form of agency law,
which as we saw, requires a certain "loyal" behavior from the agent.
Finally, some economists recently have suggested that there is a cost
utility in encouraging ethical, i.e., "altruistic" behavior. For example,
Eric Noreen in an interesting article suggests that agents in business
adopt ethical principles, because the adoption of such principles, which
stress keeping promises, meeting obligations, and acting atruistically
or even loyally, will reduce transaction costs and lead to more efficiency. He suggests that "At least some varieties of ethical behavior
are not to be scorned; they are a necessary lubricant for the functioning of markets."[18] These claims are based on studies on game
theory, which show that in some circumstances other-regarding behavior rather than competitive behavior leads to more productive
results. The fourth motivator, then, is an appeal to other-regarding
ethical principles.

Along with economists such as Noreen, there are a number of
organizational theorists for whom loyalty is productive of efficiency.
Obviously, if a principal can get the agent to take his fiduciary responsibility seriously, policing costs will be reduced and greater efficiency will result. In this vein, Paul Lawrence, the organizational theorist says, "Ideally, we would want one sentiment to be dominant in
all employees from top to bottom, namely a complete loyalty to the
organization purpose."[19]

But there is a problem with Noreen's and Lawrence's approach.
Its appeal to altruism or loyalty runs counter to the assumption of
humans as exclusively self-interested, and hence looks naive to those
adopting an opportunistic view of human beings. For hard-nosed
economists, appeals to ethical concerns such as loyalty necessarily look
naive because of the egoistic view of human motivation that they
adopt. They expect self-interested, profit-oriented behavior. Hence,
the insistence that the system be guided by the self-interested pursuit
of profit undermines all attempts such as Noreen's to bolster loyalty
or cooperation or team spirit. With respect to agency obligations,
this insistence on self-interest creates a paradox, for the agent is required to suppress his self-interest for the sake of a principal. But if
the agent is like everyone else, entirely self-interested, as the egoistic
view of the atomistic man suggests, why should or would that self-
interested agent give up her own interest for the sake of a principal's
interest, when the principal's interest conflicts with the agent's. On
this account, there is no good reason. Thus, economists are left with
the anomaly of a system that rests on self-interest needing to find a
self-interested motive for someone to give up their self-interest—a

selfish reason for not being selfish, so to speak. This is indeed para-
doxical if not downright contradictory.

GLAUCON'S PROBLEM

Thus, we see that underneath the problem of agency costs is a philosophical problem, the problem of "Why be a loyal agent?" Students
of ethics will recognize this as a perennial problem structurally similar to a problem raised first by Glaucon in Plato's *Republic,* again by
Thomas Hobbes in the seventeenth century, and recently by John
Rawls, among others, who dubbed it "the free rider" problem.

Glaucon presents the problem in the context of society as a whole,
whereas the agency problem is a problem within the economic system. Nevertheless they are structurally similar. If everyone is motivated only by self-interest, then society is held together by agreements that are entered into only for the sake of self-interest. If that
is the case, why abide by these agreements when they are not in
one's self-interest? Glaucon maintains there is no reason. If the reason for making a contract in the first place was that it would make
me better off, why abide by that contract when doing so will not
make me better off?

The seventeenth century English philosopher Thomas Hobbes who,
like Glaucon, sees our laws as the result of agreements ("social contracts") forged on the basis of self-interest, also clearly sees there is
no reason for an individual to obey the law if it is not to the individual's advantage. Still, Hobbes, like Noreen, also looks at the problem
from the point of view of society overall, and not just from the individual's point of view. He realizes that if everyone broke the contract society would be chaotic and our individual lives would be "nasty,
brutish and short." Hence Hobbes recommends strict sanctions that
will make it in the interest of the individual to follow laws. Now it is
true that life would be chaotic, if everyone looked out for themselves
alone. But without strong sanctions why should we bother with the
societal perspective that promotes concern for others, if from our
individual perspective our particular interests will not be served by
honoring the contracts we have made? But he never answers the
questions "Why not break the law if it is to my advantage?"

Ian Maitland gives a modern rendering of the Glaucon, Hobbes
problem in an insightful article called "The Structure of Business
and Corporate Responsibility." Maitland says:

> . . . minus coercion, codes of conduct are inherently unstable. The de-
> fection of even a handful of firms would undermine the social contract

on which the consent of the majority was based . . . self-regulation is of limited usefulness because of the free-rider problem.

In our atomistic market economy, firms are bound to take a partial or parochial view of their behavior and its consequences. For the most part, their own actions, seen in isolation, have imperceptible impacts for better or for worse on the general welfare. Firms may well deplore the consequences that result when all firms engage in irresponsible actions, but so long as they have no control over other firms' behavior they have no incentive to behave responsibly themselves. In such circumstances, social responsibility is not rational but irrational.[20]

Maitland reiterates the structure of Hobbes's and Glaucon's argument. People made agreements to surrender some of their interests for the well-being of society, recognizing the trouble that arises when everyone behaves self-interestedly. But, if we know everyone won't behave selfishly, then self-interested behavior is rational, because being a free-rider will be in one's interest—it will give one edge on the competition, while abiding by the rules, if there are not penalties attached to breaking them, will simply put one at a disadvantage. Thus one can justify being a free rider because after all everyone else is in this for their own interest. Others are just not clever enough to catch on.

For our purpose, it is important to reiterate that it is this egoistic view of human beings that is the view most adopted by economists. Reflecting on this view makes it clear why monetary rewards and sanctions are employed in business. Business, on this view, is a world of individuals bound together by contracts and agreements, which have force only because the violation of them can be or is externally sanctioned. There are no internal ties such as loyalty, fidelity, or gratitude to bind people together. The economist's problem is to determine how much the sanctions required to get the agent to do the principal's will will cost or, in other words, what the price of the loyalty of the "loyal" agent is and whether the price is worth it? But our answer is, if the system is construed as we have just indicated, there is no way to get a loyal agent, for loyalty cannot be bought, it is not an economic commodity.

Still, is the system as committed to the self-interested rational maximizer as we say?

THE NEOCLASSICAL POSITION THAT BUSINESS SHOULD BE BASED ON THE SELF-INTERESTED PURSUIT OF PROFIT IS EGOISTIC

Is the situation in business akin to that described by Glaucon and Hobbes? We would like to show that it is if one assumes like Fried-

man that "there is one *and only one* social responsibility of business—
to use its resources and engage in activities designed to increase its
profits so long as it stays within the rules of the game, which is to
say, engages in open and free competition without deception and
fraud."[21]

Business as a social institution and form of life is the result of
conventional agreements, i.e., it was created the way it is by human
beings. There was no such thing as a business system when the first
people either swung out of the trees or traipsed out of Eden. Since
business is an institution that human beings have developed, the
question arises, why have they developed it as a self-interested system? Why was it set up that way? The answer is long and complicated, but it is clear that the initial explanations and defenses of the
system involved central assumptions that an appeal to the self-
interested nature of man would work best for society at large. That
defense of egoism begins with Adam Smith's observation that:

> It is not from the benevolence of the butcher, the brewer or the baker,
> that we expect our dinner, but from their regard to their own inter-
> est . . .[22]

Given that observation about human beings, Smith recommends
business be set up to appeal to self-interest.

> We address ourselves not to their humanity but to their self-love, and
> never talk to them of our own necessities but of their advantages.

But Smith has a moral reason for appealing to self-interest, "to
render the annual revenue of society as great as possible."

> As every individual, therefore, endeavours as much as he can both to
> employ his capital in the support of domestic industry, and so to direct
> that industry that its produce may be of the greatest value, every individ-
> ual necessarily labors to render the annual revenue of the society as great
> as he can. He generally indeed, neither intends to promote the public
> interest, nor know how much he is promoting it. . . . and by directing
> that industry in such a manner as its produce may be of the greatest
> value, he intends only his own gain, and he is in this, as in many other
> cases, led by an invisible hand to promote an end which was no part of
> his intention. Nor is it always the worse for society that it was no part of
> it. By pursuing his own interest he frequently promotes that of the society
> more effectually than when he really intends to promote it. I have never
> known much good done by those who affected to trade for the public
> good. It is an affectation, indeed, not very common among merchants,
> and very few words need be employed in dissuading them from it.[23]

Smith and many neoclassical disciples of Milton Friedman, then, defend self-interested action because it drives the market, and a flourishing market is best for all. Hence the assumption of humans as self-interested is the cornerstone of the free-enterprise system, the system that legitimates the way business is done, a system that has been successful in creating more goods and material wealth than any other system in history. But as we have seen, holding that view generates a serious problem. Such a system, because it becomes a form of life and is internalized, carries within it the seeds of its own destruction, for the agent in a system where everyone "intends only his gain" must assume his principal and everyone else occupies a thoroughly egoistic stance, while the agent is expected to be concerned not with his own gain, but the principal's. But to be loyal in such a context is irrational. Thus agency or loyalty in such a system is unworkable in principle, and economically coercive contracts are the only rational procedure unless we can find fools for agents or restructure the profit-making goal of business.

Further, if the above view were always correct, business would be impossible. The very existence of business refutes the exclusively self-interested view of human beings. If there is no loyalty or agency, business must reduce every obligation to a contractual one, one where the only thing that motivates one to follow the contract is monetary incentive or fear. In such a situation, there is no obligation, and indeed no need or motive to do anything for the principal that was not explicitly spelled out. If my only obligation as an agent is to do what I contracted for, then I need not and probably would be foolish to do something to help my principal, if (1) it were not spelled out in my job contract, (2) I was not inclined to do it, and (3) there were no monetary reward. Something as simple as putting in an extra half-hour, if it is for the sake of the principal, is not required if it is inconvenient for the agent, absent any reward or sanctioned specification of exactly under what circumstances the agent must act. In such as situation, loyalties are bought.

Is business this cold and calculating? It would seem not, i.e., there is the existence of loyal behavior in business, and indeed loyal behavior does explain a good deal of the structure of business. But that means non-egoistic behavior explains a good deal of what does go on in business.

If the above is correct, in order for Noreen's or Lawrence's suggestions for more ethics or loyalty to be realized and agency costs to be reduced, it will be necessary to challenge the corporate ethos, the form of life, which embodies the classic model of business responsibility, and the millieu which unquestioningly agrees that business' overriding responsibility is the making of profit. The grip of this profit-oriented form of life needs to be loosened.

CHALLENGING THE CORPORATE ETHOS

Such a challenge does seem to be taking place. Note Phillip Blumberg's remarks in an article called "Corporate Responsibility and the Employee's Duty of Loyalty and Obedience." Blumberg states:

> The nature of the American corporate world is changing, reflecting changing concepts of the objectives, roles and responsibilities of business. The public corporation as a social and economic organization is undergoing a process of re-examination which has not yet run its course, and the ultimate outcome of which one may still not safely predict. There is general acceptance of the concept of corporate social responsibility with the major public corporation assuming a role of increasing significance in social problem solving. Although highly controversial and not generally accepted, there is also increasing expression of a new view of the large American corporation as a social institution to achieve social objectives, rather than as an economic institution to be operated for economic objectives for the benefit of shareholders. It is inevitable, therefore, that as a corollary, new views will also emerge with respect to the changing relationship between the corporation and the groups vitally affected by it, particularly its employees, as well as such other groups as consumers, suppliers, and the public generally.[24]

Blumberg may be correct, and we are certainly sympathetic with what he says. Hopefully our view of what happened to the concept of agency shows what has gone wrong and what needs to be done. Our contention is that reflection on the agency relationship makes it clear that business operates on a double standard, claiming only the responsibility for pursuing self-interest on their part, while expecting selflessness and loyalty on the part of the agents working on its behalf. Further, consideration of the selflessness required by agency shows that to the extent economists argue that the self-interested pursuit of profit is the sole motive for activity, they implicitly defeat their own goal of lessening transaction costs. Hopefully, a consideration of what effective agency requires, including the view of human beings it demands, will lead us necessarily to a sounder view of the function of the corporation.

THE NEO-EGOISTIC PURPOSE OF BUSINESS

What the ethical-philosophical analysis of agency suggests, then, is that defenders of the neoclassical theory of the corporation need to re-examine their use of the self-interested maximizer model, as well as the "profit-making" goal of business that arises from the use of that model, rather than altering the concept of agency to fit their paradigm. Even more, we would suggest that the original concept of agency can become the new paradigm, at least for managers. Generating profits cannot be the "sole" reason for doing business, nor efficiency for that end the sole means.

It seems that the neoclassical view of the purpose of business overlooks two important distinctions. First, there is the distinction between motivating causes and justifying reasons, both of which can be given in response to the question "Why?" Thus, if I ask why I go into business, I might respond by saying "to make a profit." But that is not a justifying reason, it is a motivating cause. A justifying reason cannot be an individual motive; it must have societal implications. A reason that justifies business is an appeal to the societal goods that business creates. Thus the purpose of business cannot be to make a profit, that's a motive. The purpose is to provide goods and services. That is why society allows business, as we will see, for profit is only the sole responsibility of business if the pursuit of profit will lead to more goods and services. Absent more goods and services, the profit motive cannot be used to justify business behavior. Where there are two ends, one must take precedence. The good of society is the end that is ethically to be preferred.

The second distinction is between motives. There are monetary goals, such as profit, but they do not always explain why businesses arise. Further, it is possible that one is motivated by concerns that do not fit the narrow self-interested category. Let us look at this question of motives using some examples.

Various concerns may motivate someone to start a company. Henry Ford began his work and hence his company with more of an interest in making cars than in making money. Making cars became a way of making money, not making money the reason for making cars. Writing, for a novelist, becomes a way of making money, but it is the poor novelist who writes solely to make money. Certainly Dostoyevski and Dickens wrote to make money. But they chose writing as the way to make money. They chose it because that's what they enjoyed doing, that's how they fulfilled themselves, that's what they were, writers, and that's what they probably would have continued to be even if they didn't make much money at it. One might claim that doing fulfilling work, an activity with goals other than economic satisfaction, is as important as, if not more important, than achieving economic goals. Indeed, some economists will point out that that is a utility function, but it is a non-measurable utility function, and it is also a self-interested goal that costs the individual.

Hence, Ford's dedication to making automobiles and Dickens's to writing novels can be seen as similar to the agent's dedication to his work. The agent is dedicated to helping a principal. But merely for money? Hardly. That would be akin to prostitution, to suppressing oneself to another, not for a good reason but purely for monetary gain. But if what we have said of Ford and Dickens and agents in general is true, we have a possible strategy with which to address the question of the goal of business.

A NEW PARADIGM FOR BUSINESS: AGENCY AND PROFESSIONALISM, THE ENLIGHTENED VIEW

What I would like to suggest is the adoption of the original agency relationship as paradigmatic of some business relationships. But since that notion is antithetical to current views of the system, we have to recast our view of the system.

As we saw, the system fails to distinguish between and hence confuses legitimating purpose with motivating goals. We have also seen that "profit" is not the sole motivation for business. What we now need to make clear is a point implicit in Friedman and Smith. Making a profit can only be the sole responsibility of business if it affects the general welfare. The purpose of business that makes its practices acceptable is producing goods and services that will benefit the general welfare. That is the only moral good that justifies self-interested behavior. Hence, self-interest, even for Friedman and Smith, as the making of a profit must be subordinated to the legitimating telos of business. The reduction of the goal of business to profit making leads to undesirable consequences. As I said in another place:

> The fact that profit determines the quality of work allowed leads to a phenomenon called the commercialization of work. The primary end of an act of building is to make something, and to build well is to make it well. A carpenter is defined by the end of his work, but if the quality interferes with profit, the business side of the venture supercedes the artisan side. Thus profit forces a craftsman to suspend his devotion to his work and commercializes his venture. The more professions subject themselves to the forces of the market place, the more they get commercialized; e.g., research for the sake of a more profitable product rather than for the sake of knowledge jeopardizes the integrity of academic research facilities.[25]

It is easy to see how such a self-interested profit motive can corrupt the agency relationship we find in professions such as teaching, law, or medicine. To teach or practice law or medicine primarily for the money is to be a bad teacher, lawyer, or doctor, for when a conflict comes up between pursuing the interests of one's principal—student, client, or patient—and making money, those devoted to money will ignore their responsibility to the principal. But beyond

seeing the corruption of those honorable professions when they become profit-oriented, one can see the corruption of profit making in
other areas. To reduce one's life primarily to the making of money
is to ape King Midas and to turn an instrument of happiness into
happiness itself. It was what religious scholars called "idolatry." We
could also add for consideration, the disillusionment of a great deal
of young men and women who entered investment banking, not for
their interest in providing investment services, but as a way to making huge amounts of money.

One can do business to make money, but it is unlikely that as a
human being one can do business "solely" and "primarily" to make
money without eroding the human spirit. Besides, as we tried to indicate, we need not say that business was primarily invented to make
money. Business as an instrument was created to help increase production of goods and services. The mistake of the egoist is to confuse the object of the action with a desirable effect of the action. The
object of business was to make goods or services. The desirable side
effect of making a profit was an incentive for more production. Since
humans are indeed self-interested, there is nothing wrong with such
incentives and rewards. But it is a mistake to confuse incentives for
good actions with the purpose of those actions. Good grades are incentives for study, but the purpose of study is primarily to learn, to
expand the mind.

In the light of these observations, let us reverse the standard classical view of the purpose of business and insist that the function of
the business man is to be a good agent and fulfill the purpose of
business, which is to produce goods and services. If we do this, we
begin to develop a new model of the business person, the business
person as agent, and consequently, the business person as professional. We will turn to that model in a moment.

So we want to suggest the agency paradigm as a model for viewing how business is run and should be organized. At least the agency
view should be on all fours with the profit maximizer paradigm. We
will call this "the enlightened view." The enlightened view reveals to
us that the agency relationship requires another purpose of the firm
at least as important as the profit motive. This is a different view of
the purpose of the business system, envisioning it as a cooperative
venture where one works toward the interest of the principal's business which has two thrusts: first, the social purpose of providing goods
or services; and second, the agent's altruistic commitment to the
principal. Profit is certainly an incentive, but as an incentive it is on
all fours with other important incentives and purposes, such as non-
economic forms of fulfillment.

The agency relationship as a paradigm also reflects the purpose of
business from society's point of view rather than from the individu-

al's point of view. We suggest that the purpose of a business might not be the same as the incentive or motive for starting one. Obviously if I buy stocks in a business, I desire a profit, so the business for me as stockbroker is seen as a profit-generating instrument. But no society would permit a business to exist if it were not perceived as beneficial to the society, i.e., were not perceived as providing a good or service. So from the societal point of view, one sees profit as an incentive offered in order to get people to do business, but the business must be beneficial to society, and society can hardly view the purpose of business as exclusively profit making. The agency paradigm, then, fits more with the societal view of the purpose of business.

Let us see what follows from adopting the societal perspective. The making of money, profit, should not be viewed as an obligation. It should be viewed as an opportunity. Stockholders are allowed to make money by the establishment of corporate law. But society developed corporations because the establishment of legal entities that allowed individual stockholders to avoid liability for the debts of the corporation proved to be an efficient way to increase the production and distribution of goods, a desideratum for society. Consequently, society's needs for goods and services and its desire for more efficient production of goods and the need for more investment capital to produce those goods gave rise to corporations. The good of society came before the good of the corporation in the development of corporate law. The type of institutions that society allowed to come into being, such as businesses and corporations, are not ends in themselves, they are instruments of society for the more efficient production of goods. But we should not treat instruments as ends in themselves. Turning Kant on his head we could maintain, "Act so as never to treat a mere instrument as an end in itself."

Our dedication and loyalty must be to worthwhile goals, not to the instruments that facilitate these goals. Hence our dedication must be to people and not to the profit motive that facilitates our work or production. To think we owe a company or corporation loyalty requires us to think of that company as a person or as a group with a goal of human enrichment. If we think of it in this way we can be loyal.

The use of the new model will be aided if we adopt an additional strategy. We need to quit talking so generically about "business persons." After all, the notion of a "business" person is an abstraction. One isn't merely a business person, one has specific roles to play. The generic notion of "the business person" arises when the context of the discourse requires a term that includes all those managers, marketers, advertisers, public relations specialists, accountants, and financiers who work for a "profit" corporation, a business. But not all managers, marketers, etc., work for a profit corporation, which means they are not all "business" persons, and further not all contexts call for the generic term's use. What all managers, those who work for a profit corporation and those who work for a non-profit corporation, have in common is managing people and services so that needed and desired goods and services are effectively produced and delivered. Keeping that in mind, it becomes clear that one does not practice business so much as one practices management, accounting, financial advising, marketing, etc. If one practices business for the sake of business, then one works for the money. But to practice management, accounting, etc., solely for the money, instead of developing well managed companies or keeping proper books, or giving good investment advice, or making wise investment decisions, or developing successful marketing programs, etc., is to be a "bad" manager, accountant, financial advisor, or marketer.

Along this line we now wish to suggest that the use of the agency model of paradigm will be facilitated if we begin to view these various "business" practices as professions just as we view medicine, law, and teaching as professions. We already saw how the introduction of profit motivation corrupts the agency relation in the more traditional professions. We now suggest that the introduction of the profit motive, as a primary goal, can corrupt the business profession. To avoid that, one needs, among other things, to re-establish the service view of the various professions one finds in business, and investigate how they can be pursued in a business community with its profit motive, without compromising themselves to the profit motive. To do this we first look at what professionalism involves.

Professionalism, according to Albert Flores, is commonly described as "a complex set of role characteristics involving specialized knowledge and training, dedication to public service, and autonomous decision making authority in matters of importance to society".[26]

> Professionals are expected to practice in ways that conform to certain prescribed ethical standards. To be a professional means, in part, to be committed to using professional skills and knowledge, in morally acceptable ways, for the benefit of society. There are several interrelated reasons, centering on the need for trust and protection against the abuse of power, that justify this interpretation.
>
> First, professionals possess the ability and power of knowing how best to deal with problems requiring professional expertise, and this creates a clear moral concern about how professionals should behave when dealing with clients. Second, clients are in the unusual position in which their need for expert assistance and their inability to satisfy this need for them-

selves makes them both dependent on and vulnerable to the professional's expertise. Hence, they have little choice but to invest the relationship with their trust, though only to the degree that this trust is reasonable.

To assure that this investment is warranted, professionals are expected to refrain from acts that would violate a client's trust.[27]

THE AGENT IN BUSINESS AS PROFESSIONAL, OR THE PROFESSIONAL AS AGENT

We suggest that the agency model of the business person is aided by viewing the business person as a professional. But such a suggestion is more than simply an heuristic device. A case can be made that to be an agent in business is to be a professional. A little reflection shows how most of the positions we have cited—managing, accounting, advising in financial matters, marketing—fulfill Flores's criteria of a profession. In all of these cases the following is true. One doesn't simply do what one is told, one has expertise, one reads and anticipates the needs and interests of the principal and operates for the principal's good. Managers, Financiers, Accountants, Ad Executives, Sales Representatives, are all agents. Agents are, qua agent, committed to good, i.e., the good of their client.

But, one might ask, isn't the good of the client the profit made? Certainly. But in business the client as a stockholder is allowed to make money because he has invested in a process that facilitates the production of a *good*. This certainly raises the special problem of the motives and responsibilities of the stockholders and owners. But we have already seen that profit, far from being the sole purpose of business, is rather the incentive or reward allowed by society to encourage the production of goods, which are desired and presumably beneficial to society. On this view it seems at least possible to blend the professional interests of agents and their principals.

What all of the above is meant to suggest is that economists rethink the rational maximizer model of the business person that they employ, as well as re-think the importance of community relationships on the economy. Their atomistic model is normatively skewed and empirically limited, leading to unreliable predictions of results. After all, a model that takes into account only monetary rewards, as a predictive model will fail to appreciate or compute the results of devotion to others, working for social goals, working for self-esteem, and other non-monetary forms of fulfillment. A firm or corporation that gives its employees or agents satisfaction in their work, because of its moral import or usefulness, and which is not simply devoted to profit maximization, should be a firm that has less transaction costs in motivating agents, for it allows these agents to view themselves as productive members of society and helps them avoid a good deal of value conflicts that "hard nosed" business men insist one must cope with.

Further, the model is normatively skewed, because it promotes narrowly self-interested behavior expecting that to lead to morally acceptable results. An often overlooked and questionable assumption that Friedman makes is that the business person should have the same goal as the business. That is too simple. The purpose of the part need not be, and in general is not, the same as the purpose of the whole, although it should, in a well working whole, contribute to it. Just as the purpose of the hand is not the purpose of the person, neither is the purpose of the bookkeeper the purpose of the entire enterprise. Hopefully the hand in fulfilling its purpose contributes to the whole person, just as the manager in managing well contributes to the purpose of the business, which, we reiterate is two-fold, the producing of goods and services to make a profit. Our suggestion, then, is that only this complex normative view does justice to the normative issue.

Let us sum up. The necessity of the existence of agents makes it impossible for business to claim that its sole purpose is profit-making. Even if profit-making were the sole purpose of the business, the purpose and function of the managers, accountants, marketers, and other functionaries should not be construed solely as fulfilling the profit-making purpose.

IS THE ENLIGHTENED VIEW ALSO NAIVE?

But how realistic are we? Aren't we as naive as Noreen? Aren't we trying to change an entire economic system with puny ideals? Is it not the case that some if not most people go into business simply make a profit?

It is certainly the case that systems, and in particular economic systems, strongly influence human behavior, because systems provide points of view that present and legitimate certain goals. Capitalism, as a form of life conceived by economists, presents and legitimates the self-interested point of view. Such a legitimation has the power to feed on itself.

Still, these systems do not *necessarily determine* human behavior, and history shows us there is some mediation of views possible, i.e., that ideals, if not ideas, can have consequences for practical life. The fact that other-regarding goals are essential to human development may not help in reforming the views of capitalism, but if not it is probably that brand of capitalism whose existence is threatened. Cooperation is essential for human development. Systems that do not encourage cooperation, or that systematically undermine it, have within them the seeds of their own destruction. Thus if ideas have consequences and our enlightened view is seen as naive, then so must the neoclassical view, for it is flawed to the extent that it does not recognize that the making of a profit is insufficient as a fulfilling goal of human life.

Plato reminds us that there are three kinds of goods. Those things good in themselves, those good for other things, and best of all those good in themselves and for other things. Profit is good for other things, as an incentive. But producing works or services for others can be rewarding both in itself and as a profit-making venture. Writing is good. Writing that is good writing and also brings monetary rewards is better. We need to apply this two-fold notion of good to business: business as good for making profit; but more importantly business as involving a creative activity good in itself, or because of the goods it produces. The purpose of business need not be construed as an either/or proposition. Profit is not and cannot be the primary, let alone the only, purpose of business as a humane system. Rather, business should be construed as a system that encourages the production of goods by utilizing the incentive of profit.

We are suggesting a view of business as an activity, found in the older sense of "being about my business," one's work, one's tasks, or one's calling. Here one has an activity that involves her in the production of goods or services and creating goods that benefit society. Just as the purpose of education is to produce learned people, from society's point of view, the purpose of business, from society's, not the individual's, point of view, is to allow a system that maximizes goods.

We think, then, that a more enlightened view would construe profit as one of the benefits that come from pursuing a "good" end. But such a view should cause economists to reform their concept of human nature and what fulfills it. Economic incentives—monetary rewards that are treated as the sole incentives—are atomizing incentives. Non-atomizing, societal dependent incentives are more adequate because they take into account the societal needs and nature of human beings, a nature implicitly recognized and required if there is to be an activity such as "being an agent" for another. Organizational theorists seem to recognize more than some economists that human beings are societal and that their full satisfaction and self-actualization is the result of a blend of their self-interest and feelings of benevolence for others. Thus they appeal to the concepts like "the team," "the family," etc.

Action on another's behalf, the key requirement of agency, cannot be achieved if the primary motives are money or fear of the law. We need to realize that motivation as well as human fulfillment is found in social acceptance, social giving, fullness as a member of a group or groups, etc., for we are partly defined in terms of how we relate to others. Our very identity is other-dependent.

In summary, business as a system requires agents. The rise of the corporation required persons acting on behalf of (in the interests of) others. However, business as a human practice has a telos that legitimates business as a system. The telos of business that legitimates it, according to neoclassical economic theory, is the pursuit of self-interest. But the pursuit of self-interest is, at least at times, incompatible with working on behalf of others. At times then, agency (construed as working for others) is incompatible with "legitimate" self-interested business concerns. To avoid the incompatibility, market economists, who study efficiency within the system, perforce alter the concept of agency, turning it from a fiduciary relationship to a contractual relationship of two self-interested individuals. Thus, the mediating power of agency is destroyed by the adoption of the neo-classical model. It can be restored by an adoption of a model of professionalism, a model that utilizes the fiduciary agency relationship, e.g., the doctor-patient relationship.

Looking at agency and its problems should suggest to us that we need to (1) reformulate the purpose and nature of business, (2) recognize the danger of generalizing business as a type of work, and (3) recognize the advisability of viewing at least some persons engaged in business as professionals, not as mere profit (money) makers.

Taking satisfaction in our work is in many ways much more important, satisfying, and fulfilling than bottom-line efficiency. John Ruskin, responding to Adam Smith's example of a pin factory, reminds us of that in the following passage.

We have much studied and much perfected, of late, the great civilized invention of the division of labor; only we give it a false name. It is not, truly speaking, the labor that is divided; but the men: Divided into mere segments of men—broken into small fragments and crumbs of life; so that all the little piece of intelligence that is left in a man is not enough to make a pin, or a nail, but exhausts itself in making the point of a pin, or the head of a nail. Now it is a good and desirable thing, truly, to make many pins in a day; but if we could only see with what crystal sand their points were polished—sand of human soul, much to be magnified before it can be discerned for what it is—we should think there might be some loss in it also. And the great cry that rises from all our manufacturing cities, louder than their furnace blast, is all in very deed for this—that we manufacture everything there except men; we blanch cotton, and strengthen steel, and refine sugar, and shape pottery; but to brighten, to strengthen, to refine, or to form a single living spirit, never enters into our estimate of advantages. And all the evil to which that cry is urging our myriads can be met only in one way: not by teaching or preaching, for to teach them is but to show them their misery, and to preach to them, if we do nothing more than preach, is to mock at it. It can be met only by a right understanding, on the part of all classes, of what kinds of labor are good for men, raising them, and making them happy; by a determined sacrifice of such convenience, or beauty, or cheapness as is to be got only by the degradation of the workman; and by equally determined demand for the products and results of healthy and ennobling labor.[28]

NOTES

I wish to thank Rosemont College and The Pew Memorial Trust for a grant enabling me to work on this issue. I also wish to thank Henry Veatch, Hugh Lacey and Norman Bowie for encouragement and critique which made me rework some important issues in this chapter. Thanks too to Manny Velasquez, Edward Freeman, John Boatwright, John Serembus, and Michael Thompson for their reading and comments, which have been extremely helpful. But they should in no way be held responsible for the shortcomings of this chapter.

1. Richard DeGeorge (1990), p. 59.
2. Douglas J. Den Uyl (1984), p. 22.
3. Milton Friedman (1970), p. 126.
4. Michael J. Metzger et. al. (1986), p. 334.
5. Metzger (1986).
6. Robert C. Clark, In Pratt and Zeckhauser (1985), p. 77.
7. William O. Douglas, Quoted in Clark (1985), p. 76.
8. Clark (1985), p. 77.
9. Michael Jensen and William H. Meckling (1976), p. 305.
10. Adam Smith (1776), (1937), p. 200.
11. John Pratt and Richard Zeckhauser (1985), p. 2.
12. Pratt and Zeckhauser (1985), p. 2.
13. Terry M. Moe (1984), p. 756.
14. Jensen and Meckling (1976), p. 303.
15. Jensen and Meckling (1976), p. 308.
16. Pratt and Zeckhauser (1985), p. 2.
17. Pratt and Zeckhauser (1985), p. 3.
18. Eric Noreen (1987), p. 3.
19. Paul Lawrence (1958).
20. Ian Maitland (1987), pp. 167–8.
21. Friedman (1970).
22. Adam Smith (1937), p. 14.
23. Adam Smith (1937), p. 14.
24. Philip Blumberg (1985), p. 291.
25. Ronald Duska (1975), p. 298.
26. Albert Flores (1988), p. 1.
27. Albert Flores (1988), p. 2.
28. John Ruskin (1968), p. 1295.

9

Integrating Ethics into Doctoral Education: The Apparent Dilemma of Agency Theory

Wanda A. Wallace

The paradigm of agency theory is prevalent in the curriculum of every doctoral program, and many master-level courses, in accounting and finance. It has become increasingly conspicuous in the economics literature and the political science journals. While it appears cloaked in different terms, including transactions economics, analytical modeling, and positive theory, it is essentially a theory that tries to analyze the incentives of various parties involved in contractual settings—both explicit and implicit. The thrust of the theory appears on first glance to be the epitome of the "dark side" of human nature. Indeed, it appears that everyone is out for him or herself, and that no reason exists to believe otherwise. Managers are described as likely to distribute all assets to stockholders despite interests by creditors, in the absence of bonding and monitoring activities that preclude such action. The politician is revealed to be void of public interest and focused on self-interest as he or she vies for political office. The principal, in turn, will price-protect to the fullest extent necessary to reflect expected moral hazard problems stemming from diverse incentives of agents. In the absence of risk-averse managers, owners would shift all risks onto the agent as a means of avoiding any ill effects from contracting.

Yet, no matter how we pursue this self-interested theory development, we run into some inexplicable scenarios. For example, some

169

creditors extend debt solely on the creditworthiness of a borrower and invoke no apparent bonding or monitoring devices in the typical form of bond covenants. Moreover, the borrowers are observed to pay back the creditors. Similarly, philanthropy is alive and well, public-spirited citizenry exists, and whistleblowers are observed to imperil their jobs, if not their lives, to thwart unethical behavior—recall the popular film *Silkwood*.

Those who understand utility theory and its interface with agency theory have little trouble reconciling these observations with modeling. The first point recognized is that every theory is a simplification and abstraction from reality. Every doctoral student in economics and business typically reads Milton Friedman's explanation of positive economics and the ability of geometry and physics to explain billiards despite the absence of such detailed knowledge by the expert billiard player. Yet, importantly, the second realization is that utility in no way translates money. While economics has a way of focusing on monetary units, as does accounting, due to its simplicity of measurement and its obvious role in most contracting activities, utility is intended to capture whatever is deemed to be in an individual's interest. For example, if one values philanthropy, character, and perquisites such as working around friends and family, that individual may easily accept a smaller amount of money in lieu of these "utility units." The paradox of agency theory is that self-interest is always viewed as precluding public interest.

The fact of the matter is that self-interest is often, if not typically, consistent with public interest. For example, the citizenry will choose to respect a set of mutually agreed upon rules and regulations largely to protect the public interest and will deem it in their personal interest to exercise mutual respect for such laws. Why? Because in the absence of some social norms, chaos would be likely and that would presumably harm each individual's interest. Indeed, people recognize such trite but important premises as "a contract is only as good as the individual signing it." The point, of course, is that there is no such thing as a perfect contract. If one required that every possible contingency be covered in a contract, the inefficiencies of contracting would likely cause costs to exceed benefits. Essentially, the specialism that facilitated the industrial revolution would disappear and self-sufficiency would become the norm.

Certain agency theorists would extract from this discussion certain informal bonding and monitoring mechanisms. For example, the fact that a "man's word" has value speaks to signalling theory and the trademark or reputation literature. The human capital market and the concept of going concern in business would require self-interested business people to retain an image of ethical behavior. Indeed, monitoring by competitors, newspapers, consumers, employees, and regulators provides a threat of discovery of unsavory behavior and an eventual demise of business operations. This leads to a pure economics-based support for ethics, aside from any inherent esoteric principle such as "trust."

AN ECONOMICS PERSPECTIVE

An interesting account of such an economics perspective is provided by Eric Noreen in his paper "The Economics of Ethics: A New Perspective on Agency Theory" (1987).[1] He recognizes the *ex ante* costs of a lack of mutual trust that causes mutually beneficial exchanges to be foregone, deadweight losses to result from monitoring costs and inefficient risk sharing, and contracts being unenforceable due to the inability to observe opportunistic behavior. He suggests that an agreement via an ethical code to abstain from opportunistic behavior can be beneficial for everyone if internalized. He stresses the inability to effectively enforce such a code through external rewards or sanctions. The point of Noreen's exposition is that sound economic reasons exist for some forms of ethical or self-constrained behavior; this is referred to as *utilitarian ethical behavior* as distinct from altruistic behavior. Adverse selection is discussed and noted to be pervasive in the absence of truthful reporting to curb the asymmetry of information. The efficiency gains from compliance with certain rules are apparent. The contention is that the resulting gains from an ethical code offset whatever losses are experienced from losses in freedom. The prisoner's dilemma is described alongside experiments that demonstrate that people cooperate when they see mutual benefit. Of course, problems arise in the time involved in learning to cooperate, and hence the development of social norms is seen as effective in guiding behavior. Noreen offers the innovative example of a norm of tipping that allows even one-time customers to obtain good service.

In closing remarks, Eric Noreen cites the unnerving possibility that business school instructors have inadvertently encouraged a social norm of unethical behavior by emphasizing the dark side of agency theory, i.e., unconstrained opportunistic behavior. He encourages us to explore the adverse consequences on the economic system of unconstrained opportunism and to clarify the necessity of ethics to the functioning of markets.

I believed that Noreen's comments are particularly insightful in the wake of insider's trading scandals and Black Monday. Many note that the small investor has become skeptical as to whether the market is a "fair game." Evidence exists that the average return of large investors is consistently higher than that of the smaller investor. Moreover, recent literature by Lev[2] contends that the reason regulation has persisted in the market place, despite the general deregulation sentiment on Capitol Hill, is the acknowledged need to demonstrate the "fairness of the game" and the prevalence of ethical behavior. Lev points to acounting regulations as primarily representing vehicles for improving the fairness of the market. By making otherwise insider information available to the public, accounting is a means of addressing problems arising from asymmetry of information. Moreover, the attestation function helps ensure the credibility of the information provided. This equity in capital markets concept is an *ex ante* ideal of equality of opportunity via equal access to information.

These perspectives of Noreen and Lev merit discussion in doctoral, as well as master-level, education. Moreover, I would suggest a few ethics articles that dovetail with scenarios for which parallels exist in business. Specifically, Ronald Duska's articles "Whistleblowing and Employee Loyalty"[3] and "Life Boat Ethics: A Problem in Economic Justice"[4] do a nice job of clarifying moral imperatives that may arise as life and death decisions are confronted in a business context. To introduce the social and political context that influences contracting as well as the role of various types of ethical behavior, an article such as Jeffrey B. Miller's paper discussing "The Big Nail and Other Stories: Product Quality Control in the Soviet Union"[5] clarifies the role of contracts, monitoring, reputation, competition, right of refusal, and codes of conduct including loyalty in the U.S. These are contrasted with the presence of less knowledgeable third parties creating shortages and providing an atmosphere that focuses on hierarchy and results in inadequate resources in the U.S.S.R. The failure of the latter setting to balance the negotiating power of producers and users is cited as leading to less effective means of grappling with bounded rationality. Essentially, Hayek's treatise on information, explaining why a dictator cannot displace the efficiency of market transactions is heard loud and clear in such expositions.

For doctoral education, another vein of background research, which I would encourage be read in reflecting on ethics, is a working paper entitled "Letting the Chat Out of the Bag: Deconstruction, Privilege, and Accounting Research" by Arrington and Francis,[6] as it introduces philosophy and logic into an analysis of paradigm development and its propriety. Such work is highly controversial but stimulates thinking as to how different fields dovetail toward an understanding of behavior and theory development.

PERCEPTUAL DIFFERENCES

Graduate students should be made aware of the highly diverse perceptions as to where responsibility for ethics and ethical training lie, as well as debates on the ability to train others in the field of ethics. As a few examples, the *New York Times* has quoted the belief that "Ethics . . . must be embedded early, at home, in grade school, in church, . . . [being] highly personal." [Felix Rohatyn] states "I doubt it can be taught in college." Yet he states that "education is a necessary part of ethical problem solving, if it is coupled with early ethical training." [7]

Lester C. Thurow, Dean at MIT, is cited as stating "society, rather than business, has the responsibility for teaching ethical behavior." He states that "most business school students are beyond the age for ethics training." However, in his list of sources for ethics training he includes colleges and employers. [8]

In 1988, researchers concluded "there is little empirical evidence to suggest that ethical behavior and decision-making are enhanced through ethical education." [9] Yet others have contended, "It has been found that codes of ethics are more likely to affect employee behavior if they are part of an on-going program at all levels within the organization." [10] The implication is that an effect is observable.

The recognition of controversy is a first step toward beginning its resolution. The most promising avenue for instruction would seem to be the identification of ethical issues. An approach that I have used with considerable success is to assign graduate students to write an ethical case for discussion based on his or her personal experiences. The cases are distributed to the class in advance and each student leads his or her case's discussion. Each student is required to turn in a "Suggested Instructor's Notes" for the case, which are permitted to be edited subsequent to the class discussion, in tandem with preparing a second draft of the case. A brief description of the cases appears in Figure 9–1.

I can predict, from my own classroom experiences, that disagreements will arise among the students as to whether an ethical dilemma even exists in some of the cases. The students will try, no doubt, to convince their peers of the problem or lack thereof. Such dialogue will require periodic intervention by the instructor to ensure the point is made: perceptions as to what constitutes ethical behavior vary and a first step toward accountability for ethical behavior is its recognition.

When interceding, agency theory can actually assist in explaining some divergence of opinion. For example, I have found that graduate students often see little wrong with copying a movie video but become angry at the thought of copies being made of intellectual

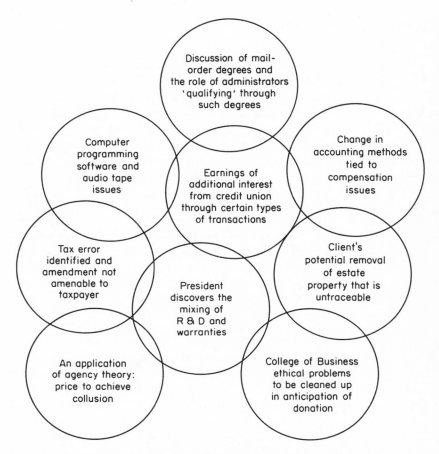

Figure 9–1. Students' Cases for Class Discussion

property such as computer programs. Apparently, the vantage point of self-interest, as to the larger probability of students authoring a program than making a video, emerges. One can also attribute the greater sensitivity to the computer software area to observed actions by regulatory bodies to "raid" business and educational settings to collect illegal copies of software. Such monitoring, in tandem with penalty functions like computer viruses—presumably more easily picked up on illegal software copies—may also account for the clearer understanding of the ethical issues.

By pointing out the irony of how ethics is sometimes better appreciated when the components of self-interest and monitoring or bonding activities are integrated in the evaluation process, one reinforces the point that ethics and agency theory are by no means at odds with one another. Moreover, agency theory can assist in identifying various parties to contracts, and others with vested interest in particular economic transactions.

RESEARCH METHODS

All of the cites to this point reflect theory and teaching tools, yet the question of method arises, particularly with respect to doctoral education. If one is interested in ethical behavior and related research, what tools are available? Eugene Szwajkowski, a management professor at the University of Illinois at Chicago has a paper entitled "The Myths and Realities of Research on Organizational Conduct." He not only provides an effective review of interdisciplinary research but suggests that all kinds of research are feasible, including hypothesis testing with large-scale samples at the organizational level. The most prevalent stream of research has been based out of Harvard and has involved presenting ethical scenarios and asking people to describe how they would behave and why.[11] Classification schemes exist whereby one can typify the degree of ethical development experienced by such an individual. As an example, a scenario can be provided whereby a loved one is dying and needs medicine. You lack the funds to purchase the medicine and the pharmacist refuses to extend credit. How do you proceed? Would you steal the drug? Explain. Essentially, behavior can evolve from a pure self-interested behavior, to a social norm behavioral, to a personal sense of right and wrong, which at times sets aside the social norm in light of higher-order considerations. To illustrate such cases' use in business, graduate students could be asked to review literature concerning auditors' ethical capacity and their resolution of independence-related conflicts.[12] It should be apparent that these research methods potentially suffer from individual's limitations in describing their personal evaluation process, much as protocol analysis has its limitations. With regard to the latter, it has been observed that when asked to describe swimming, a group of individuals failed to ever mention the word *water!* Hence, an essential consideration could well be assumed by someone telling of her ethical decision and thereby cause some misinterpretation by a researcher. Nonetheless, research to date has suggested that some reasonably reliable instrumentation exists for assessing moral behavior, and it seems to be rather resilient to individual attributes.

Having suggested at least one stream of research using a tailored tool for analysis, one must acknowledge that each of the more traditional research methods could be applied to various aspects of ethical behavior. Market research, behavioral research, modeling, and descriptive studies all hold promise. They could describe the overall return to the "economic pie" that results from some agreed upon ethical provision such as new insider trading restrictions, the individual's tendency to "cheat" such as that reflected in Russ Barefield's American Accounting Association monograph on the effect of auditing frequency on behavior,[13] the risk-sharing advantages to ethics, and the manner in which unethical behavior persists in various contracting scenarios. Yet, in the behavioral study, the ethics of subjecting people to compromising situations has to be considered. Many of you may recall the famous experiment in which individuals were asked to administer electric shock to others. A great capacity for people to do harm to others was discovered. The persistent question is what long-term effects might there have been on the individual subjects who thought they had done harm or were capable of doing harm to others in such a manner? Indeed, the most challenging aspect of ethical research in doctoral education may well be ascertaining an ethical approach to performing ethics-related research. Consider the paradox created as Harvard University recently performed tests across the U.S. in which business people were asked to discuss the ethical ramifications of certain issues and were videotaped. Many were surprisingly candid as to what were deemed "gray" areas. The question has to be asked, did they mean what was said and if not, are there long-term ill effects of having them voice their opinion off-the-cuff, yet knowing the comments are being retained for posterity?

TEACHING RESPONSIBILITIES

Getting away from research method issues that merit discussion at the doctoral level, two other goals are recommended for doctoral training and appreciation by other graduate students. One is to discuss ethics tied to teaching. The tremendous influence that professors have on students, the need for encouraging students not to cheat or otherwise act in an unethical manner, and the role model responsibility accompanying the professor's position merit discussion. In a conference I recently attended on the "Ethical Implications of Agency Theory" at the University of Delaware's Center for Values, which was attended by an eclectic group of ethicists, lawyers, economists, philosophers, and business professors, an intriguing question arose. If a company encourages lying implicitly by rewarding padding of budgets, as one example, has not that company deteriorated the ethics of its employees and undermined truthful reporting? Just as that prompted prolonged discussion on whether a tendency to report a bound on a confidence interval rather than a mean estimate constituted unethical behavior, I immediately thought of the instructional setting in which I, as a student, would get annoyed at seeing another student blatantly cheating, with an instructor, apparently oblivious of the activity, reading in the front of the classroom. Is not such implicit endorsement of rewards to cheating a similar undermining of the moral fiber of the society? Who does the enforcement of rules help? Does the monitoring of an exam process have value? I personally believe that the monitoring of exams and the taking of sanctions with respect to cheaters increases the overall "intellectual pie" of society and, eventually, its "economic pie." The responsibility of professionals in the classroom has to be ingrained in future professors and better appreciated by students, and the sole opportunity to discuss such an ethical norm and its purpose is likely to rest in doctoral education.

AWARENESS OF ETHICAL ISSUES

The second and final goal I wish to explore is to ensure that doctoral students are aware of the pervasiveness of ethical issues in business and, for our purposes, in accounting. To that end, I believe that current reading of *The Wall Street Journal* and similar press coverage should be encouraged and discussed intermittently in various doctoral seminars. Not only does this lead to an appreciation of ethics-related issues, but all of us involved in research and teaching can rarely cite either an interesting paper or an anecdote that was not inspired in some way by the media.

The themes of many past news articles bear out the "social norms" as well as incidences of non-compliance. In addition, the costs of non-compliance are apparent and their market effects and consequences within an agency framework can be discussed. First, consider general business and reputation effects. Chrysler's disconnection of odometers in certain test vehicles,[14] questionable foreign payments in companies such as International Telephone and Telegraph Corporation[15] and Anheuser-Busch,[16] prepayments to suppliers for the purpose of smoothing reported income and maximizing bonuses at H. J. Heinz Co.[17] (in 1979), and E. F. Hutton's illegal check-overdrafting scheme[18] are a few examples, in tandem with not-for-profit entities like PTL.[19] More specific to the accounting profession, consider the Grant Thornton[20] experience. Originally Alexander Grant, the CPA firm had a partner, Jose Gomez, who was accused of taking a $125,000 bribe from E.S.M. Government Securities, which led to eventual damages against Grant of almost fifty times the partner's capital. The reported interview with Gomez revealed a demise tied to ambition, a feeling of being "trapped," and a convincing of one's self that things would work themselves out. He blamed sales pressure, inexperience, and personal financial pressures. The depiction of the business environment of auditing, pressures by clients, and the implications of an individual for an entire firm are apparent in the tale of turmoil. An auditor colleague has used the media articles in graduate education, posing the question: When do you think Gomez "first stepped over the line?" Similar to the approach of discussing cases authored by students, this type of case discussion prompts contemplation and debate.[21]

Another story opens up the issue of whistleblowing by internal auditors.[22] Northrop is faced with a lawsuit filed by employees including two internal auditors who claim that after locating $400 million in false charges, the company called off the internal audit and ordered the internal auditors to turn over their working papers for shredding. One internal auditor is a former employee who claims to have copies of memoranda (which were confiscated by Northrop attorneys) warning superiors of accounting irregularities over the past two years. Such accounting-and-specific cases involving ethics merit discussion, analysis, and consideration from a pedagogical perspective at the doctoral and graduate level. What would you teach as the appropriate behavior on the part of the internal auditor? What would you have done? What can you reasonably expect from others?

The spectre of "misleading media" merits discussion. A certain backhanded compliment seems to pervade media coverage. Consider such headlines as "A 'Magician' Makes $86,000 Disappear from Cash Machines,"[23] "The Embezzler: David L. Miller Stole from His Employers and Isn't in Prison,"[24] "Borrowing Millions Without Collateral Takes Ingenuity,"[25] " 'World Class Con Men' Play Big Role in Growing Losses,"[26] and "It Takes a Hacker to Catch a Hacker as Well as Thief—Ian Murphy Helps Companies Catch Computer Pirates: But Whose Side is He On?"[27] Moreover, media have a way of suggesting pervasive fraud, almost as though it is a "social norm." For example, a survey of ethics reports that when senior executives are asked whether people are unethical in their business dealings, 66 percent say occasionally, 16 percent say seldom, 15 percent say often, and 3 percent say more often than not.[28]

Reports on retailing indicate that almost 70 percent of $12 billion in losses are due to employee theft.[29] The pervasiveness of insider trading and related Wall Street scandal is evidenced in "chronologies" of scandal.[30] The headline "Fees That Lobbyists Routinely Pay Lawmakers to Get Aquainted Raise Questions About Ethics" is self-explanatory. Honorariums in 1986 are estimated at close to $8 million, versus $2 million in 1980.[31] Articles detail "Financial Fraud: Theories Behind Nationwide Surge in Bank Swindles," quantifying the annual losses from bank fraud at over $1 billion in 1986 versus under $200 million in 1979.[32] Then, at the individual level, stories appear on "Phony Parchment: As Value of Diplomas Grows, More People Buy Bogus Credentials—Most Know Degrees Are Fake But Some Cite Experience in Life as a Justification."[33]

A number of accounting-related articles report on fraud, accounting gimmickry,[34] and efforts by the profession to respond to pressures to uncover fraud.[35] Two prevalent cases in the literature have been Wedtech[36] and ZZZZ Best.[37] Then, ironically, there is the scandal at *The Wall Street Journal* that involved the "Heard on the Street" column[38]—hence, the power of the press is evidenced on a number of dimensions.

Amid the stories of problems has arisen a recent call for ethics courses, donations for business ethics programs,[39] and a haunting question of whether an ethics course could have kept certain events from occurring.[40] Contentions have even appeared in the literature suggesting that the teaching of ethics is done in such an academic manner that its impact is limited at best. Indeed, when one considers the articles concerning ethics in investment, including divestment,[41] the point is apparent. Then, watch individuals' faces when one suggests that it might be sound policy to allow insider trading, as it would make the market more efficient.[42] Looks of dismay at the implied wealth transfers from such a policy and notions of equity and fairness are immediately cited.

It may well be that business instruction at the doctoral and other graduate levels and its focus on efficient markets, rational expectations, and self-interest, should be moderated by attention to individuals' values, societal considerations, and normative considerations beyond mere positive consequences. If normative concepts are not instilled in the minds of future professors and business people, we may have a self-fulfilling prophecy in agency theory that actually undermines the very system the theory is intended to enrich through our understanding of contracting. Such would be a most unfortunate irony.

I recently read an essay entitled "Is Capitalism Based on Greed?" The contention was that capitalism was based on greed and individualism, while socialism is based on cooperation. Some even contend that people in capitalistic societies are basically selfish and uncaring, while those in socialist societies are altruistic and community minded. An assertion is made that the concentration of wealth in private hands is almost always socially destructive, while concentrating political and economic power is socially constructive. Such notions are particularly ironic in light of Max Weber's 1904 classic text's title *The Protestant Ethic and the Spirit of Capitalism*. Indeed, the concept of capitalism in a democratic setting can be described as "man's self-interested activity for what it is: a drive to be individually self-reliant, an effort to provide for the material needs of a family, and, for many, an urge to participate in an occupation or profession which contributes to the common good." Rather than greed, democratic capitalism represents a "contemporary expression of enlightened self-interest harnessed for the advancement of the common good."[43] I suggest to you that this idea of "enlightened self-interest" is a concept worthy of development throughout the educational curriculum, and at the doctoral level, in particular, could have far-reaching implications.

The current confusion of the public as to desirable goals and behavior and the role of loyalty is perhaps best reflected in the reported survey of individuals entitled "Oliver North, Businessman? Many Bosses Say That He's Their Kind of Employee," citing leadership, charisma, missionary zeal, work ethic, and loyalty. Of course the same article cited the cutting of corners, blind following, and a character flaw that would make him an unacceptable employee.[44] While black and white choices are unusual, some guidance through the "gray" is needed so that students can begin to internalize a value system in the context of the business arena. Many of us likely feel that values are instilled at an early age; however, I suggest that people are not always effective at translating those values into a business context without some direction. Often it is as simple as drawing a poignant analogy. When you speak with those involved in uncovering frauds and litigating white-collar crimes, they quickly point out that the myth that nobody gets hurt fails to consider the number of individuals who are wiped out financially by such con men and fraud schemes. Financial harm from white collar offenses has been estimated at $100 billion per year.[45] Imagine it is your grandmother who is the investor and reconsider the consequences in a personal context. The likelihood of successful rationalization will decline and hopefully vanish.

PEDAGOGICAL TOOLS

To assist doctoral students in exploring means of integrating ethics into the classroom, discuss some available pedagogical tools. A set of suggested instructional resources are provided in Table 9–1, based on recent journal articles. A wealth of case studies and discussions of ethical dilemmas are available and can easily be updated by accessing current business periodicals. These materials develop an understanding of how rationalization, confidence of non-discovery, and a focus on ends rather than means can lead to unethical behavior. Yet, they clarify the ill consequence of such actions and the rewards to ethical behavior. These are important lessons to balance what may be false impressions gained by an unfortunate tendency to depict

Table 9–1. Suggested Instructional Resources

- Saul W. Gellerman, "Why 'Good' Managers Make Bad Ethical Choices," *Harvard Business Review* (July–August 1986), pp. 85–90.

   Manville Corporation, Continental Illinois Bank, and E. F. Hutton are profiled.

   Key points: "Executives are expected to strike a difficult balance—to pursue their companies' best interests but not overstep the bounds of what outsiders will tolerate" (p. 86).

   "Certainly part of Continental's problem was neglect of standard controls. But another dimension involved ambitious corporate goals" (p. 87).

   "A willingness to gamble thus is probably enhanced by the rationalization—true or not—that everyone else is doing something just as bad and would if they could; that those who wouldn't go for their share are idealistic fools" (p. 88) (E. F. Hutton).
- Jeffrey A. Fadiman, "A Traveler's Guide to Gifts and Bribes," *Harvard Business Review* (July–August 1986), pp. 122–36.

   Numerous examples of decisions and dilemmas are provided.
- Gordon J. Pearson, "Corporate Culture as a Management Tool," *Management Accounting* (November 1986), pp. 40–41.

   Symbols of 'executive theft' are discussed, as is an example of being approached by the boss with an improper suggestion.
- Roy Hill, "Should a Manager Advance Money to a Government Official?" *International Management* (November 1987), pp. 17, 18.

   A case is provided for discussion purposes.
- Roy Hill, "Should Executives Blow the Whistle or Stay Silent and Hope for the Best?" *International Management,* (June 1986), pp. 21, 22.

   A case is provided for discussion purposes.
- Chris Welles, "What Led Beech-Nut Down the Road to Disgrace," *Business Week* (February 22, 1986), pp. 124–26, 128.

   Details fraud, employees' justification of their conduct, and consequences for Beech-Nut.
- Ann J. Rich, "The Controller Who Said 'No' " *Management Accounting* (February 1985), pp. 34–36.

   Recounts an individual's professional battle (a true story) concerning whether to report a wrongdoing and related risks.
- "Standards of Ethical Conduct for Management Accountants," *Management Accounting* (January 1985), p. 66; Robert G. Morgan, Jalaleddin Soroosh, and Charles J. Woelfel, "Are Ethics Dangerous to Your Job?" *Management Accounting* (February 1985), pp. 25–32.

   Presents the Standards for Ethical Conduct in tandem with survey results on their importance, propriety, strengths, and weaknesses.
- Rita J. Hopewell, Eileen S. Klink, and Reuben W. Coleman, "Facing the Ethics Involved in Technical Obsolescence," *Management Accounting* (December 1984), pp. 26–29.

   Discusses the dilemma of fair presentation of inventory value in the midst of a proposed merger.
- Eric Evans, "Fraud and Incompetence in Purchasing," *Management Accounting* (November 1986), pp. 20–21.

   Provides six case studies for discussion and suggests a monitoring system to achieve an effective purchasing operation. Problems in differentiating between fraud and incompetence are explored.

Table 9–2. Approaches to Integrating Ethics in Academia

- Discussion of published cases
- Drafting of cases by students
- Analysis of media events
- Exploration of ethical perspectives regarding familiar experiences—Steven M. Cahn's book (published by Rowman & Littlefield, 1986) *Saints and Scamps: Ethics in Academia;* a "lifeboat" analogy; the "padding of budgets" phenomenon
- Consideration of research and related presumptions regarding behavior:
    Agency Theory (Eric Noreen's AOS article)
    Relevant Findings to Date (E.F. Hutton, the "Fraud Scale", SEC enforcement actions, legal cases)
    Conducting ethics-related research: experimental subjects' rights

---

defrauders as heroes in the media. The gravity of these individual's actions becomes apparent as details, rather than headlines, are explored. Table 9–2 presents an overview of many of the ideas explored herein.

In accounting and auditing, our product is our reputation. We cannot afford replications of the Gomez experience, as the attestation's value relies upon the trust of the investment community and other information users. Ethics have always been a facet of auditing education, but I suggest that we work hard at integrating ethical considerations into every dimension of instruction. When we find ourselves cynically asking "whose ox was gored" by a particular FASB, let us temper such a stand with the stated position of the board of striving to capture economic substance while balancing political factions. Let's discuss the constraints on behavior that are voluntarily accepted by various parties, none of whom are constantly on the winning side.

NOTES

1. Eric Noreen (1987). This has since been published in *Accounting Organizations and Society.*
2. Baruch Lev (1988), pp. 1–22.
3. Ronald Duska (1975).
4. Ronald Duska (n.d.).
5. Jeff B. Miller (1984), pp. 43–57. Journal renamed to *Comparative Economic Studies.*
6. C. Edward Arrington and Jere R. Francis (1987).
7. F. G. Rohatyn (1987).
8. Ralph E. Welton and James R. Davis (1989).
9. M. S. Lane, D. Schaupp, and B. Parsons (1988), pp. 223–229.

10. R. E. Berenbeim (May 1986), pp. 14–19.

11. Kohlberg and Colby (1986); Jim Rest, (1979), pp. 214–216. (Also, note Harvard's Center for Moral Development, which scores research results independently.)

12. Lawrence A. Ponemon and David L. Gabhart (1989).

13. Russell Barefield (1975).

14. "Dear Chrysler. . ." (1987), Joseph B. White (1987).

15. Laura Landro (1982).

16. Robert Johnson, John Koten, and Charles F. McCoy (1987).

17. Thomas Petzinger, Jr. (1979).

18. Andy Pasztor and Scott McMurray (1985), Chris Welles (1986).

19. Jack Kelley and Nels Johnson (1987).

20. Lee Berton (1986), Martha Brannigan and Richard Koenig (1986), Martha Brannigan (1987), Martha Brannigan (1987).

21. Professor Karen Pincus of the University of Southern California has used this approach.

22. Eileen White Read (1988).

23. William Power (1987).

24. Bryan Burrough (1986).

25. Ed Cony (1987).

26. Charles McCoy (1987).

27. Dennis Kneale (1987).

28. McFeely Wackerle Jett (1987).

29. David J. Solomon (1987), Similarly, see Lynn Adkins (1982). pp. 67–76.

30. "A Chronology of the Wall Street Scandal," *The Wall Street Journal* (February 13, 1987), p. 16; George Russell (1986). pp. 48–56.

31. Brooks Jackson (1987), p. 54; Reported by David Beckwith and written by Evan Thomas (1986), pp. 26–36.

32. Charles F. McCoy (1987), p. 15.

33. John R. Emshwiller (1987), pp. 1, 12.

34. Leon E. Wynter (1986), p. 10.

35. Lee Berton (1985), p. 7; Lee Berton (1987a), p. 13; Karen Slater (1988), p. 21.

36. Lee Berton (1987b), p. 4; (1987c), p. 6; (1987d), p. 41.

37. "ZZZZ Best Co.," *The Wall Street Journal* (June 5, 1987), p. 48; "ZZZZ Best Co. Says Outside Accountant Quit, Successor Hired," *The Wall Street Journal* (June 18, 1987), p. 45; Daniel Akst (1987a), p. 33; Daniel Akst (1987b), p. 4; Daniel Akst (1987c), pp. 1, 12; Nancy Jeffrey (1987), p. 5; "ZZZZ Best's Founder Files for Personal Bankruptcy," *The Wall Street Journal* (August 13, 1987), p. 12; "Detective in ZZZZ Best Probe Charges SEC's Lack of Resources Hindered Case," *The Wall Street Journal* (January 28, 1988), p. 6; Thomas E. Ricks (1988), p. 10; Daniel Akst and Lee Berton (1988), p. 17.

38. R. Foster Winans (1986a), p. 9; (1986b), p. 2, Sec. 4; (1986d), p. 2, Sec. 4; (1986c), Sec. 4; (1986e), p. 2, Sec. 5.

39. Irving Kristol (1987).

40. David Vogel (1987), p. 24.

41. S. Parker Hall, III (1986), pp. 7, 10; Leslie Pittel (1986), p. 136.

42. S. David Young (1985), pp. 178–83.

43. John W. Cooper (1987), pp. 1, 10, 11.

44. "Oliver North, Businessman? Many Bosses Say That He's Their Kind of Employee," *The Wall Street Journal* (July 14, 1987), p. 33.

45. Eugene Szwajkowski (n.d.).

IV

CAN AGENCY THEORY HELP EXPLAIN A CONFLICT OF INTEREST?

10

Conflict of Interest: An Agency Analysis

John R. Boatright

An agency theory is a theory that uses the model of the agency relation to describe or explain some aspect of human behavior. The most successful applications of the agency relation have occurred in theories about organizational behavior, especially those aspects of the behavior of corporations that are of concern to economists. By assuming that individuals, both inside and outside a corporation, are induced in some way to act in the interest of others, it is possible to understand a great deal about corporate structure and governance, financial strategies, responses to regulation, and many other matters.

Can the agency model be used to gain a similar understanding of ethical issues involving corporations, including the ethical relation between individuals who are assumed to stand in the relation of principal and agent? Certainly, agency theory, as it has been developed by economists and others, does not justify any specific rights or duties of agents or serve any of the other roles that we expect of ethical theories. Agency theory is no substitute for ethical theory. But the agency relation can be of use to ethical theory by providing a model for understanding some of the roles that people occupy in business and the duties and rights that attend these roles.

My aim in this chapter is to show how the agency relation can be used to give an analysis of one specific concept that is very prominent in discussions about ethics in business, namely the concept of a conflict of interest. Various analyses of conflict of interest have been proposed, but none of them entirely captures the way in which the concept of conflict of interest is actually used in the world of business. My focus is on the use of the concept in the business world and not on conflict of interest among professionals, such as lawyers, and among public officials, who are not agents of others, but public servants. There is an important difference, I believe, between conflict of interest in public and private life.

I

It may be helpful at the outset to clarify the sense in which I propose to give an agency analysis of conflict of interest and the bearing of my analysis on agency theory. Agency theory has been developed by economists purely for the purpose of explanation, and as an explanatory tool it makes no ethical judgments, either about the motivation that is presupposed or about the means used to achieve efficiency. Strictly speaking, there is not a single agency theory; rather, there can be theories about an indefinite number of relations that can be modeled on the agency relation. The model of the agent-principal relation, however, has its origin in the law and more specifically in the law of agency, which specifies the reciprocal rights and duties of agents and principals. The law of agency is justified, moreover, on the grounds that the relation of agent and principal is created by a contractual agreement between consenting parties.

The agency relation, as opposed to agency theory, thus has an inescapable ethical dimension. Not only does it gain its legally binding force from the contractual nature of the agreement between an agent and a principal, but in the law of agency, as well as in other areas of contract law, there are moral limits to the agreements that can be made. Contracts are valid only when they result from voluntary consent and do not unjustifiably harm the rights or interests of others.[1] A contract to commit a crime, for example, is invalid, as are contracts obtained by fraud or coercion. The same restrictions apply in law to the agency relation; the law of agency prevents agents from having an obligation to act in ways that unjustifiably harm the rights or substantial interests of themselves or others.

Agency theory in economics, however, operates with only the most rudimentary concept of the agency relation. The mere fact that one person is induced to act in the interest of another is generally sufficient for purposes of explanation, and there is usually no need in economics to include the ethical dimension of the agency relation. I suspect that some economists would go further and say that the ethical dimension *must* be excluded, since any acknowledgment of it would entail that people in an agency relation are acting for moral reasons and not merely on the basis of self-interested calculation, which is counter to a methodological assumption of the theory. I hold that this position is mistaken, since the ethical dimension of the agency relation can be viewed as a restraint on self-interested behavior, so that it is possible to accept the ethical dimension without assuming some alternative motivating force for human beings. It is possible, in other words, to construct a Hobbesian theory of ethics in which purely egoistic individuals rationally accept some restraints on the pursuit of self-interest.

I stress that my analysis of conflict of interest uses the agency *relation* as it is found in the law of agency and does not draw specifically on the agency *theory* of economists. Since agency theory incorporates at least the rudimentary concept of the agency relation, however, an agency analysis of conflict of interest may be of some use to economists working on the agency theory. I believe this to be the case, and the last section of this chapter contains some remarks on the implications of my analysis for the economic theory of agency.

II

The term "conflict of interest" is used rather freely to describe a broad range of morally questionable situations that occur in the course of business activity. Corporate policy statements on conflict of interest generally focus on the pursuit of outside financial interests that have a bearing on an employee's relation to the company, but it is also generally considered to be a conflict of interest for an employee to use his contacts or position in the company for the employee's own financial gain, even when the company is not affected. Outside business activity that is in direct competition with an employee's firm is clearly a conflict of interest. There is also a conflict when an employee has an interest in a company with which there is some business arrangement in which the employee participates or is able to exert some influence, since the employee may be in a position to advance her own interests over that of the company. In the same way, an employee's judgment may be compromised by gifts from suppliers or customers, not to mention kickbacks and bribes, which create obvious conflict of interest situations. Unrelated outside interests are not prohibited by most companies except insofar as they tend to interfere with an employee's obligation to devote full time and attention to his job with the company.

In each of these cases there is a personal interest that comes into conflict with the interest of another party, usually a business firm. It would be incorrect, however, to define a conflict of interest merely as a clash between competing interests. Such a definition is given in a report prepared for the Twentieth Century Fund Steering Committee on conflict of Interest in the Securities Markets, in which it is stated that the term "conflict of interest" denotes "a situation in which two or more interests are legitimately present and competing or conflicting."[2] This definition is surely too broad, since it could be ex-

tended to cover virtually every business relation. In the relation between buyer and a seller, for example, each party strives to advance
his or her own interest at the expense of the other, but neither party
faces a conflict of interest.

Norman Bowie has also characterized a conflict of interest as the
presence of conflicting legitimate interests with the further stipulation that only one of the interests can be fulfilled, as opposed to
"competing interests," which permit the balancing and partial satisfaction of different interests.[3] According to Bowie, an example of a
conflict of interest as opposed to competing interests is represented
by a company whose product poses a serious danger while an alternative produced by another company does not. In this case there is
no justification for balancing the interests of the company and the
welfare of the consuming public, since there is an alternative.

The distinction between conflicting and competing interests is taken
from an analysis given by Joseph Margolis.[4] However, Margolis introduces a distinction between conflicts of interests and conflicting
interests (which Bowie prefers to call "competing interests") precisely
in order to make the point that a conflict of interest is not to be
confused with the mere presence of different interests or even opposed obligations. Margolis is correct, I believe, to insist that Anti-
gone—who was torn between her duty to bury her slain brother and
Creon's command that he not be given a proper burial—faced conflicting or opposed obligations but did not face a conflict of interest.
Bowie's distinction should be viewed, I think, as a distinction among
Margolis's conflicting interests and not as part of a definition of
"conflict of interest."

Although the Twentieth Century Fund report describes the relation between buyer and seller in general, a conflict of interest arises
in the securities market (which is the concern of the report) when a
person or an institution operates as a fiduciary and has a fiduciary
responsibility to a client.

> It is important to distinguish the relation between fiduciary and client
> from that between ordinary buyer and seller. A used car salesman has
> much narrower obligations to his customers than a fiduciary has to his
> client. Of course, sellers have obligations of truthfulness—for example,
> the used car dealer has a duty not to set back the odometer—and in some
> situations sellers may have special duties, such as when a buyer relies upon
> a seller to select an article for particular use. But except for such limited
> duties, neither party is obligated to serve the other's interest.[5]

A conflict of interest occurs not merely when there is a conflict but
when an interest of some kind conflicts with an obligation that a
person has to others. Tom Beauchamp recognizes this when he writes,

"Conflict of interest involves either a conflict between role obligations and personal interests or a conflict between two role obligations."[6] It is not sufficient, however, to speak of role obligations as being in conflict with personal interest without some qualification. A husband who commits adultery has a role obligation of faithfulness that comes into conflict with a personal interest in an extramarital affair, but we would not say that he has a conflict of interest. Similarly, a salesman who pads his expense account puts his own interest above his obligation to the firm without being in a conflict-of-interest situation.

Also, I do not think that merely having two conflicting role obligations is sufficient to make a situation a conflict of interest. A vivid example of this point is provided by what John Beach calls the Catch-22 of the accounting profession, whereby an accountant is simultaneously under an obligation to keep information confidential and to disclose information when important matters of public interest are at stake. An accountant has obligations to different parties, to clients and to the public, but I would not characterize this situation as a conflict of interest but rather, following Margolis, as one of conflicting obligations.[7]

III

The conflict in a conflict of interest, then, is not merely a conflict between conflicting interests, although conflicting interests are involved. The conflict occurs when a personal interest comes into conflict with an obligation of a certain kind or when two obligations of a certain kind come into conflict. The kind of obligations in question can be characterized as role obligations, as Beauchamp suggests, but a further qualification is needed. The qualification is that the obligation in a conflict of interest is an obligation to act in the interest of another. This kind of obligation exactly coincides with the obligation in an agency relation. It is the obligation that an agent owes a principal. Role obligations include the obligations of agents, but they extend more broadly to include other kinds of obligations, including those of principal to agent as well as obligations that have nothing to do with the agency relation. These other kinds of obligations may enjoin the performance of specific acts which may be *to* the benefit of a person, but they are not specifically obligations to act *in* that person's interest.

As a preliminary definition, then, a conflict of interest may be described as a conflict that occurs when a personal interest interferes with a person's acting so as to promote the interest of another *when the person has an obligation to act in that other person's interest.* This is equivalent to asserting that a conflict of interest arises when a personal interest interferes in the performance of an agent's obligation to a principal. This is a definition of one kind of conflict of interest, namely when a personal interest interferes with the performance of an obligation. Conflicts between two obligations can be similarly defined as situations in which a person has conflicting obligations to act in the interest of two different parties. This definition differs from the one given by Beauchamp in the stipulation that both obligations in question must be those that arise in an agency relation.

One writer who recognizes the connection between conflict of interest and the agency relation is Robert E. Frederick, who writes, "A conflict of interest in the corporate setting arises when an agent has an interest that influences his judgment in his own behalf or in behalf of a third party, and which is contrary to the principal's interest."[8] This definition is not entirely accurate, however, for several reasons. One is that the influencing of judgment, while a common feature of conflict of interest situations, is not always present. I argue in a later section that a conflict of interest can exist where there is not opportunity for exercising judgment. A second reason is that a conflicting interest need not actually influence an agent but only have a tendency to exert an influence. All that is required for a conflict of interest is that an interest interfere, either actually or potentially, with the performance of an agent's duty. Furthermore, the interest that creates the conflict need not be contrary to the principal's interest. It frequently is contrary, but abuse of position, for example, or the use of confidential information, constitutes a conflict of interest, even when a principal's position is not affected adversely. To exploit an agency relation for personal gain is to violate the bond of trust that is an essential part of the relation.

A definition should also be given for "personal interest." Roughly, a person has an interest in something when the person stands to gain some benefit or advantage from that thing. A person can also "take an interest" in someone else's interest, especially when that person is a family member or a close associate, in which case the benefit or advantage accrues to someone else. In most cases, however, the person taking an interest in the well-being of another also gains in some way. The benefit or advantage is usually restricted to a financial gain of some kind and should be limited to something tangible. Merely satisfying a desire, for example, would not seem to be enough, for otherwise a lawyer who detests a client and secretly hopes that the client will be convicted would face a conflict of interest, as would a lawyer who prefers to play golf rather than spend the time adequately representing a client. The benefit or advantage also has to be substantial enough to interfere significantly with a person's performance of an obligation.

It is necessary to qualify the definition that has been given to avoid cases of the following kind. Lawyers are regarded in the law not only as agents of a client but also as agents of the court. In this dual role, a lawyer might find that delaying a trial unnecessarily is to the advantage of a client. Doing so, however, would be an abuse of the court system and a violation of the lawyer's duty to the court. Public accountants face a similar conflict, which is described in a previous section as the Catch-22 of the accounting profession. I would be reluctant to say that cases of this kind involve conflict of interest, mainly because the term "conflict of interest" implies some wrongdoing that an agent has an obligation to avoid. The cases just described involve systematic features of situations that professionals, such as lawyers and accountants, individually cannot alter. This kind of case can be excluded from the definition by stipulating that none of the agency obligations in a situation arise because of unavoidable systematic features of that situation. What is "unavoidable and systematic" may be open to interpretation, but the term "conflict of interest," like any term, has borderline areas of application.

The definition that I have given must be modified to account for the conflict of interest that arises for organizations. In the agency relation, the agent is typically a person acting for a principal, which may be another person or an organization, but organizations can also be agents for a principal. Thus, an accounting firm or an advertising agency is an agent for some client, which is usually another organization. Accounting firms have discovered that it is very profitable to provide management services to companies that they also audit, but there is great concern in the profession that this dual function endangers the independence and objectivity of accountants, even when the work is done by different divisions of a firm.[9] Advertising agencies that have clients with competing products face a similar kind of conflict of interest. Investment banking houses have also been accused of conflict of interest for financing takeovers of companies with whom they have had long-standing relations, and many banks have an investment banking department and a department or affiliate working on mergers and acquisitions. It is generally considered a conflict of interest for large law firms, as well as for individual lawyers, to accept clients with competing interests, even when the work is done by different departments within the firm.

For an accountant to provide managerial services to a company that he also audits is a clear conflict of interest. But why is it a conflict when these functions are performed by different persons in different departments of a firm? One answer is that an accounting firm also has an interest that is shared by every member of the organization. When management services are more lucrative than auditing, firms have an incentive to conduct audits in ways that favor their clients. The creative work for competing advertising accounts is generally done by independent groups, but there is also an incentive to commit greater resources and talent to more valuable accounts. In addition, advertising campaigns involve very sensitive information about product development and marketing strategies, which it may be difficult to keep confidential.

Another more subtle reason why organizations can be in conflict-of-interest situations is that when an organization, such as an advertising agency, accepts a client, there is an organizational commitment to serve the interest of the client that goes beyond merely delivering agreed upon services. To take on a client is to make a commitment of loyalty. For an organization to work for and against a client at the same time is incompatible with this kind of organizational commitment. Some of the conflicts perceived by clients suggest a desire to prevent a company from aiding their competitors and to punish them when they do. For example, the giant tobacco and food conglomerate RJR Nabisco took away from Saatchi & Saatchi accounts valued between seventy and eighty million dollars for producing television commercials announcing Northwest Airline's new smoking ban. There is some merit, however, to the position expressed by an official of RJR Nabisco who said that the company thought it important to deal with advertising agencies "that have a wholly consistent philosophical approach to its plans and programs".[10]

There is no consensus among clients and advertising agencies about what constitutes a conflict, and disagreement can and does arise. For example, Young & Rubicam lost a forty million dollar account from Hallmark Cards for taking on a twenty million dollar account from AT&T Communications long-distance telephone service, since Hallmark perceived a conflict. Young & Rubicam attributed the loss to a belief by Hallmark that the agency "should not do personal, emotional and motivating advertising for two different companies." The agency found this to be too "broad and general a concept" to constitute a conflict.[11]

Conflict of interest that is genuinely organizational in nature and not merely an instance of individuals within an organization facing a conflict of interest can occur, therefore, in organizations. Although it is important to recognize this point, it raises no difficulty for the definition that has been presented, since organizations as well as individuals can be agents and can have organizational obligations and interests that are not necessarily the same as those of the individuals who compose an organization. The term "person" can simply be expanded in this instance to include organizations without entering into the lively debate over whether organizations are persons.

IV

Support for an agency analysis can be given by showing how it accommodates the many features of conflict of interest situations better than alternative analyses. Some of these features can be brought out by a critical examination of an analysis of conflict of interest that has been called "the lawyer's analysis." Michael Davis offers this analysis of conflict of interest, which he finds in the American Bar Association's *Code of Professional Responsibility* and in the literature on legal ethics.[12] The central notion in this analysis is that of an interest that interferes with a person's exercising judgment on behalf of another. Davis's rough formulation is as follows:

> A person has a conflict of interest if (a) he is in a relationship with another requiring him to exercise judgment in that other's service and (b) he has an interest tending to interfere with the proper exercise of judgment in that relation.[13]

Davis clarifies the nature of the relationship and the standards for the proper exercise of judgment in a fuller definition, but the rough formulation is sufficient for present purposes, since my criticisms are not altered by his clarifications.

This analysis seems to be ideally suited to the situation of lawyers and other professionals, such as accountants and engineers, whose stock in trade is a body of specialized knowledge that is the basis for making judgments. Not only are professionals paid for their use of this knowledge in making judgments, but part of the value of their services lies in the confidence that can be placed in a professional's judgment. Accountants do not merely examine a company's financial statement, for example; they attest to the accuracy of that statement and to its compliance with generally accepted accounting principles or GAAP. The National Society of Professional Engineers' *Code of Ethics for Engineers* stipulates that engineers shall not submit plans or specifications that are not safe and in conformity with accepted engineering standards.[14] So an engineer's signature on a blueprint is also a warrant of its quality. The analysis also fits the situation of other kinds of employees who make decisions that involve judgment, since judgment is not exclusively a feature of professional work.

However, there are some conflicts of interest for which the lawyer's analysis is not adequate. First, there is the conflict of interest that arises when an employee competes directly with her employer where there is no question of impaired judgment. Consider this case, which is taken from a policy statement issued by the Xerox Corporation:

> The wife of a Xerox tech rep inherits money. They decide it would be profitable to open a copy shop with her money and in her name in a suburban city. The territory they choose is different from his. However, there are several other copy shops and an XRC in the vicinity. She leases equipment and supplies from Xerox on standard terms. After working hours, he helps his wife reduce costs by maintaining her equipment himself without pay. He also helps out occasionally on weekends. His job performance at Xerox remains as satisfactory as before. One of the nearby competitive shops, also a lessee of Xerox equipment, writes to his manager complaining that the employee's wife is getting free Xerox service and assistance.

The conflict of interest in this case consists solely in the fact that the employee's work outside of his employment at Xerox places him in direct competition with his employer. It is not the investment itself that creates the conflict. The territory is different from his own, and so he would never have to exercise judgment on the job that could be compromised by his wife's business. The conflict results from his servicing of the equipment, which results in unfair competition to other customers of Xerox and indirectly harms the company. This kind of example can be understood as a conflict of interest only under the assumption that the tech rep has an obligation not to compete with his employer and that this obligation is independent of any exercise of judgment in the role of a technician. As long as he is employed by Xerox, his skill as a technician, which is in part the result of company training, belongs, in a sense, to the company, and he would be free to exercise these skills only by leaving the employment of Xerox.

The lawyer's analysis also does not fit conflict of interest involving misuse of position. Another case given in the Xerox policy statement is the following:

> A supervisor's wife works for a real estate firm. When it is determined that a Xerox employee from out of state will be brought in as one of his subordinates, he makes it a point to introduce this subordinate to his wife and suggests that she can help him find a house.

What is the justification for calling this a conflict of interest? The company is not materially harmed, and the supervisor's judgment is not impaired. There is not even a conflict in the sense that the interest of the company and that of the employee are opposed. The conflict of interest consists rather in the improper use of his position in the company to advance his own interests. As a supervisor, his obligation in that role is to serve the interests of the company exclusively. Thus, the supervisor is not filling his role as an employee of the company. Instead he is acting outside the scope of his corporate role and using this role to his own advantage.

This way of looking at the matter assumes that an employee has an obligation to act *only* in the fulfillment of a role and not to advance his own interests in the course of being employed to serve the interests of another. It might be replied that the supervisor's judgment was affected in that steering itself was an instance of bad judgment on his part. That is, his outside interest affected his judgment as a supervisor when he decided to introduce new subordinates to his wife. This reply begs the question, however, for it is the fact that the steering is a conflict of interest that makes the judgment bad, and so the conflict must lie in something other than his judgment as a supervisor to engage in steering.

The analysis of conflict of interest that I have developed can be extended to show how the utilization of information acquired in the course of employment, including insider trading, constitutes a conflict of interest. The case of R. Foster Winans, who wrote the column "Heard on the Street" for *The Wall Street Journal,* is instructive here. Winans admitted to the SEC and to his employer that he had violated the newspaper's code of ethics regarding conflict of interest, which prohibits a reporter from misusing his or her position for private gain. The code states in part:

> It is not enough to be incorruptible and act with honest motives. It is equally important to use good judgment and conduct one's outside activities so that no one—management, our editors, an SEC investigator with power of subpoena, or a political critic of the company—has any grounds for even raising the suspicion that an employee misused a position with the company.[15]

The conflict of interest inherent in the use of information acquired in the course of employment for one's own benefit is not due necessarily to any impairment of an employee's judgment but to the obligation of an employee to use this information only in the interest of the firm. There is no suggestion, for example, that Winans allowed his financial interests to influence the content of his column in *The Wall Street Journal.* A journalist who allowed personal financial interests to affect the content of news stories would be guilty of a conflict of interest for the reason that his or her objective and independent judgment would be compromised. But there is also a conflict of interest when a reporter has information prior to publication and can capitalize on the expected results. There is no need for the writer's judgment to be compromised for a conflict to exist. The conflict consists rather in using the information in a way that is not a part of the role of a reporter and that may also harm the interests of the newspaper company.

A third feature of conflict of interest is that it may occur even after a person is no longer in a role that calls for judgment on behalf of another party. This point is illustrated by the attempt of American Express to acquire the McGraw-Hill Book Company in a hostile takeover. The President of American Express, Roger H. Morley, was a director of McGraw-Hill, and in that capacity he was privy to a great deal of information that could aid American Express in planning the acquisition. It would certainly be a conflict of interest for the president of a company to attempt a takeover of another company in which he served as a director. Mr. Morley relinquished his role as a director prior to the takeover bid, but he was charged by Harold McGraw of McGraw-Hill with a conflict of interest in planning the takeover while he was still serving as a director.[16] Suppose, for the sake of argument, that the takeover was planned only after Mr. Morley had left the board. Would there no longer be a conflict of interest? A director in Mr. Morley's position has an obligation not to use information confidentially acquired against the interest of a company even after he leaves the board of that company. To use information in this way involves a person in a conflict of interest. After leaving a board of directors, a person is no longer in a position to exercise judgment on behalf of the company in question, and so there is no question of a person's judgment being compromised. But the possibility of a conflict of interest remains in the obligation not to misappropriate confidential information.

The persistence of the obligations of an agent is recognized in the American Bar Association's *Model Rules of Professional Conduct*. Section 1.9 on conflict of interest involving former clients reads:

A lawyer who has formerly represented a client in a matter shall not thereafter:

(a) represent another person in the same or a substantially related matter in which that person's interests are materially adverse to the interests of the former client unless the former client consents after consultation; or

(b) use information relating to the representation to the disadvantage of the former client except as Rule 1.6 would permit with respect to a client or when the information has become generally known.

A lawyer who represents two clients with opposed interests at the same time faces an obvious conflict of interest. The judgment that is exercised on behalf of one is liable to be compromised by the commitment that the lawyer has to serve the interests of the other. When clients are represented one at a time, however, this kind of conflict is not present. If compromised judgment were essential to conflict of interest, then there would be no reason on the lawyer's analysis for prohibiting this kind of activity as a conflict of interest, since a lawyer would be able to exercise competent judgment in representing both clients.

The justification for Rule 1.9 is, I suggest, that the obligation of a lawyer to a former client does not cease with the end of the lawyer-client relation. Even when a lawyer is no longer being paid to exercise judgment on the client's behalf, the lawyer has an obligation not to harm the former client's interests. The reason is that the lawyer, in virtue of the past relation, has confidential information along with contacts, experience, and other advantages, which were acquired in the course of representing the former client and which the lawyer is in a position to exploit for the benefit of a new client. As a result, a lawyer has an obligation not to exploit the past relation in this way, even though there is no present relation in which the lawyer is called upon to exercise judgment.

An attempt to save the lawyer's analysis from this kind of objection might be made by arguing that in representing a new client a lawyer is still exercising judgment that may bear on the interests of a former client. Competent judgment, according to Davis, is judgment that benefits a person to the degree that a person is justified in expecting in virtue of another's role. The benefit that a client is justified in expecting from a lawyer may then be interpreted to include the lack of future harm resulting from the past relation. However, this attempt distorts the concept of judgment exercised in the service of another in a way that makes it dangerously vague and inclusive. When such distortion is the price of uniformity—to use H.L.A. Hart's phrase—it is a sign that the analysis is faulty and ought to be replaced rather than patched up in an ad hoc fashion.

V

The objections that I make against the lawyer's analysis all stem from a common source, namely that the concept of judgment competently exercised for the benefit of another is too narrow to encompass the diversity of conflict-of-interest situations. This does not mean that the analysis is wrong and that the concept of judgment does not have a place in an adequate analysis of conflict of interest. I suggest rather that the concept is not central and that the relevance of judgment is due to some more inclusive analytic framework of which the concept of judgment is only a part.

The problem of direct competition, where an employee's service to an employer is unimpaired is easily accommodated on an agency analysis. The law of agency clearly recognizes an obligation of loyalty that extends to activities outside an employee's work. An agent has a duty not to acquire a competing interest or to act for others who are in competition with the principal. Section 394 of the *Restatement of Agency* specifically prohibits an agent from acting "for persons whose interests conflict with those of the principal in matters in which the agent is employed." The moonlighting technician is prohibited by the law of agency from servicing Xerox equipment, whether the equipment is in his wife's shop or the shop of another Xerox customer. If the technician did not service equipment, however, but did (say) the bookkeeping for his wife's business, there would be no conflict of interest, since bookkeeping is not concerned with "matters in which the agent is employed." Working in any capacity for a direct competitor of Xerox, even in a non-technical capacity, would be a conflict of interest, but using his Xerox skills in an unrelated business, such as working on weekends in a camera repair shop, would probably not constitute a conflict of interest. These fine distinctions are easily made by referring to the duty of loyalty that an agent owes a principal, but they cannot be accounted for by the lawyer's analysis or other proposed definitions of "conflict of interest."

Abuse of position of the kind represented by the supervisor who introduces new employees to his real estate agent wife can easily be accounted for by the provision that agents have an obligation to act only as authorized while carrying out the duties of an agent. In all of his business dealings with new employees, the supervisor is an agent of the company and is obligated in all job-related activity to perform only those acts that are within the scope of the job. An employee may have a great deal of latitude in determining what is within the scope of a job, but steering business to his wife is surely not what the supervisor is hired by Xerox to do.

The duty to act only as authorized can also serve to prohibit the use of confidential information and insider trading, but the law of agency specifically imposes an obligation of confidentiality that applies to such cases. Section 395 of the *Restatement* prohibits the use of information "acquired by him during the course of or on account of his agency . . . to the injury of the principal, on his own account or on behalf of another." For a reporter or a financial writer to capitalize on the effect of a news story is to use information acquired as a result of working for a publication and is clearly covered by the duty of confidentiality.

The possibility of conflict of interest when a person no longer occupies a role is due principally to the duty of confidentiality. The president of American Express has an obligation according to the law of agency not to use information acquired while serving as a director for McGraw-Hill either during the term of his service or later. The information covered by the duty of confidentiality includes all information acquired by him as an agent that is used to the detriment of the principal, even when the information "is *not* connected with the subject matter of his agency."[17] This broad interpretation of what constitutes information prohibits the use not only of confidential information provided to a director by the company but also all other non-public information about a company that would be useful for a person planning a takeover.

An agency analysis is better suited than the lawyer's analysis or any other definition to account for organizational conflict of interest. The judgment of individual members of an accounting firm or an advertising agency may be compromised by serving competing clients or by offering different services. But even when such problems are kept to a minimum by having the work performed by different departments or groups within an organization, there remains the problem of organizational commitment. An advertising client has some justification for holding that giving an account to an advertising agency commits the agency to serve only the client's interest and not to acquire competing interests. Similarly, the public, which trusts accounting firms to render reliable audits, has a right to feel that providing management services compromises the reliability of a firm's audits. In addition, it may be objected that providing management services means that a public accounting firm is no longer serving only the public.

Finally, an agency analysis explains why certain kinds of conflicting obligations are not conflicts of interest. Although at least one writer has labeled the conflict which John Beach calls the Catch-22 of the accounting profession a conflict of interest, I hold that it is simply a case of conflicting obligations of the kind described by Joseph Margolis. The theory of agency recognizes many limits to the obligations of agents. The duty to serve an agent is limited, for example, by the law and by business and professional ethics.[18] I do not think that we want to say that accountants face a conflict of interest between serving a client's interest and observing GAAP. GAAP places a clear limit on an accountant's obligation to a client. An agent no longer has a duty of confidentiality, according to the *Restatement,* when information is revealed to protect a "superior interest." The decision in the Alexander Grant case, for example, holds that the interests of the public may on occasion be such a "superior interest."

> Although the duty of confidentiality implied in the accountant-client relationship is favored, this court recognizes that such a duty is not absolute. Overriding public interests may exist to which confidentiality must yield.[19]

Conflicting court rulings about the obligations of accountants with regard to confidential information have made the exact boundaries of these obligations uncertain, but it would be a mistake, I think, to confuse uncertainty about obligations with conflict of interest.

VI

The analysis that is presented in this chapter uses the agency relation as it is found in the law of agency and makes little reference to the economic theory of agency. Since agency theory is built on the agency relation, however, the law of agency and related matters such as conflict of interest are potentially relevant. For the legal obligations of agents, corporate policies on employee conduct, professional codes of ethics, and the like, are factors in the efficiency of agency relations. The reason why they are factors is simply that conflict of interest disrupts the agency relation by inducing agents to act in their own interest rather than the interest of another, and eliminating conflict of interest promotes efficiency in agency relations.

Agency theory assumes that individuals and firms are motivated solely by considerations of self-interest, but this assumption is compatible with the use of normative restraints on conduct as long as they derive their efficacy from considerations of self-interest. It may be desirable to loosen the egoistic assumption of agency theory to allow for agents acting on normative as opposed to self-interested reasons. But a company that has a policy prohibiting employees from accepting gifts or favors and enforces this policy with effective sanctions has designed a system of control that operates by preventing one source of conflict of interest. The accounting systems of firms also operate in part by rules and procedures that seek to eliminate conflict of interest. Conflict of interest can also be controlled in more informal ways. Advertising agencies, for example, are under no legal or moral obligation not to have competitors as clients, but advertisers frequently avoid doing business with an agency when a conflict of interest is perceived. Such avoidance constitutes an informal control.

It can be seen from these examples that some considerations involving conflict of interest are relevant to the description and explanation of many different kinds of control systems using the theory of agency. Some systems deal with conflict of interest merely by rules and procedures that involve no explicit reference to the concept of a conflict of interest, while others rely on laws, policy statements, and codes of ethics that explicitly prohibit conflict of interest. These latter means of control are as amenable to treatment by agency theory as are the former, and greater attention to them might help expand the power and scope of agency theory.

NOTES

1. See Anthony T. Kronman (1980), 472–97.

2. *Abuse on Wall Street: Conflicts of Interest in the Securities Markets* (Westport, CT: Quorum Books, 1980), 4.

3. Norman E. Bowie (1982), 103. Bowie continues to hold this view in a more recent paper (1988), 59–73.

4. Joseph Margolis (1979), 361–72.

5. *Abuse on Wall Street*, 5.

6. Tom L. Beauchamp and Norman E. Bowie (1988), 472.

7. Bowie, using his definition, does characterize the accountants' dilemma as a conflict of interest. Bowie, "Accountants, Full Disclosure, and Conflicts of Interest," 63–64.

8. Robert E. Frederick (1983), 125.

9. See Abraham J. Briloff (1987), 22–29.

10. "Cigarette Maker Cuts Off Agency That Made Smoking-Ban TV Ads," *New York Times*, April 6, 1988.

11. "Conflict a Hallmark for Y&R," *Advertising Age*, 55 (May 10, 1984), 5.

12. American Bar Association, *Code of Professional Responsibility* (Chicago: National Center for Professional Responsibility, 1980), EC 5-1.

13. Michael Davis (1982), 21. For a criticism of Davis and an analysis of conflict of interest that is similar to my own, see Neil R. Luebke (1987), 66–81. This article was published after the completion of my paper, so that I was unable to take advantage of its many insights.

14. National Society of Professional Engineers, *Code of Ethics for Engineers*, 1987, III, 2, b.

15. "Media Policies Vary on Preventing Employees and Others from Profiting on Knowledge of Future Business Stories," *The Wall Street Journal*, March 2, 1984, p. 8. While admitting to a conflict of interest, Winans denied that he had engaged in insider trading or had done anything illegal. The SEC has generally prosecuted insider trading under regulations that require that there be full disclosure of all material facts when securities are bought and sold, so that insider trading constitutes a kind of fraud rather than conflict of interest. However, the SEC view has been developed in order to deal with the practical problem of regulating the securities market and is not intended to be an ethical analysis.

16. The charge is contained in an open letter to the directors of American Express published in *The Wall Street Journal*, January 81, 1979. The case is discussed by Bowie in *Business Ethics* (1982).

17. *Restatement of Agency*, Sec 395. (Emphasis added.)

18. *Restatement of Agency*, Sec 385. (Emphasis added.)

19. *Wagenheim v. Alexander Grant & Co.* 10th District, Court of Appeals, Ohio (1983), 3393.

11

Agency, Conflicts of Interest, and Creditors' Committees: A Case Study

William E. Lawson

Two related concepts receive a great deal of attention in the business ethics literature: conflict of interest and agency theory. As a topic of research, conflict of interest has been discussed longer in the history of business ethics. Traditionally, as Robert Frederick notes, a conflict of interest in the corporate setting arises when an agent has an interest that influences his judgment in his own behalf or in behalf of a third party, and that is contrary to the principal's interest. The moral and legal basis of conflicts of interest is relatively clear.[1] The usual problems cited as examples of conflict of interest center around acts of personal enrichment. Acts such as graft, insider trading, and influence peddling come immediately to mind.

One goal of theorists of conflict of interest is to articulate the conditions under which laws and codes can be formulated to resolve such conflicts.[2] However, business ethicists are now aware that conflicts of interest occur in business settings that do not involve personal enrichment. For example, an employee may find himself torn between his duty to the company and his duty to the public good. This is often the issue in whistle-blowing cases. This type of conflict of interest forced business ethicists to examine the relationship of the worker as an agent to the employer as principal.

> Via the work contract the agent agrees to further the principal's interest. If the agent acts for himself or a third party in a manner contrary to the principal's interest, he breaks his contract with the principal. Contract

204

breaking is unfair to the principal, and, if generally practiced, would undermine the institution of business, with attendant social disutility. Given the asymmetry in the law of agency, however, which places obligations of loyalty, obedience, and confidentiality on the agent, and given that the employer typically sets the majority of the provisions of the work contract, it seems morally, if not legally, incumbent on the employer to clearly specify in the contract what constitutes a conflict of interest.[3]

"The model of the agent-principal relation, . . . has its origin in the law and more specifically in the law of agency, which specifies the reciprocal rights and duties of agents and principals."[4]

One intriguing area of concern for principal-agent theorists is the situation in which a single agent has obligations to two different principals and these principals have conflicting interests. The agent faces a conflict of interest. Since one goal of the research on agency is to provide an analysis of the agency relationship that can be used to provide codes, policies, and laws that help resolve possible conflicts of interest between agent and principal, the research on conflict of interest and agency overlap.

In this regard, the Federal Bankruptcy Code pertaining to service on a court-appointed creditors' committee provides an interesting problem for both our understanding of conflict of interest and agency relationships in business, particularly in our understanding of the agent's obligations to principals with conflicting interests.

It is my contention that a member of a creditors' committee who is at the same time an employee of one of the businesses affected by the bankruptcy proceeding is an agent for two different principals. I think that this situation creates a conflict of interest because the Bankruptcy Code is written in such a manner that it implies a principal-agent relationship. I will point out why an appeal to the restatement of agency does not resolve this conflict of interest. Finally, I will argue that our understanding of the nature of the principal-agent relationship in the creditors' committee case has significant bearing on court-appointed fiduciary relationships.

I

The creditors' committee tends to be an important but seldom discussed part of the bankruptcy proceeding. The following citations from the Bankruptcy Law Manual shows the importance of the creditors' committee, as a protector of the public interest, in a Chapter 11 bankruptcy reorganization.

A basic assumption that underlies American bankruptcy law is that it is often preferable to encourage and facilitate rehabilitation of businesses in financial trouble instead of providing for liquidation only. From a broad perspective, rehabilitation is better for the economy because it minimizes unemployment and waste of business assets. It is much more productive to use assets in the industry for which they were designed instead of selling them as distressed merchandise at liquidation sales. Also, rehabilitating a business is in the best long-term interest of creditors and shareholders.[5]

Although in most reorganization cases existing management continues to conduct the debtors' business, in the ordinary course after the petition is filed, creditors want to look over the debtor's shoulder carefully to make sure that their interests are being protected. Of course, it is unwieldly, if not impossible, for every creditor to keep a close eye on the debtor's operation. For this reason, the code provides for a mechanism that assures that creditors will be able to oversee the operation and to voice their thoughts throughout the Chapter 11 case. This mechanism involves the appointment of committees of creditors and equity security holders.[6]

Under Sec.1102(a) of the Bankruptcy Code, the court appoints a creditors' committee of those creditors holding unsecured claims. This committee generally consists of the seven largest creditors. The committee considers whether a trustee is needed and whether the size of the committee should be increased to be more representative of the types of claims peculiar to that bankruptcy estate.

The code specifies which creditors are to be appointed to the committee. Sections 1103 and 1104 deal with the appointment and duties of the trustee, if one is to be appointed, and the debtor in possession about the bankruptcy. The committee should investigate the acts, conduct, assets, liabilities, and financial condition of the debtor and help formulate a plan of reorganization. The committee is also empowered to perform other services in the interest of the parties represented.[7]

Richard Niles Chassin notes that:

The concept of creditors committees under Chapter 11 evolved from the need to give the creditors of a bankrupt debtor some voice in the administration of the case. Typically, committees are designed to represent classes of creditors that are too large to speak effectively for themselves. Accordingly, in exercising the committee function, each member has a fiduciary duty to the class of creditors the committee represents. Ideally, creditors of the class represented on any given committee can be assured that their interests are being represented adequately by members who share common interests.

The committee cannot function effectively as the representative of a given class of creditors unless its members share a common interest with those creditors it seeks to represent. For example, the most commonly appointed class is unsecured creditors. Ideally, since unsecured creditors share the fact of not possessing a security interest in the debtors property, acting in his own self-interests, a committee member inadvertently and necessarily acts in the best interest of the other class members.[8]

All committee members act in a representative capacity and have fiduciary obligations. Each member of the committee acts for the best interest of its constituents, not in its own private interest.[9]

The goal of the creditors committee is to devise a reorganization plan that will not only save the company but will also return to the creditors some part of their debts.[10]

The basic qualifications necessary to serve on a creditors' committee were outlined in *In re Vermont Real Estate.* The party seeking membership on an unsecured creditors' committee must be: (1) a creditor who holds an unsecured claim against the debtor, and (2) one who is unsecured.[11] The court does allow companies to send their company credit managers to serve as members of the creditors' committee. When one of these credit managers agrees to be a member of the creditors' committee does she now take on obligations that override her obligations to the company that sent her to the creditors' committee meeting? This question is the heart of this chapter.

It is generally realized that some members of a creditors' committee have dual roles,[12] first as a member of the creditors' committee and then as an employee of one of the creditors. As such, an individual has two opportunities to vote on a plan of reorganization.

The first occurs as a committee member representing all the creditors. This is where it is important that an individual put aside the influences and biases that result because of who he works for and what his employer's interest may be. This is hard to do, but certainly not impossible.[13]

The second vote is made in the individual's role as an employee of his company. When the ballot for his company arrives, he can permit all parochial influences to affect his decision and vote accordingly.[14]

There are at least three possible reasons for not supporting the plan at the company level. First, the debtor has been a bad client and has been a source of problems over and above the inability to make payments on time. It is the company's wish to be rid of the debtor, even if it means that other creditors lose money. Second, the debtor is a competitor of the company and, again, it is the company's wish to get rid of the debtor. Third, the company accounting department has informed the representative that the company would get a better return if the debtor's company were liquidated. Again other creditors may not fare as well.

What is the obligation of the member of the creditors' committee at this point? Thomas J. McDonnell thinks that working on a creditors' committee means making an honest effort to work out a good plan for all involved. "However, to work on the committee with the knowledge you will not support your own plan would not be ethical."[15] McDonnell does not tell us why such behavior is not ethical.

James Seaholm recognizes that members of creditors' committee have a dual role in the acceptance of a reorganization plan. However, he thinks that a vote as a committee member could be cast in favor of a plan of reorganization that represents the best deal for all creditors as a body while the same person could vote against the plans as not being in the best interests (or desires) of his company.[16]

> Seaholm is ambiguous here for he later states that if a committee member supports the proposed plan of reorganization, he usually should be prepared to campaign for its acceptance. Some plans call for significant loss by trade creditors and often encounter reluctance if not outright opposition . . .[17]

The member of the committee appears to have two conflicting sets of obligations. If he takes seriously his position as a member of a creditors' committee, he should support the plan. However, as an employee he will be under pressure to do what his employer thinks is best for the company, which may not be in the best interest of all other creditors.

II

Is the creditors' committee case a case of conflicting interests rather than a conflict of interest? It may be argued that what we have here is only a case of conflicting interests and not really a conflict of interest. The employee has competing interests. He has an interest in keeping a good working relationship with his employer and he wants to fulfill his duties as a member of the creditors' committee. He can only do both when his employer agrees that the reorganization plan is acceptable. If his employer does not like the plan, he has to decide if he should continue to support the plan and argue for its acceptance. At this point his interests no longer compete, but conflict.

How does this situation arise? The answer to this question turns out to be dependent on the answer to the question: What is the relationship of the member of the creditors' committee to the committee? If it turns out that the employee becomes an agent for the creditors' committee when he sits on the creditors' committee, then his support for the reorganization plan would conflict with his principal-agent relationship with his employer. Is he an agent for the committee?

If we admit that some members of the committee have dual roles, it is possible to see how the Bankruptcy Code and Manual give us some rationale for thinking that membership on a creditors' committee is a principal-agent relationship. According to the Bankruptcy, members of a creditors' committee have a fiduciary relation to the committee.

All committee members act in a representative capacity and have fiduciary obligations. Each member of the committee acts for the best interest of its constituents, not in its own private interest.[18] One is said to be in fiduciary relation by a person having a duty, created by his undertaking, to act primarily for another's benefit in matters connected with such undertaking.[19] It is characterized as a trust.

Second, members of the creditors' committee are expected to work out a reorganization plan that will ensure the best possible return for all creditors. Third, the plan, once accepted by the creditors' committee, must be approved by the creditors.

The members of the committee, having read the Bankruptcy Code and Manual, would see themselves as agents for the committee and thus obligated to support the plan and to expect that other members of the committee will support the plan. When we add to the language of the Bankruptcy Code the understanding that

> Chapter 11 of the U.S. Bankruptcy Code is designed to rehabilitate and reorganize financially distressed individuals and organizations. The statutory aims of the formal reorganization proceeding include the following: preservation of the property and assets that the debtor requires to maintain itself as a going concern; avoidance of forced and destructive liquidation of the debtor's assets; protection of the interests of creditors, both secured and unsecured; and restructuring of the debtor's debts and finances such that the debtor will be able to retain those assets necessary to rehabilitate its finances while quickly reimbursing creditors at the greatest amount possible.[20]

It is not difficult to understand why a member of the creditors' committee would feel that she has an obligation to support the plan, as a member of the committee. We can now understand why McDonnell believes that not voting for the plan is acting unethically. The goal of the committee is to save the company and return to the creditors some part of their debts. The goal is directly connected to interests pertaining to society as a whole: the public interest.[21]

I noted earlier that a basic assumption of the Bankruptcy Code was that it is better to rehabilitate a business in financial trouble rather than to liquidate its assets. It is thought that this process serves the public interest much better. So important is this commitment to the public interest that the Bankruptcy Code includes a cram-down clause.

> The creditor may accept or reject the plan. However, if the class holding two-thirds of the amount and more than one-half of claims approves the

plan, it will be confirmed. Sections 1126 and 1129 contain the provisions for cram-down if it is in the best interest of the parties and the estate. The plan and its provision are crammed down a party's throat despite objections.[22]

Thus if it is at all possible, the goal is to save the business, and we can understand why it is in the best interest of the state, businesses, and the public to have a legal mechanism that prevents mean-spirited businessmen from putting other business out of business.

The assumption that it is better to save a business is tied directly to another important assumption that underlies the Bankruptcy Code. It seems to assume that all persons on the committee are in the same relationship to the other members of the committee. That is, they are all creditors. However, it turns out that large companies will often send representatives (agents) to serve on the committee. These agents are employees of the company and according to the laws of agency have an obligation to their employers. If it is the case that a number of small creditors have the same interest, the representative of the large company have a different agenda.

These employees will have personal interest. They will want to do what is in their self-interest. This may mean not going against the desires of their employers, an action that may cause one to be fired. They must keep in mind the organization interest. And yet, their membership on the creditors' committee is tied directly to the public interest, an interest that is not totally at odds with the organization interest, that is, to keep businesses doing business.

I have already cited three possible reasons for a company to veto a plan. If the employee goes with his employer, he has betrayed the other members of the creditors' committee who believed that his effort to develop the plan was a good faith one. Is there a way to resolve this conflict?

Philosophers like Boatright, Frederick, and Davis have made appeals to the restatement of agency as a way to understand the agency relationship. Boatright, in particular, wants to focus on an analysis of conflict of interest that makes use of the agency relation as it is found in the law of agency and does not draw specifically on the agency theory of economics.[23]

It is unclear that in this case an appeal to the restatement of agency helps to clarify the issue. In fact, the restatement seems to present another problem for understanding the relationship between committee members who are employees and the creditors' committee. The restatement of agency states "that a person appointed by a court to manage the affairs of others is not an agent of the others."[24] The Bankruptcy Law Manual states "the court is obligated to appoint a committee of creditors holding unsecured claims 'as soon as practicable' after the order for reorganization relief under Chapter 11."[25]

In a sense an appeal to the restatement of agency would resolve the apparent conflict of interest. The employee is really an agent for his employer. His or her obligations are tied directly to the interest of the employer. But this interpretation also has the effect of undermining the integrity of the creditors' committee.

The language of the Bankruptcy Code implies that an agency relationship exists between the members of the committee and the debtor. This relationship is necessary given the public commitment to not forcing people out of business when the business can be rehabilitated. While it may be in the general long-term interest of any company to help to keep other businesses in business, this long-term interest may conflict with other short-term interests of a company. It is clear that there will be some businesses that will have interests that conflict with the interest of the creditors' committee. Individuals who are employees of creditors are caught between their commitment to the language and purpose of the Bankruptcy Code and their role as agent for their employer.

This problem has to be resolved because it calls into question the authority of any court-appointed agent to manage the affairs of others. Do court-appointed roles override that principal-agent relationship? If court-appointed roles do override, then they seem to undermine the principal-agent relationship spelled out in the restatement of agency. If they do not override, the committee has no force.

A survey of the literature of conflict of interest does not seem to help. Consider for example, Michael Davis's discussion of conflict of interest. Davis is concerned with applying insights gained from the legal profession to general cases of conflict of interest. Legal ethics long ago worked out an analysis of conflict of interest as a situation tending to undermine independent professional judgment. The knowledge that one remains first and foremost an agent for one's employer would tend to undermine independent professional judgment as a member of creditors' committee.[26]

This debate is further complicated by the knowledge that literature on conflict of interest in bankruptcy is limited. When conflict of interest is discussed, it is generally in the context of insiders on the creditors' committee, that is, persons who have an interest that supports the debtor; a wife or family member; persons who have other legal liens against the debtor and want the plan to fail because some other financial interest will be served; professionals, such as lawyers, accountants, or other professionals, whose access to information about the debtor would be used in non-professional ways.[27] Little attention is given to the employee sent to represent a company at a creditors' committee meeting. The focus on the legal principal-agent relationship has expanded the traditional boundaries of conflict of interest research. These expanded boundaries are still not broad enough to encompass all the conflicts of interest that occur in the business setting.

NOTES

1. Frederick (1983), p. 125.
2. Frederick, p. 130.
3. Frederick, p. 125.
4. Boatright, p. 3.
5. Weintraub and Resnick (1986).
6. Weintraub, pp. 8–60.
7. Myer (1986), p. 446.
8. Chassin (1984), p. 107.
9. See In re Rea Holding Corp., 8 Br75, 81 (SDNY 1980) ("Those who serve on a creditors committee owe a fiduciary duty to all creditors which they fulfill by advising creditors of their rights and of the proper course of action in the bankruptcy proceeding.")
10. McDonnel, Thomas J., "Your First Creditors' Committee," *Credit & Financial Management*, November 1981, p. 24.
11. Chassin p. 115.
12. Seaholm (n.d.), unpublished manuscript, p. 29.
13. Seaholm, p. 29.
14. Seaholm, p. 29.
15. McDonnell, p. 32.
16. Seaholm, p. 29.
17. Seaholm, p. 30.
18. Weintraub, pp. 8–61.
19. Black (1979), p. 563.
20. Malin (1985), p. 25.
21. Macklin (1983), p. 245.
22. Myers, p. 447.
23. Boatright, "Conflict of Interest: An Agency Analysis," p. 4.
24. Restatement, Sec.14F.
25. 11 USC Sec. 1102(a)(1).
26. Davis (1982), p. 20.
27. Chassin, p. 123.

BIBLIOGRAPHY

Abuse on Wall Street: Conflicts of Interest in the Securities Markets (1980), Westport, Conn.: Quorum Books.

Adkins, L. (1982), "The High Cost of Employee Theft," *Dun's Business Month* (October).

Akerlof, G. (1980), "A Theory of Social Custom, of Which Unemployment May Be One Consequence," *Quarterly Journal of Economics,* Vol. 95, No. 4, pp. 749–75.

Akst, D. (1987c), "Fallen Star: How Whiz-Kid Chief of ZZZZ Best Had, and Lost, It All," *The Wall Street Journal* (July 9).

Akst, D. (1987b), "ZZZZ Best Investigates Financial Data; Minkow Resigns as Chief and a Director," *The Wall Street Journal* (July 6).

Akst, D. (1987a), "ZZZZ Best Plans to Seek Protection under Chapter 11," *The Wall Street Journal* (July 7).

Akst, D., and L. Berton (1988), "Accountants Who Specialize in Detecting Fraud Find Themselves in Great Demand," *The Wall Street Journal* (February 26).

Alchian, A. (1965), "The Bases of Some Recent Advances in the Theory of Management of the Firm," *Journal of Industrial Economics* (November). Reprinted in W. Breit and H. M. Hochman (eds.) (1971), *Readings in Microeconomics,* 2nd ed., New York: Holt, Rinehart and Winston, pp. 131–39.

Alchian, A., and H. Demsetz (1972), "Production, Information Costs and Economic Organization," *American Economic Review* (December), Vol. 62, No. 5, pp. 777–95.

American Bar Association (1980), *Code of Professional Responsibility,* Chicago: National Center for Professional Responsibility.

American Law Institute (1958), *Restatement of Agency,* Second, Philadelphia.

Aoki, M. (1984), *The Co-Operative Game Theory of the Firm,* Oxford: Oxford University Press.

Aristotle, *Nichomachean Ethics.* Book I, Chapter I, with an English translation by H. Rackham, London: W. Heineman, Ltd., 1972.

Aristotle, *The Politics.* Book I, Chapter I. Revised and represented by T. Saunders, Harmondsworth, England; New York, N.Y.: Penguin, 1981.

Arnason, R. J. (1982), "The Principle of Fairness and Free-Rider Problems," *Ethics* (July), pp. 616–33.

Arrington, E., and J. R. Francis (1987), "Letting the Chat out of the Bag:

213

Deconstruction, Privilege, and Accounting Research," University of Iowa working paper.

Arrow, K. J. (1985), "The Economics of Agency," in J. Pratt and R. Zeckhauser (eds.), *Principals and Agents*, Boston: Harvard Business School Press, pp. 37–51.

Arrow, K. J. (1974), *The Limits of Organization*, New York: W. W. Norton & Company.

Arrow, K. J. (1970), "The Organization of Economic Activity: Issues Pertinent to the Choice of Market versus Non-market Allocation," in R. H. Haveman and J. Margolis (eds.), *Public Expenditures and Policy Analysis*, Chicago: Markham, pp. 59–73.

Arrow, K. J. (1973), "Social Responsibility and Economic Efficiency," *Public Policy*, Vol. 21, pp. 303–17.

Arrow, K. J. (1963), "Uncertainty and the Welfare Economics of Medical Care," *The American Economic Review*, Vol. 53, No. 5, pp. 941–73.

Arthur, J., and W. Shaw (eds.) (1978), *Justice and Economic Distribution*, Englewood Cliffs, N.J.: Prentice-Hall.

Atiyah, P. S. (1981), *Promises, Morals, and Law*, Oxford: Oxford University Press.

Axelrod, R. (1984), *The Evolution of Cooperation*, New York: Basic Books.

Azumi, K. (1972), "Environmental Needs, Resources, and Agents," in K. Azumi and J. Hage (eds.), *Organizational Systems*, Lexington, Mass.: D.C. Health, pp. 91–100.

Baiman, S. (1982), "Agency Research in Managerial Accounting: A Survey," *Journal of Accounting Literature* (Spring), Vol. 1, pp. 154–213.

Baiman, S., and B. L. Lewis. (1987), "An Experiment Testing the Behavioral Equivalence of Strategically Equivalent Employment Contracts," mimeo (November).

Banfield, E. C. (1975), "Corruption as a Feature of Governmental Organization," *Journal of Law and Economics*, Vol. 18, No. 3 (December), pp. 587–605. See also comments by M. W. Reder and S. Rottenberg, pp. 607–15.

Banfield, E. C. (1958), *The Moral Basis of a Backward Society*, New York: The Free Press of Glencoe.

Barber, B. (1983), *The Logic and Limits of Trust*, New Brunswick, N.J.: Rutgers University Press.

Barefield, R. (1975), *The Impact of Audit Frequency on the Quality of Internal Control*, Studies in Accounting Research # 11, Sarasota, Fla.: American Accounting Association.

Barnard, C. I. (1938), *The Functions of the Executive*, Cambridge, Mass.: Harvard University Press.

Barry, V. (1986), *Moral Issues in Business*, 3rd ed., Belmont, Calif.: Wadsworth Publishing Co.

Baumol, W. J. (1986), *Superfairness*, Cambridge, Mass.: M.I.T. Press

Beauchamp, T. L., and N. E. Bowle (eds.) (1988), *Ethical Theory and Business*, 3rd ed., Englewood Cliffs, N.J.: Prentice-Hall.

Beckwith, D. and E. Thomas (1986), "Peddling Influence," *Time* (March 3).

Berenbeim, R. E. (1986), "An Outbreak of Ethics," *Across the Board* (May).

Berle, A. A., and G. C. Means (1932), *The Modern Corporation and Private Property*, New York: Macmillan.

Berton, L. (985), "Accounting Group to Disclose Plans for Panel on Fraud," *The Wall Street Journal* (February 12.).

Berton, L. (1987b), "Former Auditor at KMG Main is Investigated," *The Wall Street Journal* (February 9).

Berton, L. (1986), "Grant Thornton Finds Itself in Turmoil—Suit over ESM Shows Partners' Vulnerability," *The Wall Street Journal* (April 14).

Berton, L. (1987a), "Panel to Recommend Stiffer Penalties, More Audit Safeguards to Fight Fraud," *The Wall Street Journal* (April 27).

Berton, L. (1987d), "Wedtech Files Suits Against Auditors for $105 Million," *The Wall Street Journal* (April 14).

Berton, L. (1987c), "Wedtech Used Gimmickry to Prosper," *The Wall Street Journal* (February 23).

Black, D. (ed.), (1984), *Toward a General Theory of Social Control*, Vols. 1 & 2, Orlando, Fla.: Academic Press.

Black, H. C. (1979), *Black's Law Dictionary*, St. Paul, Minn.: West Publishing Co.

Blumberg, P. I. (1985), "Corporate Responsibility and the Employee's Duty of Loyalty and Obedience: A Preliminary Inquiry," in J. R. DesJardins and J. J. McCall (eds.), *Contemporary Issues in Business Ethics*, Belmont, CA: Wadsworth Publishing Co.

Boatright, J. (n.d.), "Conflict of Interest: An Agency Analysis."

Bohm, P. (1962), "Estimating Demand for Public Goods: An Experiment," *European Economic Review*, Vol. 3, pp. 111–30.

Bowie, N. (1988), "Accountants, Full Disclosure, and Conflicts of Interest," *Business and Professional Ethics Journal*, Vol. 5, No. 3–4 (1988), pp. 59–73.

Bowie, N. (1982), *Business Ethics*, Englewood Cliffs, N.J.: Prentice-Hall.

Brannigan, M. (1987), "Aftermath of Huge Fraud Prompts Claims of Regret," *The Wall Street Journal* (March 4).

Brannigan, M. (1986), "Auditor's Downfall Shows a Man Caught in the Trap of His Own Making," *The Wall Street Journal* (March 4).

Brannigan, M., and R. Koenig (1986), "Nine are Indicted in Collapse of ESM; U.S. Charges Firm Hid Its Huge Losses," *The Wall Street Journal* (April 4).

Breton, A., and R. Wintrobe (1982), *The Logic of Bureaucratic Conduct: An Economic Analysis of Competition, Exchange, and Efficiency in Private and Public Organizations*, Cambridge: Cambridge University Press.

Briloff, A. (1987), "Do Management Services Endanger Independence and Objectivity?" *CPA Journal*, Vol. 57 (August), pp. 22–29.

Burrough, B. (1986), "The Embezzler: David L. Miller Stole from His Employers and Isn't in Prison," *The Wall Street Journal* (September 19).

Butler, J. (1726), "Preface" and "Sermon One" in *Fifteen Sermons Preached at the Rolls College Chapel*, London: Reprinted 1835, Thomas Tegg & Son.

Carmichael, L. (1983), "Firm-Specific Human Capital and Promotion Ladders," *Bell Journal of Economics*, Vol. 14, pp. 251–58.

Chassin, R. N. (1984), "Judicial Misrepresentation of Creditors' Committee," *Bankruptcy Developments Journal*, Vol. 1.

Chatfield, M. (1974), *A History of Accounting Thought*, Hinsdale, Ill.: Dryden Press.

"A Chronology of the Wall Street Scandal," (1987), *The Wall Street Journal*, (February 13).

Clark, P., and J. Q. Wilson (1961), "Incentive Systems: a Theory of Organizations," *Administrative Science Quarterly* (September), Vol. 6, pp. 129–66.

Clark, R. C. (1985), "Agency Costs versus Fiduciary Duties," in J. Pratt and R. Zeckhauser (eds.), *Principals and Agents: The Structure of Business*, Boston, Mass.: Harvard Business School Press, pp. 55–79.

Coase, R. H. (1937), "The Nature of the Firm," *Economica* n.s. 4, pp. 386–405. Reprinted in G. J. Stigler and K. E. Boulding (eds.) (1952), *Readings in Price Theory*, Chicago: Richard D. Irwin for the American Economic Association.

Colby, A., and L. Kohlberg (1986), *The Measurement of Moral Judgment*, Cambridge: Cambridge University Press.

Coleman, J. S. (1974), *Power and the Structure of Society*, New York: W. W. Norton.

Coleman, J. S. (1982), *The Asymmetric Society*, Syracuse, N.Y.: Syracuse University Press.

Coleman, J. (1985), "Market Contractarianism," *Social Philosophy and Policy*, Vol. 2, pp. 69–114.

Conard, A., Knauss, R., and S. Siegel (1987), *Agency, Associations, Employment and Partnerships*, Fourth Edition, Mineola, N.H.: The Foundation Press.

Cony, E. (1987), "Borrowing Millions Without Collateral Takes Ingenuity," *The Wall Street Journal* (March 23).

Cook, K. (1982), "Network Structures from an Exchange Perspective," in P. V. Marsden and N. Lin (eds.), *Social Structure and Network Analysis*, Beverly Hills, Calif.: Sage Publications, pp. 177–99.

Coombs, F. S. (1980), "The Bases of Non-compliance with a Policy," *Policy Studies Journal*, Vol. 8, No. 6 (Summer), pp. 885–92.

Cooper, J. (1987), "Is Capitalism Based on Greed?" *Integer* (Summer/Fall).

Curtler, Hugh, (ed.) (1986), *Shame, Responsibility, and the Corporation*, New York: Haven Publishing Co.

Cyert, R. M., and J. G. March (1963), *A Behavioral Theory of the Firm*, Englewood Cliffs, N.J.: Prentice-Hall.

Davis, M. (1982), "Conflict of Interest," *Business & Professional Ethics Journal*, Vol. 1, No. 4 (Summer).

Davis, N. J., and B. Anderson (1983), *Social Control: The Production of Deviance in the Modern State*. New York: Irvington Publishers.

"Dear Chrysler: Outsiders' Advice on Handling the Odometer Charge" (1987), *The Wall Street Journal* (June 26), p. 19.

DeGeorge, R. T. (1986), *Business Ethics*, 2nd ed., New York: Macmillan.

DeGeorge, R. T. (1983), "Social Reality and Social Relations," *The Review of Metaphysics*, XXXVII, pp. 3–20.

DeGeorge, R. T. (1992), "Agency Theory and the Ethics of Agency," this volume, Oxford University Press.

Demski, J. (1982), "Managerial Incentives,: in A. A. Rappaport (ed.), *Information for Decision Making*. New York: Prentice-Hall, pp. 348–57.

Demski, J. (1986), "The Principal-Agent Model," Teaching Note, Yale School of Management.

Den Uyl, D. J. (1984), *The New Crusaders: The Corporate Responsibility Debate*, Bowling Green: Social Philosophy and Policy Center, 1984.

"Detective in ZZZZ Best Probe Charges SEC's Lack of Resources Hindered Case" (1988), *The Wall Street Journal*, (January 28).

Dickens, C. (1868), *Hard Times for These Times*, New York: The Works of Charles Dickens, Books, Inc.: 1910.

DiMaggio, P., and W. W. Powell (1983), "The Iron Cage Revisited; Institutional Isomorphism and Collective Rationality in Organizational Fields," *American Sociological Review*, Vol. 48, pp. 147–60.

DiMento, J. (1986), *Environmental Law and American Business: Dilemmas of Compliance*, New York: Plenum Press.

Diver, C. S. (1980), "A Theory of Regulatory Enforcement," *Public Policy*, Vol. 28, No. 3 (Summer), pp. 257–99.

Dornbusch, S. M., and W. R. Scott with the assistance of B. C. Busching and J. D. Laing (1975), *Evaluation and the Exercise of Authority*, San Francisco: Jossey-Bass.

Dow, G. K. (1987), "The Function of Authority in Transaction Cost Economics," *Journal of Economic Behavior and Organization*, Vol. 8, pp. 13–38.

Dunsire, A. (1978), *Control in a Bureaucracy*, New York: St. Martin's Press.

Duska, R. (n.d.), "Life Boat Ethics: A Problem in Economic Justice," Rosemont College.

Duska, R. (1975), "Whistleblowing and Employee Loyalty," in J. DesJardins and J. McCall (eds.), *Contemporary Issues in Business Ethics*, Belmont, CA: Wadsworth Publishing Co., 1985.

Easterbrook, F. (1985), "Insider Trading as an Agency Problem," in J. Pratt and R. Zeckhauser (eds.), *Principals and Agents: the Structure of Business*, Boston, Mass.: Harvard Business School Press, pp. 81–100.

Eavey, C., and G. Miller (1984), "Fairness in Majority Rule Games with a Core," *American Journal of Political Science*, pp. 570–86.

Eccles, R. (1985), "Transfer Pricing as a Problem of Agency," in J. Pratt and R. Zeckhauser (eds.), *Principals and Agents: the Structure of Business*, Boston, Mass.: Harvard Business School Press, pp. 151–86.

Eckstein, H., and T. R. Gurr (1975), *Patterns of Authority: A Structure Basis for Political Inquiry*, New York: Wiley-Interscience.

Eisenhardt, K. A. (1985), "Control: Organizational and Economic Approaches," *Management Science*, Vol. 31, No. 2 (February), pp. 134–49.

Eisenstadt, S. N., and L. Roniger (1984), *Patrons, Clients, and Friends: Interpersonal Relations and the Structure of Trust in Society*. Cambridge: Cambridge University Press.

Emerson, R. M. (1981), "Social Exchange Theory," in M. Rosenberg and R. H. Turner (eds.), *Social Psychology: Sociological Perspectives*, New York: Basic Books, pp. 30–65.

Emshwiller, J. (1987), "Phony Parchment: As Value of Diplomas Grows, More People Buy Bogus Credentials," *The Wall Street Journal* (April 2).

Epstein, R. A. (1985), "Agency Costs, Employment Contracts, and Labor Unions," in J. Pratt and R. Zeckhauser (eds.), *Principals and Agents: the Structure of Business*, Boston: Harvard Business School Press, pp. 127–48.

Etzioni, A. (1961), *A Comparative Analysis of Complex Organizations: On Power, Involvement, and Their Correlates*, New York: Free Press.

Etzioni, A. (1988), *The Moral Dimension: Toward a New Economics*, New York: Free Press.

Evan, W. and R. Freeman (1988), "A Stakeholder Theory of the Modern Corporation: Kantian Capitalism," in T. Beauchamp and N. Bowie (eds.), *Ethical Theory and Business*, 3rd ed., Englewood Cliffs, N.J.: Prentice-Hall.

Evans, J. H., and J. M. Patton (1983), "An Economic Analysis of Participation in the Municipal Finance Officers Association Certificate of Conformance Program," *Journal of Accounting and Economics*, Vol. 5, pp. 151–75.

Fadiman, J. A., "A Traveler's Guide to Gifts and Bribes," *Harvard Business Review* (July–August 1986), pp. 122–36.

Fama, E. F. (1983b), "Agency Problems and Residual Claims," *Journal of Law and Economics*, Vol. 26, No. 2 (June), pp. 327–49.

Fama, E. F. (1980), "Agency Problems and the Theory of the Firm," *Journal of Political Economy*, Vol. 88, No. 2 (April), pp. 288–307.

Fama, E. F., and M. C. Jensen (1983a), "Separation of Ownership and Control," *Journal of Law and Economics*, Vol. 26, No. 2 (June), pp. 301–25.

Feinberg, J. (1986), *Harm to Self; Volume Three of the Moral Limits of the Criminal Law*, Oxford: Oxford University Press.

Feinberg, J. (1988), *Harmless Wrongdoing: Volume Four of the Moral Limits of the Criminal Law*, Oxford: Oxford University Press.

Ferson, M. (1954), *Principles of Agency*, Mineola, N.Y.: The Foundation Press.

Flores, A. (1988), *Professional Ideals*, Belmont, Calif.: Wadsworth Publishing Co.

Frank, R. H. (1988a), *Passions Within Reason: The Strategic Role of the Emotions*, New York: W. W. Norton & Company.

Frank, R. H. (1988b), "Social Forces in the Workplace," presented at the Conference on the Enforcement of Social Norms, University of Delaware, June 1988.

Frankel, M., ed. (1987), *Values and Ethics in Organization and Human Systems Development: An Annotated Bibliography*, Washington, D.C.: American Association for the Advancement of Science.

Frederick, R. (1983), "Conflict of Interest," in M. Snoeyenbos, R. Almeder, and J. Humber (eds), *Business Ethics: Corporate Values and Society*, Buffalo: Prometheus Books.

French, P. (1984), *Collective and Corporate Responsibility*, New York: Columbia University Press.

Fried, C. (1981), *Contract as Promise: A Theory of Contractual Obligation*, Cambridge: Harvard University Press.

Friedman, M. (1962), *Capitalism and Freedom*, Chicago: University of Chicago Press.

Friedman, M. (1985), "The Social Responsibility of Business Is to Increase Its Profits," in J. DesJardins and J. McCall (eds.), *Contemporary Issues in Business Ethics*, Belmont, Calif.: Wadsworth Publishing Co.

Friedman, M. (1970), "The Social Responsibility of Business Is to Increase Its Profits," *New York Times Magazine*, September 13, 1970.

Galaskiewicz, J. (1985), *Social Organization of an Urban Grants Economy: A Study of Business Philanthropy and Nonprofit Organizations*, Orlando, FL: Academic Press.

Gambetta, D. (ed.) (1988), *Trust: Making and Breaking Cooperative Relations*, Oxford: Basil Blackwell Ltd.

Gauthier, D. (1986), *Morals by Agreement*, Oxford: Oxford University Press.

Gibbs, J. P. (1981), *Norms, Deviance, and Social Control: Conceptual Matters*, New York: Elsevier; distr. by Greenwood Press, Westport Press, Conn.

Gibbs, J. P. (ed.) (1982), *Social Control: Views from the Social Sciences*, Beverly Hills: Sage Publications.

Goldberg, V. P. (1976), "Regulation and Administered Contracts," *Bell Journal of Economics*, Vol. 7, No. 2 (Autumn), pp. 426–48.

Goodin, R. E. (1985), *Protecting the Vulnerable: A Reanalysis of Our Social Responsibilities*, Chicago: University of Chicago Press.

Green, J. and J. J. Laffont (1986), "Partially Verifiable Information and Mechanism Design," *Review of Economic Studies*, LIII, pp. 447–56.

Hall, S. P. III (1986), "Ethics in Investment: Divestment," *Financial Analysts Journal* (July–August).

Hardin, R. (1988), *Morality and the Limits of Reason*, Chicago: University of Chicago Press.

Harsanyi, J. C. (1977), "Morality and the Theory of Rational Behavior," *Social Research*, Vol. 44, No. 4, pp. 623–56.

Hart, H. L. A. (1955), "Are There Any Natural Rights?" *Philosophical Review*, Vol. 64, pp. 175–91.

Hart, O. (1983), "Optimal Labor Contracts Under Asymmetric Information: An Introduction," *Review of Economic Studies*, Vol. L, pp. 3–35.

Hart, O., and B. Holmstrom (1987), "The Theory of Contracts," in T. Bewley (ed.), *Advances in Economic Theory: Fifth World Congress*, Cambridge: Cambridge University Press, pp. 71–155.

Higgins, E. T., and C. D. McCann (1984), "Social Encoding and Subsequent Attitudes, Impressions, and Memory: Context-Driven and Motivational Aspects of Processing," *Journal of Personality and Social Psychology*, Vol. 47, pp. 36–39.

Hirschman, A. O. (1981), "Morality and the Social Sciences: a Durable Tension," as reprinted in *Essays in Trespassing: Economics to Politics and Beyond*, Cambridge: Cambridge University Press, pp. 294–306.

Hobbes, Thomas (1651), *Leviathan*, edited by A. R. Waller, Cambridge: Cambridge University Press, 1904.

Hollis, M. (1987), *The Cunning of Reason*, Cambridge: Cambridge University Press.

Holmes, Jr., O. W. (1891), "Agency," *Harvard Law Review*, Volume 4.8 pp. 346–64.

Holmes, Jr., O. W. (1891), "Agency II," *Harvard Law Review*, Volume 5.1, pp. 1–23.

Holmstrom, B., and J. Richart-Costa (1986), "Managerial Incentives and Capital Management," *Quarterly Journal of Economics*, Vol. 101, pp. 835–60.

Holmstrom, B., and J. Tirole (1987), "The Theory of the Firm," in R. Schmalensee and R. Willig (eds.), *Handbook of Industrial Organization*, New York: Elsevier.

Hornstein, H., H. Masor, K. Sole, and M. Heilman (1971), "Effects of Sentiment and Completion of Helping Act on Observer Helping," *Journal of Personality and Social Psychology*, Vol. 17, pp. 107–112.

Howton, F. W. (1969), *Functionaries*, Chicago: Quadrangle.

Jackson, B. (1987), "Fees That Lobbyists Routinely Pay Lawmakers to Get Acquainted Raise Questions about Ethics," *The Wall Street Journal* (December 17).

Jeffrey, N. (1987), "ZZZZ Best Name, Inventory Attract $62,000 Auction Bid," *The Wall Street Journal* (July 27).

Jelinek, M. (1981), "Organization Structure: The Basic Conformations," in M. Jelinek, J. A. Litterer, and R. E. Miles (eds.), *Organizations by Design: Theory and Practice*, Plano, Tex.: Business Publications.

Jensen, M. C. (1983), "Organization Theory and Methodology," *Accounting Review*, Vol. 50 (April), pp. 319–34.

Jensen, M. C., and W. H. Meckling (1976), "Theory of the Firm: Managerial Behavior, Agency Costs and Ownership Structure," *Journal of Financial Economics*, Vol. 3, No. 4 (October), pp. 305–60.

Jett, McF. (1987), "A Question of Ethics," *The Wall Street Journal* (September 18).

Johnson, K., and H. Jaenicke (1980), *Evaluating Internal Control*, New York: John Wiley and Sons.

Johnson, R., J. Koten, and C. McCoy (1987), "State of Shock: Anheuser-Busch Cos. Is Shaken by Its Probe of Improper Payments," *The Wall Street Journal*, (March 31).

Kahneman, D., J. Knetsch, and Thaler (1986), "Fairness and the Assumptions of Economics," in R. M. Hogarth and M. W. Reder, *Rational Choice: The Contrast Between Economics and Psychology*, Chicago: University of Chicago Press, pp. 101–16.

Kahneman, D., J. Knetsch, and R. Thaler (1986), "Fairness as a Constraint on Profit Seeking," *American Economic Review*, pp. 728–41.

Kahneman, D., P. Slovic, and A. Tversky (eds.) (1982), *Judgment Under Uncertainty: Heuristics and Biases*, Cambridge: Cambridge University Press.

Kaufman, H., with the collaboration of M. Couzens (1973), *Administrative Feedback: Monitoring Subordinates' Behavior*, Washington, D.C.: The Brookings Institute.

Kelley, J., and N. Johnson (1987), "Audit: PTL Spent Lavishly," *USA Today*, (July 24).

Kiesler, S., and L. Sproull (1982), "Managerial Responses to Changing Environments: Perspectives on Problem Sensing from Social Cognition," *Administrative Science Quarterly*, Vol. 27, pp. 548–70.

Klitgaard, R. (1988), *Controlling Corruption,* Berkeley: University of California Press.

Kneale, D. (1987), "It Takes a Hacker to Catch a Hacker as Well as a Thief," *The Wall Street Journal* (November 3).

Knight, F. (1921), *Risk, Uncertainty, and Profit,* New York: Houghton, Mifflin (Hart, Schaffner & Marx Prize Essays, 31), reprinted with new prefaces in 1933, 1948, and 1957.

Knoke, D., and C. Wright-Isak (1982), "Individual Motives and Organizational Incentive Systems" in *Research in the Sociology of Organizations,* Vol. 1, Greenwich, Conn.: JAI Press, pp. 209–54.

Kohlberg and Colby (1986), *The Measurement of Moral Judgment,* Cambridge University Press.

Kreps, D. (1984), "Corporate Culture and Economic Theory," unpublished, August.

Krislov, S., K. O. Boyum, J. N. Clark, R. C. Shaefer, and S. O. White (eds.) (1972), *Compliance and the Law: A Multidisciplinary Approach,* Beverly Hills, Calif.: Sage Publications.

Kristol, I. (1987), "Ethics Anyone? Or Morals," *The Wall Street Journal,* (September 15).

Kronman, A. T. (1980), "Contract Law and Distributive Justice," *The Yale Law Journal,* Vol. 89, No. 3, pp. 472–511.

Lancaster, K. (1979), *Variety, Equity and Efficiency,* New York: Columbia University Press.

Landa, J. T. (1981), "A Theory of the Ethnically Homogeneous Middleman Group: An Institutional Alternative to Contract Law," *Journal of Legal Studies,* Vol. 10 (June), pp. 349–62.

Landro, L. (1982), "Analysis of ITT's Report Shows Problems in Halting Questionable Foreign Payments," *The Wall Street Journal* (June 3).

Lane, M. S., D. Schaupp, and B. Persons (1988), "Pygmalion Effect: An Issue for Business Education and Ethics," *Journal of Business Ethics,* 7.

Langer, E. J., R. S. Bashner, and B. Chanowitz (1985), "Decreasing Prejudice by Increasing Discrimination," *Journal of Personality and Social Psychology,* Vol. 49, pp. 113–20.

Lawrence, P. (1958), "The Changing of Organizational Behavior Patterns: A Case Study of Decentralization," Boston: Division of Research, Harvard Business School, as quoted in K. Walters (1975), "Your Employee's Right to Blow the Whistle," *Harvard Business Review,* Vol. 53, No. 4 (July–August).

Lazear, E., and S. Rosen (1981), "Rank-Order Tournaments as Optimum Labor Contracts," *Journal of Political Economy,* Vol. 89, pp. 1045–64.

Leibenstein, H. (1976), *Beyond Economic Man: A New Foundation for Microeconomics,* Cambridge: Harvard University Press.

Leibenstein, H. (1987), *Inside the Firm: The Inefficiencies of Hierarchy,* Cambridge: Harvard University Press.

Lepper, M. R., and D. Greene (1975), "Turning Play Into Work: Effects of Adult Surveillance and Extrinsic Rewards on Children's Intrinsic Motivation," *Journal of Personality and Social Psychology,* Vol. 33, pp. 25–35.

Lev, B. (1988), "Toward a Theory of Equitable and Efficient Accounting Policy," *The Accounting Review*, Vol. 63 (January).

Levinthal, D. (1988), "A Survey of Agency Models of Organizations," *Journal of Economic Behavior and Organization*, Vol. 9, pp. 153–85.

Luebke, N. R. (1987), "Conflict of Interest as a Moral Category," *Business and Professional Ethics Journal*, 6.

Macklin, R. (1983), "Conflicts of Interest," in T. Beauchamp and N. Bowie (eds.), *Ethical Theory and Business*, 2nd ed., Englewood Cliffs, N.J.: Prentice-Hall.

Maitland, I. (1987), "The Structure of Business and Corporate Responsibility," in S. Sethi and C. Falbe (eds.), *Business and Society*, Lexington, Mass.: D. C. Heath and Co., pp. 167–74.

Malin, J. (1985), "Why Sit on a Creditors' Committee," *Cashflow*, (August).

March, J. G., and J. P. Olsen (eds.) (1976), *Ambiguity and Choice in Organizations*, Bergen, Norway: Universitetsforlaget.

March, J. G., and H. A. Simon (1958), *Organizations*, New York: Wiley.

Margolis, H. (1982), *Selfishness, Altruism, and Rationality*, Chicago: University of Chicago Press.

Margolis, J. (1979), "Conflicts of Interest and Conflicting Interests," in T. Beauchamp and N. Bowie, *Ethical Theory and Business*, Englewood Cliffs, N.J.: Prentice-Hall.

Marsden, P. V. (1982), "Brokerage Behavior in Restricted Exchange Networks," in P. V. Marsden and N. Lin (eds.), *Social Structure and Network Analysis*, Beverly Hills, Calif.: Sage Publications, pp. 201–18.

Marwell, G., and R. Ames (1981), "Economists Free Ride, Does Anyone Else?" *Journal of Public Economics*, Vol. 15, pp. 295–310.

Maser, S., and J. Coleman (1988), "A Bargaining Theory Approach to Default Provisions and Disclosure Rules in Contract Law," mimeo.

Mautz, R. (1972), *Effect of Circumstance on the Application of Accounting Principles*, New York: Financial Executives Research Foundation.

McCloskey, D. (1990), *If You're So Smart: The Narrative of Economic Expertise*, Chicago: University of Chicago Press.

McCloskey, D. (1986), *The Rhetoric of Economics*, Brighton: Wheatsheaf.

McCoy, C. (1987), "Financial Fraud: Theories Behind Nationwide Surge in Bank Swindles," *The Wall Street Journal* (October 2).

McCoy, C. (1987), "World Class Con Men Play Big Role in Growing Losses," *The Wall Street Journal* (October 2).

McDonnell, T. (1981), "Your First Creditors' Committee," *Credit & Financial Management* (November).

NcNeil, I. (1980), *The New Socal Contract*, New Haven: Yale University Press.

Means, E. (1962), "Vicarious Liability for Agency Contracts," *Virginia Law Review*, Vol. 48, pp. 50–57.

Metzger, M., et al., (eds.) (1986), *Business Law and the Regulatory Environment*, Homewood, Ill.: Richard D. Irwin.

Meyer, J. W., and B. Rowan (1977), "Institutional Organizations: Formal Structure as Myth and Ceremony," *American Journal of Sociology*, Vol. 83, pp. 340–63.

Milgram, S. (1963), "Behavioral Study of Obedience," *Journal of Abnormal and Social Psychology*, Vol. 67, pp. 371–78.

Milgram, S. (1974), *Obedience to Authority*, New York: Harper and Row.

Mill, J. (1957), *Utilitarianism* (Chap. IV), Indianapolis: Bobbs-Merrill Library of Liberal Arts.

Miller, G. G. (1987) "Administrative Dilemmas: The Role of Political Leadership," Political Economy Working Paper #118, Washington University, June.

Miller, J. (1984), "The Big Nail and Other Stories: Product Quality Control in the Soviet Union," *The ACES Bulletin*, Vol. XXVI (Spring), pp. 43–57. Journal renamed *Comparative Economic Studies*.

Mintzberg, H. (1983), *Power in and around Organizations*, Englewood Cliffs, N.J.: Prentice-Hall.

Mitnick, B. M. (1984), "Agency Problems and Political Institutions," Paper presented at the 1984 Annual Meeting of the Midwest Political Science Association, Chicago, April 12–14.

Mitnick, B. M. (1982), "Agents in the Environment: Managing in Boundary Spanning Roles," Paper presented at the 42nd Annual Meeting of the Academy of Management, New York, N.Y., August.

Mitnick, B. M. (1985), "Agents of Legitimacy: Pantheonic Directorates and the Management of Organization Environments," Paper presented at the Fifth Annual Sunbelt Social Networks Conference, Palm Beach, Fla., February 14–17.

Mitnick, B. M. (1973), "Fiduciary Rationality and Public Policy: The Theory of Agency and Some Consequences," Paper presented at the 1973 Annual Meeting of the American Political Science Association, New Orleans, La.

Mitnick, B. M. (1980), *The Political Economy of Regulation: Creating, Designing, and Removing Regulatory Forms*, New York: Columbia University Press.

Mitnick, B. M. (1976), "The Theory of Agency: A Framework," Paper presented at the 1976 Annual Meeting of the American Sociological Association, New York, N.Y.

Mitnick, B. M. (1987), "The Theory of Agency and Organizational Analysis," *Working Paper Series*, Pittsburgh: University of Pittsburgh (May).

Mitnick, B. M. (1974), "The Theory of Agency: The Concept of Fiduciary Rationality and Some Consequences," unpublished Ph.D. dissertation, Department of Political Science, University of Pennsylvania.

Mitnick, B. M. (1975a), "The Theory of Agency: The Fiduciary Norm," Paper presented at the 1975 Annual Meeting of the American Sociological Association, San Francisco, Calif.

Mitnick, B. M. (1975b), "The Theory of Agency: The Policing 'Paradox' and Regulatory Behavior," *Public Choice*, Vol. 24 (Winter), pp. 27–42.

Mitnick, B. M., and R. W. Backoff (1984), "The Incentive Relation in Implementation," in G. C. Edwards, III (ed.), *Public Policy Implementation*, Vol. 3 of S. Nagel (ed.), *Public Policy Studies: A Multi-Volume Treatise*, Greenwich, Conn.: JAI Press, pp. 59–122.

Moe, T. M. (1984), "The New Economics of Organization," *American Journal of Political Science*, Vol. 28 (November), pp. 739–77.

Moore, B., Jr. (1978), *Injustice: The Social Bases of Obedience and Revolt*, New York: M. E. Sharpe, distr. by Pantheon Books.

Myer, L. (1986), *Debtor-Creditor Relations Manual and Forms*, Colorado Springs, Co.: Shepard's/McGraw-Hill.

National Society of Professional Engineers (1987), *Code of Ethics for Engineers*, Washington, D.C.

Namazi, M. (1985), "Theoretical Developments of Principal-Agent Employment Contracts in Accounting: the State of the Art," *Journal of Accounting Literature*, pp. 113–62.

Newton, L., "To Whom is the Nurse Accountable? A Philosophical Perspective," *Connecticut Medicine Supplement*, 43 (10), pp. 7–9 (October 1979).

Nichols, A. L., and R. J. Zeckhauser (1986), "The Perils of Prudence: How Conservative Risk Assessments Distort Regulation," *Regulation*, Vol. 10, No. 2, pp. 13–24.

Nisbett, R. E., and L. Ross (1980), *Human Inference: Strategies and Shortcomings of Social Judgment*, Englewood Cliffs, N.J.: Prentice-Hall.

Noreen, E. (1987), "The Economics of Ethics: A New Perspective on Agency Theory," Seattle: University of Washington (April 2).

Nozick, R. (1974), *Anarchy, State, and Utopia*, New York: Basic Books.

"Oliver North, Businessman? Many Bosses Say That He's Their Kind of Employee" (1987), *The Wall Street Journal*, (July 14).

Oster, S. (1988), "The Goals of Reorganizations," Mimeo of a chapter in her forthcoming book on corporate strategy to be published by Oxford University Press.

Ouchi, W. G. (1980), "Markets, Bureaucracies, and Clans," *Administrative Science Quarterly*, Vol. 25 (March), pp. 120–42.

Parker, R. (1965), "Lower of Cost or Market in Great Britain and the United States: An Historical Perspective," *Abacus*, pp. 156–72.

Pasztor, A., and S. McMurray (1985), "Hutton's Vice Chairman, 2 Others Agree to Step Down Following Check Probe," *The Wall Street Journal* (September 6).

Penno, M. (1984), "Assymmetry of Pre-Decision Information and Managerial Accounting," *Journal of Accounting Research*, Vol. 22, No. 1 (Spring), pp. 177–91.

Penno, M. (1988) "A Discussion of 'Economic Effects of a Mandated Audit in a Contingent-Claims Economy' ", *Contemporary Accounting Research*, Vol. 4, No. 2 (Spring), pp. 389–91.

Perrow, C. (1986), *Complex Organizations: A Critical Essay*, 3rd ed., New York: Random House.

Petzinger, T., Jr. (1979), "Heinz to Probe Prepayments to Suppliers by Using Outside Lawyers, Accountants," *The Wall Street Journal* (April 30.)

Pittel, L. (1986), "Divested Stocks Aren't Cheap," *Forbes* (February 24).

Ponemon, L. A., and D. L. Gabhart (1989), "Auditor Independence Judgments; A Cognitive Developmental Model and Experimental Evidence," State University of New York working paper, subsequently published in the *1989 Contemporary Accounting Research (CAR) Conference Issue*.

Posner, R. A. (1986), *Economic Analysis of Law*, 3rd ed., Boston: Little, Brown, and Company.

Power, W. (1987), "A 'Magician' Makes $86,000 Disappear From Cash Machines," *The Wall Street Journal* (May 18).

Pratt, J. W., and R. Zeckhauser (eds.) (1985), *Principals and Agents An Overview*," in *Principals and Agents: The Structure of Business*, Boston: Harvard Business School Press, pp. 1–36.

Pratt, J. W., and R. Zeckhauser (eds.) (1985), *Principals and Agents: The Structure of Business*, Boston: Harvard Business School Press.

Radner, R. (1987), "Decentralization and Incentives," in T. Groves, R. Radner, and S. Reiter (eds.), *Information, Incentives, and Economic Mechanisms: Essays in Honor of Leonid Hurwicz*, Minneapolis: University of Minnesota Press.

Radner, R. (1981), "Monitoring Cooperative Arrangements in a Repeated Principal-Agent Relationship," *Econometrica*, pp. 1127–48.

Rawls, J. (1971), *A Theory of Justice*, Cambridge: Harvard University Press.

Read, E. (1988), "Northrup Faces Inquiry Over Bomber Billing," *The Wall Street Journal*, (February 25).

Rest, J. (1979), *Development in Judging Moral Issues*, Minneapolis: University of Minnesota Press.

Ricks, T. (1988), "ZZZZ Best Auditors Testify Law Firm Warned Them Not to Disclose Suspicions," *The Wall Street Journal*, (February 2).

Roberts, J. (n.d.), "Moral Hazard and the Principal-Agent Problem," Teaching Note, Stanford University, Graduate School of Business.

Rohatyn, F. G. (1987), "Ethics in America's Money Culture," *New York Times* (June 3, 1987), p. A27.

Rorty, R. (1989), *Contingency, Irony and Solidarity*, New York: Cambridge University Press.

Rose, D., M. Miller, and C. Agnew (1984), "Reducing the Problem of Global Warming," *Technology Review*, Vol. 87 (May–June), pp. 48–58.

Rose-Ackerman, S. (1978), *Corruption: A Study in Political Economy*, New York: Academic Press.

Ross, S. A. (1973), "The Economic Theory of Agency: The Principal's Problem," *American Economic Review*, Vol. 62, No. 2 (May), pp. 134–39.

Royko, M. (1987), "It's Time to Tame Rampaging Trucks," *Chicago Tribune* (July 8), p. 3.

Ruskin, J. (1968), "The Stones of Venice," in M. Abrams, et al. (eds.), *The Norton Anthology of English Literature*, Vol. 2, New York: W. W. Norton.

Russell, G. (1986), "Going After the Crooks," *Time* (December 1), pp. 48–56.

Schelling, T. C. (1978), *Micromotives and Macrobehavior*, New York: Norton.

Schelling, T. C. (1960), *The Strategy of Conflict*, Harvard University Press.

Scott, W. (1988), "Economic Effects of a Mandated Audit in a Contingent-Claims Economy," *Contemporary Accounting Research*, Vol. 4, No. 2 (Spring), pp. 354–88.

Seaholm, J. (n.d.), "The Duties, Functions and Responsibilities of an Unsecured Creditors' Committee Under Chapter 11," an unpublished manuscript.

Sen, A. (1986), *On Ethics and Economics*, New York: Blackwell.

Sen, A. (1981), *Poverty and Famines: An Essay on Entitlement and Deprivation*, Oxford: Oxford University Press.

Sen, A. (1977), "Rational Fools: A Critique of the Behavioral Foundations of Economic Theory," *Philosophy and Public Affairs,* Vol. 6, pp. 317–44.

Shapiro, S. P. (1987), "The Social Control of Impersonal Trust," *American Journal of Sociology,* Vol. 93, No. 3 (November), pp. 623–58.

Simon, H. A. (1957b), "A Behavioral Model of Rational Choice," in H. Simon, *Models of Man: Social and Rational,* New York: Wiley, pp. 241–60.

Simon, H. A. (1957a), "A Formal Theory of the Employment Relation," in H. Simon, *Models of Man: Social and Rational,* New York: Wiley, pp. 183–95.

Slater, K. (1988), "Accounting Board Clears Rules Ordering Auditors to Watch for Corporate Fraud," *The Wall Street Journal* (February 10).

Smith, A. (1776), *An Inquiry into the Causes of the Wealth of Nations,* edited by E. Canan, New York: Random House, 1937.

Snoeyenbos, M., R. Almeder, and J. Humber (eds.) (1983), *Business Ethics: Corporate Values and Society,* Buffalo: Prometheus Books.

Solomon, D. (1987), "Hotlines and Hefty Rewards: Retailers Step Up Efforts to Curb Employee Theft," *The Wall Street Journal* (September 17).

Spence, A. M., and R. Zeckhauser (1971), "Insurance, Information, and Individual Action," *American Economic Review,* Vol. 61, No. 2 (May), pp. 380–87.

Stigler, G., and G. Becker (1977), "De Gustibus Non Est Disputandum," *American Economic Review,* Vol. 67 (March), pp. 76–90.

Stiglitz, J. (1986), "Common Values and Multiple Equilibria?" unpublished presentation at the University of Pennsylvania, October.

Stinchcombe, A. L. (1975), "Norms of Exchange: Status, Authority, and Fiduciary Norms in Organizations," paper delivered at the 1975 Annual Meeting of the Public Choice Society, Chicago.

Stout, R., Jr. (1980), *Organizations, Management, and Control: An Annotated Bibliography,* Bloomington, Ind.: Indiana University Press.

Swanson, G. E. (1971), "An Organizational Analysis of Collectivities," *American Sociological Review,* Vol. 36, No. 4 (August), pp. 607–24.

Szwajkowski, E. (n.d.), "The Myths and Realities of Research on Organizational Misconduct," Working Paper W605, University of Illinois of Chicago.

Taylor, M. (1987), *The Possibility of Cooperation,* Cambridge: Cambridge University Press.

Thompson, F., and L. R. Jones (1986), "Controllership in the Public Sector," *Journal of Policy Analysis and Management,* Vol. 5, No. 3, pp. 547–71.

Tirole, J. (1986), "Hierarchies and Bureaucracies: On the Role of Collusion in Organizations," *Journal of Law, Economics, and Organization,* Vol. 2, No. 2 (Fall), pp. 181–214.

Varian, H. R. (1975), "Distributive Justice, Welfare Economics, and the Theory of Fairness," *Philosophy and Public Affairs,* Vol. 4, pp. 223–47.

Vaughan, D. (1983), *Controlling Unlawful Organizational Behavior: Social Structure and Corporate Misconduct,* Chicago: University of Chicago Press.

Verne, J. (1958), *The Begum's Fortune,* New York: Ace Books.

Vogel, D. (1987), "Could an Ethics Course Have Kept Ivan from Going Bad?" *The Wall Street Journal* (April 27).

Wallace, W. A. (n.d.), "The Economic Role of the Audit in Free and Regulated Markets," Touche Ross and Co. Aid to Education Program.

Wallace, W. A. (1986), "Agency Theory and Governmental and Nonprofit Sector Research," unpublished paper.

Watts, R. L., and J. L. Zimmerman (1979), "The Demand for and Supply of Accounting Theories: The Market for Excuses," *The Accounting Review*, Vol. 54, No. 2, pp. 273–305.

Watts, R. L. (1983), "Agency Problems, Auditing, and the Theory of the Firm: Some Evidence," *Journal of Law and Economics*, Vol. 26, No. 3 (October), pp. 613–33.

Weintraub, B., and A. Resnick (1986), *Bankruptcy Law Manual*, revised ed., Boston: Warren, Gorham & Lamont.

Welles, C., "Why the E.F. Hutton Scandal May be Far from Over," *Business Week* (February 24, 1986), pp. 98–101.

Welton, R. E., and J. R. Davis (1989), "Improving Professional Ethics: Can Ethical Behavior Be Changed?" (Working paper, Clemson University).

White, H. C. (1985), "Agency as Control," in J. Pratt and R. Zeckhauser (eds.), *Principals and Agents: The Structure of Business*, Boston: Harvard Business School Press, pp. 187–212.

White, J. (1987), "Chrysler Pleads No Contest to Charges in Odometer Case, To Pay $16.4 Million," *The Wall Street Journal* (December 15).

Willer, D., and B. Anderson (eds.) (1981), *Networks, Exchange, and Coercion: The Elementary Theory and its Applications*, New York: Elsevier; distr. by Greenwood Press, Westport, Conn.

Williamson, O. E. (1985), *The Economic Institutions of Capitalism: Firms, Markets, Relational Contracting*, New York: The Free Press.

Williamson, O. E. (1964), *The Economics of Discretionary Behavior: Managerial Objectives in a Theory of the Firm*, Englewood Cliffs, N.J.: Prentice-Hall.

Williamson, O. E. (1975), *Markets and Hierarchies: Analysis and Anti-trust Implications*, New York: The Free Press.

Williamson, O. E. (1983), "Organization Form, Residual Claimants, and Corporate Control," *Journal of Law and Economics*, Vol. 26, No. 2 (June), pp. 351–66.

Williamson, O. E., and W. G. Ouchi (1981), "The Markets and Hierarchies Program of Research: Origins, Implications, Prospects," in A. Van de Ven and W. Joyce (eds.), *Perspectives on Organization Design and Behavior*, New York: Wiley, pp. 347–70.

Williamson, O. E., M. L. Wachter, and J. E. Harris (1975), "Understanding the Employment Relation: The Analysis of Idiosyncratic Exchange," *Bell Journal of Economics*, Vol. 6 (Spring), pp. 250–80.

Wilson, J. Q. (1973), *Political Organizations*, New York: Basic Books.

Wimsatt, W. C. (1986), "Heuristics and the Study of Human Behavior," in D. Fiske and R. Shweder, *Metatheory in Social Science: Pluralisms and Subjectivities*, Chicago: University of Chicago Press, pp. 293–314.

Winans, R. (1986b), "After Deal Made, Rules Begin to Change," *Houston Chronicle* (October 20).

Winans, R. (1986c), "Overwhelming Evidence Prompts Call from SEC," *Houston Chronicle* (October 22).

Winans, R. (1986a), "Seduction and Scandal at the Journal," *Houston Chronicle* (October 19).

Winans, R. (1986d), "Stockbroker Brant Starts Cashing in on Reporter's Tips," *Houston Chronicle* (October 21).

Winans, R. (1986e), "There Was Just One Alternative: Tell the Truth," *Houston Chronicle* (October 23).

Wynter, L. (1986), "Bank Board Allowed Accounting Device to Bolster Weakened Thrifts' Statement," *The Wall Street Journal* (April 24).

Young, S. (1985), "Insider Trading: Why the Concern?" *Journal of Accounting, Auditing & Finance"* (Spring).

Zald, M. N. (1978), "On the Social Control of Industries," *Social Forces,* Vol. 57, No. 1 (September), pp. 79–102.

Zimmerman, J. L. (1977), "The Municipal Accounting Maze: An Analysis of Political Incentives," *Journal of Accounting Research,* Vol. 15 (Supplement), pp. 107–44. Also, comments by J. Gould and A. Mandolini, pp. 145–55.

Zucker, L. G. (1986), "Production of Trust: Institutional Sources of Economic Structure, 1840–1920," in B. Staw and L. Cummings, *Research in Organizational Behavior,* Vol. 8, Greenwich, Conn.: JAI Press, pp. 53–111.

"ZZZZ Best Co." (1987), *The Wall Street Journal* (June 5).

"ZZZZ Best Co. Says Outside Accountant Quit, Successor Hired" (1987), *The Wall Street Journal* (June 18).

"ZZZZ Best's Founder Files for Personal Bankruptcy" (1987), *The Wall Street Journal* (August 13).

INDEX

White-collar crimes, harm from, 180
Willer, D., 91, 92, 93
Williamson, O.E., 36, 76, 77, 78, 82, 84,
    89, 92
Wilson, J.Q., 81, 92, 121
Wimsatt, W.C., 30
Winans, R. Foster, 197, 203n15
Wintrobe, R., 91
Wittgenstein, 144
Woelfel, C.J., 181
Work
  commercialization of, 160
  satisfaction in one's, need for, 167–68
Worker safety, 122
  in terms of profit-maximizing
    behavior, 119–20

trust and trustworthiness of firm and,
    124
Wright-Isak, C., 81

Xerox Corporation, 195–986
  abuse of position policy at, 19

Young & Rubicam, 194

Zald, M.N., 91
Zeckhauser, R., 3, 21n4, 40, 56n5, 80,
    93, 147, 151
Zimmerman, J.L., 78–79
ZZZZ Best, 179